Boxed In

Helen Baehr lectures in Media Studies at the Polytechnic of Central London. She has written extensively about women and the mass media and her study of women and local radio, *Shut Up and Listen! A View from the Inside*, appeared in 1984. She has been involved in the production of TV programmes since 1980 and was a founder member of the Women's Broadcasting and Film Lobby. She researched several programmes for Channel 4's current affairs series, *Broadside*, and in 1985 produced a series of eight international documentaries, *Female Focus*, for Channel 4.

Gillian Dyer has taught in further, higher and adult education in the areas of women's studies and media studies. She is the author of *Advertising as Communication* (Methuen, 1982) and has written articles on television drama documentary, interviews on television, and marketing signs and semiotics. She is currently writing a workbook on women and communication for bridging/fresh start courses and producing a video to accompany the book.

Boxed In

Women and Television

Edited by Helen Baehr
and Gillian Dyer

New York and London

First published in 1987 by
Pandora Press
(Routledge & Kegan Paul Ltd)
11 New Fetter Lane, London EC4P 4EE

Published in the USA by
Pandora Press
(Routledge & Kegan Paul Inc.)
in association with Methuen Inc.
29 West 35th Street, New York, NY 10001

Set in Ehrhardt and Rockwell
by Columns of Reading
and printed in The British Isles
by The Guernsey Press Co. Ltd
Guernsey, Channel Islands

Library of Congress Cataloging in Publication Data

Boxed in.
  (Pandora Press popular culture)
  Includes index.
  1. Women in television.   2. Women in the television
industry.   3. Television programs for women.   I. Baehr,
Helen.   II. Dyer, Gillian.   III. Series.
PN1992.8.W65B6   1987   791.45′088042   87–9113

British Library CIP Data also available

ISBN 0–86358–112–9 (c)
      0–86358–216–8 (p)

Contents

Contents

Illustrations

Contributors

Charlotte Brunsdon teaches Film Studies at the University of Warwick and is editor of *Films for Women*.

Rosalind Coward lectures in Media Studies at Reading University and is author of *Female Desire*.

Julie D'Acci lectures at the University of Wisconsin-Madison and is writing a doctoral dissertation on *Women and Prime-Time American Television*.

Margaret Gallagher is co-ordinator of the Steering Committee on *Women and Television* for the Commission of the European Communities. She has also directed projects on women and media in Europe, Asia and Africa.

Ann Gray teaches and is working on a DPhil at the University of York on women and popular culture.

Patricia Holland is a freelance writer and film-maker. She is co-editor of *Photography, Politics, Two*.

Jill Hyem started her career as an actress. She has written several television plays, including episodes of *Angels*, *Nanny*, *Sharing Time*, and *Howards Way*, and was co-writer of the *Tenko* series.

Joy Leman lectures in Film, Television and Media Studies at the London College of Printing, The London Institute.

Loretta Loach is Vice-Chair of the Council of the Campaign for Press and Broadcasting Freedom. She is a freelance journalist.

Contributors

Gillian Skirrow teaches Film and Television Studies at the University of Strathclyde and was formerly an educational producer with Thames Television.

Angela Spindler-Brown works as an independent producer and teaches and writes on the media.

Sue Stoessl is Head of Marketing at Channel 4 Television.

Acknowledgments

Many people have contributed to this book. We would like especially to thank the authors of the individual essays for their efforts and encouragement. We are grateful to the many women, both inside and outside television, who have influenced the ideas, purpose and scope of the project. Our thanks to Philippa Brewster and Candida Lacey at Pandora Press for their editorial advice, David Child and John Woodward for their help throughout, and our friends and families for their constant support and patience.

Figures 5.1 and 5.2 © BBC Hulton Picture Library; Figure 5.3 © BBC; Figure 11.1 © BBC Enterprises Ltd; Figures 12.1, 12.2 and 12.3 © Thames TV; Figure 13.1 © Ms. and Steve Shapiro; Figure 13.2 © CBS Television. Figure 13.3 © Orion Television.

Introduction

This book has been compiled in order to fill a gap we feel has existed for far too long in the Media/Communication/Women's Studies field. Despite an encouraging growth in interest in women and the medium of television, there was no one book that brought together issues of women's employment, representation and viewing in relation to the small screen. Published work on the subject tends to be scattered over a wide number of sources and this may be inevitable given the interdisciplinary nature of television and media studies. We hope that by putting this collection of original essays under a single cover, we have brought the question of women and television into sharper focus. The book encompasses a number of topics and issues and the work indicates a diversity of theoretical and methodological perspectives. We have included essays by women practitioners to hear the views of women working in the industry. They offer insights and knowledge based on practical experience not always available to the rest of us. As editors, we have chosen to present a plurality of approaches in order to show the richness and range of women's writing on television and open up the way to further exploration and study. The essays relate primarily to British television culture although Margaret Gallagher's survey of new communications technology in relation to women does present a global picture, and Julie D'Acci's study of *Cagney and Lacey* concerns the production of a popular prime-time American TV series which enjoys international distribution.

The work presented emerges within the context of a developing feminist television criticism. From its beginnings, the women's liberation movement has reacted critically, often angrily, to what is sometimes rather loosely called 'sexism in the media'. Feminist activity within media organisations and Media Studies in

1

schools and colleges has been steadily responding to television programmes and programming policies and to the industry's employment practices which still discriminate against women. The involvement of women studying, teaching and working in television has opened up the question of their special relationship to the medium as a primary definer of social significance and cultural meanings. Recent research on women's genres, the manner in which we watch television, the 'flow' of TV programmes and the fragmentation of rhythms of text and reception all represent highly fruitful and legitimate lines of enquiry and assert a timely re-evaluation of women's culture and pleasures. The television soap opera and family melodrama have, in particular, attracted a good deal of criticial attention and a welcome body of writing exists elsewhere on these genres. There are important subjects which we would like to have included in this volume, for instance work about black women's relationship to television culture. In our search for contributions on studies of the representation and employment of women from the ethnic communities in television, we found that little work is currently being carried out in these areas. If women are to achieve an equal status in television the linked prejudices of racism and sexism have to be addressed. Overall, much work remains to be done to bring together the correspondences between women employed in television and the representations of women produced.

The book is divided into three sections. Part One 'Women and Communications Technology' deals broadly with the future and the developing technologies of cable, satellite and video. Part Two 'Programming Strategies', raises the question of women's programming, and Part Three 'On the Screen', deals more specifically with programmes. It is hard to be sanguine about the so-called communications revolution and what it means for women. Part One shows that, on the whole, women do not necessarily benefit from the new communications technology. Margaret Gallagher discusses the scale and global interconnected-ness of the new information and entertainment systems and suggests that powerful business conglomerates are unlikely to consider women's interests other than in strictly commercial terms. There are already examples of unregulated TV stations in Europe which transmit a basic diet of pornographic material. The new technology has also meant an increase in home-centred entertainment, the video cassette recorder potentially offering women more control and choice over the content and context of viewing. But, as Ann Gray shows, the meanings and pleasures of the home video are heavily circumscribed by existing family power relations. On a more public front, it is important to recognise the need to campaign in the light of changes resulting from new technology. Loretta Loach argues that women are in danger of losing what little ground they have gained in employment and conditions of service in the television industry. A watchful eye and positive action remain necessary strategies in a situation of rapid technological change, increased casualisation of labour and crisis management.

Debates about women's programming are hardly new, and Part Two opens with Joy Leman's fascinating picture of resistance to the idea of programmes for women in the early days of television. Using material gathered from the BBC Written Archives Centre she argues that then, as now, powerful economic, organisational and ideological constraints operate to influence the nature and content of programmes designed for women. Issues around women and Channel 4 are a feature of this Part. When the channel was set up, it brought what many people feel may have been the last public debate about programme content. Developments around cable and satellite are essentially about distribution, not programmes. Channel 4 went on air in November 1982 with its brief to innovate, experiment and produce programmes for audiences not catered for by ITV and many disenfranchised groups, including women, took heart. They felt that their views would finally be taken seriously and their interests and concerns catered for. In many respects Channel 4 is new and refreshing, but there are signs that its commitment to 'difference' is diminishing. Rosalind Coward accuses it of being half-hearted in its approach to women's programmes. She argues that whilst men's programmes are taken for granted, programmes especially addressed to women have so far been 'allowed to fail'. At the time of writing Channel 4 has just announced plans for a new women's magazine programme. It is still too soon to say if this will fare differently from its predecessors. Sue Stoessl, Head of Marketing at Channel 4, provides an inside view of programming policy and strategy. She writes that the channel aims to provide programmes in 'areas of interest' and that they have to be enjoyable for men as well as for women. Minority groups are not necessarily defined in terms of sex, age or ethnic origin. Helen Baehr and Angela

Spindler-Brown highlight the contradictions that exist between professionalism and feminism in relation to programme-making. They chart the history of *Broadside*, Channel 4's first women's current affairs series, and show the difficulties encountered in challenging existing production practices.

The contributions in 'On the Screen' deal with changes in imagery and representation and with struggles over the construction of the meanings of 'woman', particularly in drama production. Charlotte Brunsdon analyses the successful TV crime series *Widows* which represented a response to feminist critiques and made a bid to address the 'independent woman' in the audience. But the essay argues that the constraints of genre finally triumphed over attempts to produce different, popular and recognisable representations of women and ultimately destroyed some of the pleasures of the series. Gillian Skirrow approaches the question of meaning and reading the text through an examination of the performances and attitudes of the actresses in two police series with female protagonists. Using material gathered through interviews with the leading actresses in *Juliet Bravo* and *Widows*, she suggests that they were crucial in injecting feminism, even in a modified form, into the productions and that concessions made to the actresses derived partly from a respect for 'authenticity'. In the chapter 'Entering the arena', Jill Hyem describes her experiences as a writer for television and some of the difficulties she has encountered in writing strong parts for women. She met with resistance from male colleagues during the production of her successful series *Tenko*, which not only featured women centrally but also revived popular memories of women's contributions to the war effort in the 1940s. The police detective series *Cagney and Lacey* draws its inspiration from the women's movement and the male buddy movies of the 1970s. Julie D'Acci examines the way the series grapples with feminist issues within the limitations of commercial TV production in the United States. Within the sphere of actuality programming, there has been a significant increase in the number of women newsreaders seen on our television screens in recent years. The way they are dealt with by television is the subject of 'When a woman reads the news' which shows how the appearance of equality on the screen conceals the imposed limits of 'femininity' in the hard world of news reporting.

We hope that this collection of work will provide some new

insights into women and television. We hope, too, that it will encourage and extend the debates on the issues raised and contribute to both teaching and learning in the area.

1 Women and television: an overview

Gillian Dyer

Feminist television criticism is an emerging body of work which examines the representation of women on television, women's readings and spectatorship of television and related issues of employment and feminist production practices. It is concerned too with exploring the notion of feminine discourse and feminine pleasures in relation to television. It is being developed by women working within academic disciplines such as Media, Film and Cultural Studies and by the women's movement and feminist media practitioners. That television is an important source of insights into the beliefs and assumptions about women and their sexuality in contemporary society is axiomatic to this critique. Television provides entertainment and information, and as a discursive practice and producer of cultural meanings it is a major force in the production of dominant images of women. In addition, market research indicates that overall the majority of TV viewers in western cultures are women.

From its beginnings in the 1960s, the women's liberation movement identified the basic pattern of power that exists in the mass media. Men own and control the media and it is their ideas, viewpoints and values which dominate the systems of production and representation in broadcasting, the press and advertising. This power has not gone unchallenged. Women have reacted against the traditional representations which centre on women's domestic and sexual roles because they are limited and limiting; they undermine the way women think about themselves and also constrain how others think of them. Television, of all the media, seems to offer the most 'real' images. They are readily available, for the initial layout of the cost of a television set and a licence fee – often they appear to be 'live', conforming to 'real time' and are, for the most part, consumed within the domestic environment.

But this 'reality' is deceptive. Television does not present innocent, neutral pictures of the world; rather its views are selective, schematic and constructed. The women's movement understands the extent to which our consciousness is shaped by powerful, simplified images and has exerted some pressure on the media, in order to combat cultural stereotyping of women and their experience. Over the past two decades, feminist activity in media practice and in media studies has increased. There have been calls for equal opportunities in employment and a challenge mounted to discredit sexist content. Alternative images have been created which develop and expand women's consciousness of themselves instead of limiting it. The media has had to recognise the criticisms and demands of women. In some cases they have accommodated a women's perspective and women's issues; they have also seen the commercial and ideological potential of creating a new cultural stereotype: the 'new woman'. The 'new woman' has become the new media cliché overtaking the traditional domestic image of the 1950s. As Helen Baehr remarks, 'Female sexuality, often confused with female liberation, has become big business' (Baehr, 1980, p.31). One of the tasks of feminist media criticism, then, is to analyse the reconstruction and accommodation of feminism and feminist issues as well as the more outdated views of women.

Television is increasingly taking women seriously and there are a number of programmes, or types of programme, that feature women in a more central way. Even the women's liberation movement has become safe and been given a legitimacy in contrast to earlier, hysterical representations of 'women's libbers'. Women's issues have arrived on the media agenda – documentaries, discussion programmes and dramas on female topics such as infertility, cervical and breast cancer, rape, etc. The female audience is in some cases becoming recognised as a distinct grouping, and afternoon magazine programmes such as *Mavis on 4* often address a woman who is no longer satisfied with a diet of fashion, cookery and celebrity interview.

Yet there are sections of programming which stubbornly cling to degrading and trivialising views of women. For example, the game show *3–2–1* features a hostess who is dressed in little more than sequins and who has the non-job of escorting participants on and off stage. Sports programming is an area which is the preserve of men. Not only is it dominated by masculine sports and male commentators, it occupies a privileged position in the schedules. Sports coverage celebrates the male values of competition, toughness, endurance and physical prowess and, above all, the male body, but for the appreciation of the male viewer. Women's sporting activity is all but excluded from our screens because it doesn't fit into the mythic values of male sport. Sports commentators and reporters devalue women participants with their condescending and trivialising use of the term 'girls' to refer to mature and experienced athletes. Men are clearly targeted by the scheduling of television sports in their leisure times (i.e. at weekends) and, by and large, women are regarded as outsiders or a third party of the 'genre's' mode of address. They are involved neither in the rules/science of the game nor in the celebration of male values and physique. The development and application of new communication technologies indicate that there will be an increase in televised sports over the next decade.

Women have made significant advances in television in recent years in the sphere of factual production. However their increased visibility and activity have to be regarded as a mixed blessing. Female newsreaders and reporters have, it is true, emerged as an essential element of news programmes and women presenters often 'front' news bulletins. News and current affairs are still, however, the preserve of men, on and off screen. There are many more women who have influence in television than in the 1970s but their numbers are insignificant compared to the many male editors, producers and executives, and they generally remain isolated. It is also doubtful if the few high-flyers have influenced access and training at lower levels. News gathering is competitive and hierarchical – a job for the boys hunting in packs – and deeply implicated in the male worlds of politics, economics, business and industry. In terms of styles of reporting and allocation of items, the news is male. No wonder that women find the going tough within news production and that many female viewers feel alienated by the current form and content of news broadcasts (Hobson, 1980). Feminist critics regard the increased visibility of women, particularly on serious programming, as tokenism or 'window dressing'. The problem of increased recognition and representation goes beyond counting how many more females are on the screen. As Helen Baehr has noted, 'There is all the difference in the world between encouraging more women to become media professionals – "window-dressing the set" – and organising a real feminist challenge against media structures and professional practices which reproduce the subordinate role of women' (Baehr, 1981). More female newsreaders does not mean that issues of sexism and oppression will be raised and challenged or that the women's movement will be adequately and fairly treated. Television news coverage of Greenham Common and the women's peace movement, analysed in the Glasgow Media Group's work, *War and Peace News*, was far from neutral or objective.[1] It is also necessary to point out that in Britain, at least, the women newsreaders on the national bulletins are young, conventionally attractive and, with the exception of Moira Stewart, white. As Anna Coote and Beatrix Campbell so trenchantly put it, 'Men can be short fat, ageing, bald, have misshapen noses and crooked teeth, warts and specs and straggly beards – and still spend hours in front of television cameras' (Coote and Campbell, 1982, p.198).

Changes in the presentation of women have also appeared in the fictional sphere, and in TV commercials there has been a proliferation of the 'new woman' stereotype to add to the previous advertising stereotypes of dutiful, caring mother and glamorous, efficient hostess. While this new image may be more superficially in tune with reality and, it could be argued, is a source of identitification and pleasure for women, it is one that is contradictory. The liberated woman is strongly marked by signs of her femininity and sexuality – she is well made-up, her clothes are up-to-date, she works outside the home but more often than not she appears in the context of consumption rather than production. She is active, lively and sexy. Although she appears competent and independent, her liberation and well being are strongly equated with material consumption. This dynamic is of course at the core of the advertisement's repressive work: to create an ideal body image which sets in motion our desire to consume. And this more liberated stereotype again puts us under the microscope of self-scrutiny and the male gaze. The advertisers have put a lot of effort into accommodating women's liberation; they clearly see that there is a potential market in the liberated and upwardly mobile woman. Equally, they have sought, in some cases, to ridicule or to redress the effects of the women's movement. This process of negating or defusing challenges to historically dominant meanings of gender – 'recuperation' – is not of course confined to advertising. A similar concept is Barthes's

9

notion of inoculation. It is a process by which the dominant ideology is able to ensure its continuance by neutralising threats from oppositional ideologies, through acknowledging some of their elements in an apparent show of tolerance; as Barthes has said, 'One immunises the contents of the collective imagination by means of a small inoculation of acknowledged evil; one then protects it against the risk of a general subversion' (Barthes, 1972, p.150).

The new, successful woman in commercials does little by way of examining the basic social power structures and limits the difference, with regard to the representation of women, to previously defined male positions. A similar process can be found in the use of role-reversal, where men are shown doing the cooking, bathing babies, etc. A number of advertisements try a different tack and romanticise women, thus working to 'compensate' (although not intentionally) for lack of opportunities or lack of power in more 'real' public spheres. The romanticisation of motherhood is a well-known feature of ads for household products, patent medicines, etc. The needs and desires of women are depicted in terms of her nurturing and caring role within the family. A mother is complete if her children have gleaming, white clothes and the dishes sparkle. She is shown in soft, dreamy focus in the bosom of the ideal family.

In the sphere of popular drama, the demand for more women's parts has resulted in a gradual increase in the number of women as central characters in the police and crime genre. This development, although in many ways refreshing, raises new contradictions in the portrayal of power and gender for, ironically, 'strong' women policewomen, lawyers, etc. are invariably shown enforcing the patriarchal laws which oppress them. Women police series are not necessarily progressive and the 'feminism' is usually personalised and depoliticised. For example, the Cagney and Lacey characters in the series of that name play engaging female detectives but they represent, in the words of Elizabeth Cagan, 'a "safe" outlet for "fantasies of liberation"' (Cagan, 1978, p.6). The 1980s have seen a number of such series with heroic women supplanting heroic men and this indicates the way that the media have incorporated certain aspects of the woman question into the dominant culture. But this 'separatist strategy' (Skirrow, 1985) does not question the aesthetics and conventions of the male crime series through which meanings are in part realised. In

Britain, the series *Juliet Bravo* is significant in this respect; it leaves undisturbed the framework of male police structures of the crime series and does not enable the questioning of women's relationship to the law and consensus morality.[2] It was introduced at a time when women's liberation had become a safe media topic and when the image of policing was in need of reassessment. The American and the British versions of the action police series had been criticised for their alleged excessive violence and the BBC, at least, felt that police series needed some softening up. *Juliet Bravo* was in part a response to the 'unholy alliance' of the women's movement, the National Viewers' and Listeners' Association and the Police Federation. Shifting police work and the ideology of law and order from the male to the female was in part a response to the climate of the time. It also worked to portray the police in compassionate and caring terms, at a time when there was some cynicism about police methods in the wider society. The idea of a woman-centred police series with family appeal also fulfilled the institutional function of giving an old formula a new angle.

One of the most distinctive television forms, and one that has attracted feminist critical work, is that of the long-running, continuous serial. Several recent studies have looked at the TV soap opera as a woman's genre, focusing particularly on the way their narratives are constructed around women and the female point of view, but also raising the question of audience readings, gendered spectatorship and female pleasures. Much early critical work on narrative stemming from textual semiotics, psychoanalysis and audience research, was predicated on a passive and powerless viewing subject. Semiotics and psychoanalysis were concerned to show how meaning is structured in the text and how the viewer is drawn into the text's subject positions. In terms of the text, narrative, in a novel or a film, is organised around equilibrium, disequilibrium, resolution – an initial situation is disrupted and the narrative works to restore balance and harmony through the resolution and tidying up of tensions and contradictions. Classic psychoanalytic film theory suggests that female discourses/female sexuality are the threats which disturb the narrative and it is these which must be contained through narrative closure. The reader or viewer of a narrative is involved in the pursuit of resolution and the closure, when the initial problematic is rendered harmless, is satisfying. The effect of the narrative is not only pleasure but also

11

creates a sense of inevitability: the closure seems to be predestined, tidy and without contradiction. Some feminist film theorists have in the recent past argued that classic narrative films are organised around the male spectator or male gaze, that the female is the object of look/desire and that a female subject position is impossible. Cinema spectatorship, it is suggested, involves masculine identification for spectators of either gender. Other feminist theorists have argued that while in a patriarchy female desire and a female point of view are difficult, they are, on some occasions, contradictory. For example, the plot, characters and visual discourse of women's pictures such as melodrama are characterised as excessive and indicate the genre's tendency 'to [pose] problems for itself which it can scarcely contain' (Cook quoted in Kuhn, 1984, p.20).

The issue of female subjectivity and narrative theory's stress on resolution and coherence are important in the consideration of soap opera. Classic narrative theory cannot, for instance, account for tensions and contradictions that remain unresolved, particularly as regards audiences of different gender. Nor can it account for narratives that do not close, like the long-running soap opera on TV. Soap opera offers the viewer a far more open structure through a complex organisation of time, temporary resolutions and a proliferation of enigmas. Christine Geraghty in her discussion of *Coronation Street* as a continuous serial has shown that the soap opera:

> provides us with the feeling of an unwritten future while giving
> necessary access to the past. We are constantly left wondering what
> will happen next – occasionally with a real cliffhanger. It presents us
> with endless variations on regular patterns and provides a range of
> characters which is both varied and limited. (Geraghty, 1981, p.26)

Other writers have argued that the form of the domestic soap opera, and the glossy melodramatic versions like *Dallas* and *Dynasty*, in their offering of temporary resolutions and by leaving contradictions unresolved, overturn classic narrative structure. Jane Feuer, for instance, argues that television melodramas offer a potentially progressive form because the multiple plot structures do not allow for clear-cut ideological positions and constructions. Marriage, for instance, is rarely viewed as a happy ending – an excuse for narrative closure. Rather we know that every marriage is headed for divorce.

Since no action is irreversible, every ideological position may be countered by its opposite. Thus the family dynasty sagas may be read as either critical of the dominant ideology of capitalism or as belonging to it, depending upon the position from which the reader comes at it. (Feuer, 1984, p.15)

The continuing uncertainty specific to the genre creates a kind of freedom for viewers to construct their own readings of the text, sometimes against the grain. The Joan Collins character in *Dynasty* is interesting in this respect, since as a strong, beautiful and scheming woman at the centre of the drama who initiates much of the action, she invites admiration and a certain subversive pleasure as well as providing a villainess and a foil to the weaker Krystle. Tania Modleski is similarly optimistic about the potential of soap operas to create a feminist aesthetic, construct feminine subject positions and transcend patriarchal modes of subjectivity. Her argument is that the characteristic narrative form of soap operas, i.e. endless deferred resolutions and climaxes, connect with women's work in the home and the kinds of rhythms women experience in their daily lives, where there is also no resolution, constant repetition and interruption. The soap opera is constructed around multiple plot lines and offers a number of identifications, mini-problems and their resolutions. Thus no one story is absorbing for too long and this reflects the state of constant distraction that the housewife has to cope with from children, other adults, the telephone, the doorbell, preparing meals, etc. Soap operas bring to the foreground skills typically associated with women, such as those which involve interpersonal relations, personal and domestic crises. They 'train' women to become 'ideal readers' not just of the text but of people. Through the constant, claustrophobic use of close-up shots, they help train women to 'read' other people, to be sensitive to their (unspoken) feelings. The use of the close-up, Modleski says, 'contrasts sharply with other popular forms aimed at masculine visual pleasure, which is often centred on the fragmentation and fetishisation of the female body' (Modleski, 1982, p.99). Thus the construction of a female point of view and the validation of female subject positions give the soaps their appeal and also their pleasure. Although not progressive, they do offer some opposition to patriarchal modes of subjectivity.

Charlotte Brunsdon's work on the British soap opera *Crossroads* extends Modleski's work by putting less stress on the formal properties of the text and looking at the social and cultural context of consumption. She draws a distinction between the subject position proposed by the soap opera *Crossroads* and the social subject who may or may not take up the position. For Brunsdon the spectator addressed by soap opera is constructed within culture, rather than by representation. Viewers must possess a certain cultural capital or cultural codes to draw on in order to make sense of the soap opera. In other words the spectator must be familiar with the plots and characters of a serial and with the genre, but also have access to wider cultural competences of marriage, family and personal life. She states:

> The ideological problematic of soap opera – the frame or field in which meanings are made . . . – is that of 'personal life'; more particularly personal life in its everyday realisation through personal relationships . . . constituted primarily through representations of romances, families . . . it is the sphere of women's 'intimate oppression'. (Brunsdon, 1981, p.34)

The text implies and requires a feminine reader who must be skilled in the 'rules' of romance, marriage and family life. These moral and ideological frameworks which inform the character's dialogue are aimed at 'constructing moral consensus about the conduct of personal life' (Brunsdon, *op. cit.*, p.35).

In her critique of *Coronation Street*, Terry Lovell argues that while we should not be too optimistic about the revolutionary potential of some forms of popular culture, a series like *Coronation Street* is situated ambiguously and in contradictory ways in relation to feminism and patriarchy. It is a relatively 'open' text. It offers women a validation and celebration of those interests and concerns which are theirs, and through its highlighting of strong, middle-aged independent women it represents 'an important extension of the range of imagery which is offered to women within popular forms, and as such, is welcome' (Lovell, 1981, p.52). It remains to be seen if the newer soap operas, *EastEnders* and *Brookside*, with their large and heterogeneous casts and where women seem to be seen primarily in relation to their husbands and children, can claim to address the female audience in quite the same way.[3]

It is perhaps easy to be pessimistic about the representations of women in mainstream television and to wish for a greater and more rapid involvement of women in the industry's creative and decision-making areas. Certainly, the women's movement has exerted pressure from within and without television, so that there is a more conscious and concerted effort to tackle inequality of opportunity and a greater willingness to include women's issues in programmes. Equally important are those television narratives, some of which embody a feminist critique, which allow some play with conventions and meanings and open up the possibility of feminist readings. Critical writing on soap operas has also shown the polysemic possibilities of women's readings of television and while the genre is still 'rubbished' (and sneakily watched) by men, the recognition is there, that it is an important aspect of women's culture. The rapid expansion in the use of the home video recorder also opens up interesting possibilities for women. The context of viewing is changing and there is potentially a greater choice of texts available. While these have their negative aspects, and by and large women's use of video is circumscribed by the family context, there are possibilities for women to negotiate viewing and control the reception of video. However, the gains in terms of increased recruitment into television and a greater equality and wider variety of representations of women on television must be set against the drawbacks: the spectre of more privatised broadcasting systems and an increasingly timid and retrenched public broadcasting service.

Notes

1 See Glasgow Media Group (1985), chapter 6, for an analysis of TV news coverage of Greenham Common and the women's peace movement.
2 See Gillian Skirrow's (1985) essay on '*Widows*' and the series' challenge to the constraints of crime fiction, its progressiveness and its different kinds of pleasure for women. She also makes the point that it was the first TV production to raise questions about the representation of women 'out of the margins and into the mainstream' (p.184).
3 See Christine Geraghty's (1983) discussion on women in relation to their place in the 'new realism' of *Brookside*.

References

Baehr, H. (ed.) (1980), *Women and Media*, Oxford, Pergamon Press.
Baehr, H. (1981), 'Women's employment in British television: programming the

future?', *Media, Culture and Society*, vol.3, pp.125–34.

Barthes, Roland (1972), *Mythologies*, Jonathan Cape.

Brunsdon, C. (1981), 'Crossroads: notes on a soap opera', *Screen*, vol.22, no.4, pp.32–7.

Cagan, E. (1978), 'The selling of the women's movement', *Social Policy*, no.8, pp.4–12.

Coote, A. and Campbell, B. (1982), *Sweet Freedom*, London, Picador.

Feuer, Jane (1984), 'Melodrama, serial form and television today', *Screen*, vol.25, no.1, pp.4–16.

Geraghty, C. (1981), 'The continuous serial: a definition', in R. Dyer *et al.* (eds), (1981), *Coronation Street*, Television Monograph, London, British Film Institute, pp.9–26.

Geraghty, C. (1983), '*Brookside* – no common ground', *Screen*, vol.24, nos 4–5, pp.137–41.

Glasgow Media Group (1985), *War and Peace News*, Milton Keynes, Open University Press.

Hobson, D. (1980), 'Housewives and the mass media' in *Culture, Media, Language*, London, Hutchinson.

Kuhn, A. (1984), 'Women's genres' in *Screen*, vol.25, no.1, pp.18–28.

Lovell, T. (1981), 'Ideology and *Coronation Street*' in Dyer, *op.cit.*, pp.40–52.

Modleski, T. (1982), *Loving with a Vengeance*, Hamden, Connecticut, Shoe String Press.

Skirrow, G. (1985), '*Widows*' in M. Alvarado and J. Stewart (eds) (1985), *Made for Television: Euston Films Limited*, London, British Film Institute.

PART ONE
Women and Communications Technology

2 Redefining the communications revolution

Margaret Gallagher

> The twentieth century marks the onset of the communications revolution. The human environment has been transformed by a panoply of electronic technologies. World satellite systems now make distance and time irrelevant. . . . Networks of telephones, telex, radio and television have exponentially increased the density of human contact. (*The Communications Revolution*, Frederick Williams, 1982, pp.230–31)

> *Communications revolution*: . . . far from entering a brave new world, many women find themselves in a false dawn, facing new and unfamiliar forms of old stereotypes . . . and, as new fields develop, struggling not only to gain a foothold but even to hold their own. (*A Feminist Dictionary*, Cheris Kramarae and Paula Treichler, 1985, p.102)

For at least the past decade, it seems, the 'communications revolution' has been just around the corner. 'The wired nation' and 'the electronic cottage', however familiar they may have become as concepts, retain an element of futuristic fantasy – Utopian or Orwellian, depending on one's interpretation of technological and economic trends. Especially in Britain, where discussions about cable and satellite development seem to have dragged on interminably, the only really visible sign of disturbance to a pattern of television broadcasting laid down thirty years ago has been the introduction of Channel 4, and programmes first aired in the 1950s and 1960s (*Panorama*, *Coronation Street*) still occupy regular time-slots. The average viewer might seem justified in concluding that the communications revolution remains, in the late 1980s, more a media construct, directed by vested interests, than a reality.

Seen from elsewhere – the United States, Canada, Japan or

indeed much of continental Europe – the picture looks quite different. Take the Netherlands. In the early 1970s, Anthony Smith wrote of Dutch broadcasting that 'apart from Britain, scarcely any country is more boastful of the system of organisation and control it has evolved, in many ways justly so' (Smith, 1973, p.268). Public service broadcasting in the Netherlands has traditionally been renowned for its openness (organisations with 150,000 members are assured access to broadcasting time on one of the two television channels) and its controlled commercialism (advertising is concentrated in blocks before and after news programmes, amounting to about thirty minutes daily, with none permitted on Sundays). Yet 'by the end of the 1970s and the beginning of the 1980s . . . neither new technological developments nor commercial influences could be kept out any longer' so that, little over a decade after Smith's assessment, according to a recent analysis, 'writing about broadcasting . . . in the Netherlands is like contributing to yesterday's paper' (Brants, 1985, pp.114,104). With well over 12,000 independent cable systems in operation and 80 per cent of homes connected, the Netherlands is – after Belgium – the second most densely cabled country in Europe. There is also an increasing supply of programmes via satellite from British-based transnational commercial stations such as Sky Channel and Music Box. Twenty per cent of Dutch homes have video recorders, and about 10 per cent of all television sets now in use are equipped for teletext (Bardoel, 1985; Brants, op.cit.; Brants and Jankowski, 1985).

The pattern is similar throughout Western Europe. The Commission of the European Communities estimates that by 1989 there will be ninety satellite and cable channels in its twelve member states, in addition to the existing networks. According to the Commission £6.6 billion is being invested in new cable developments in West Germany, £8 billion in France, and £2.7 billion in Britain. Sky Channel, which introduced commercial satellite television to Europe in 1982, by 1986 was reaching five million viewers in twelve countries. In some of these, for example the Scandinavian countries, national broadcasting systems, on which advertising is not permitted, are now having to compete with commercial programming over which there is little or no national control.

Almost imperceptibly in Britain, and with little of the public debate which surrounded the introduction of the fourth channel, the television landscape has been changing since the early 1980s. The Thatcher government's 1983 White Paper on cable development adopted a market-led, 'lightly regulated' policy towards the expansion of British broadcasting. As a result, by the middle of 1986 seven new broadband (multi-channel) cable systems were in operation and more than a million households – an all-time high – were connected to independent cable services. Twelve satellite television stations, with programmes originating daily from the United States, France, Belgium, Switzerland, Luxembourg, Ireland, West Germany, Italy and the Netherlands, as well as from Britain itself, were available to these cable operators. The announcement of the merger between Music Box and Superchannel marked the definite entry of the ITV companies into the new cable market. The privatised British Telecom had become the largest single provider of satellite transmission in Europe, had shares in four of the new British broadband cable systems and – with its new film channel, Star – had begun to move into programme services. Direct broadcasting by satellite (DBS) came closer to realisation with the re-opening by the IBA (following withdrawal of the BBC from a joint venture) of bidding for the operating franchise. Radical change in the financing and control of British broadcasting was called for by the 1986 Peacock Report, whose recommendations reflected a belief in commercial forces and privatisation as a way towards a 'full broadcasting market . . . in which viewers and listeners can express preferences directly . . . as consumers'.

Development of new communication technologies is frequently justified in terms of their presumed benefits to users – increased choice, encouragement of interactive and participatory approaches, reflection of minority and community interests. The technological cornucopia thus appears to promise a new world, in which electronic democracy is assured by the availability of thirty or so television channels which, between them, will offer 'something for everyone'. The magic carpet of the communications revolution has, according to enthusiasts, the power to transport us to this world. But just where is this magic carpet leading women? Are we in fact 'going along for the ride'? Or are we simply being taken for one?

Communication developments in context

The 'communications revolution' is being shaped by a powerful array of inter-related technological, economic and political influences. In the first place, technological convergence is dissolving the barriers between the various media. The familiar conceptual and analytical categories of mass media research, based on an understanding of the various communication media – for example, television, film, print, telephone – as separate entities, each providing its own distinct service, are becoming rapidly redundant. In the new broadband telecommunications systems, the same 'wire' can deliver via our television screens not just traditional television programming, but individualised subscriber programming (pay-TV), videotex news, consumer catalogue and reference information, as well as specialised services such as electronic mailing, electronic shopping, home banking, security alarm systems, and so on. In other words, the television screen is becoming the common delivery station around which a wide range of formerly separate business, information and communications enterprises are converging.

Consequently, it is becoming impossible to speak of 'the future of television' except as part of the wider future of information technology. The new 'information economy' is seen by almost all Western governments as the key to industrial growth. Thus Britain's decision to foster the development of cable television is simply a means to a greater end, which is 'to develop and exploit the most modern telecommunications infrastructure to meet the needs of commerce and industry while simultaneously meeting the social and domestic needs of all parts of the country' (Home Office, 1983). British broadcasting policy has now become part of a broader discussion which encompasses consideration of industrial expansion, employment and consumerism.

The development of information and communication technologies in Europe since the early 1980s is inescapably, and somewhat paradoxically, linked with economic crisis and recession. The new technologies are seen as a key to industrial recovery in terms of modernisation, international competitiveness, and jobs. In 1982 Kenneth Baker, then Minister for Information Technology, spoke of the development of the cable television network in Britain as being part of a technological revolution equivalent in significance to the development of the railway network in Victorian England. New technologies are also part of a fundamental restructuring which has been taking place in most European economies over the same period. New strategies of rationalisation, computerisation and automation of production processes and jobs, particularly in the service sector, are part of what has come to be known as 'the flexibilisation of labour', often a euphemism for shedding jobs, cutting real wages, increasing inequality and job insecurity, and reducing social security protection. Women are the principal losers in this process. For example, Hacker (1979) found that technological change at American Telephone & Telegraph (the equivalent of British Telecom) in the late 1970s resulted in 13,000 new jobs for men, while 22,000 women were made redundant. Eurostat (the statistical agency of the European Economic Community) figures for March to August 1986 show a fall in male unemployment, but a static female unemployment rate. The indications are that women constitute the largest section among the 'new poor' of Britain, France, West Germany and the United States (Mies, 1986; Scott, 1984).

This phenomenon is linked to a 'roll-back strategy', itself prompted by the economic recession, in which government policy re-emphasises the family, the ideology of motherhood, and women's responsibility for housework and for the care of children, the elderly and the chronically sick. The pro-family movement rejects the feminist call for governments (at the state level) and men (at the individual level) to recognise their responsibilities in relation to child-rearing and home-making and returns the family to private territory outside the realm of public policymaking. 'Nothing is more intimate or mysterious than the family. . . . Family policy belongs at home' (Samuelson, 1986). The public resanctification and mystification of the family in ideological terms is, of course, in harmony with a great deal of standard media output which has traditionally depicted family life from a highly idealised perspective (Gallagher, 1981). It is likely that new 'market-led' media developments will reinforce this ideology. According to Silvio Berlusconi, who has a near monopoly of private, commercial television in Italy, 'Commercial television is a little like the advertising which nourishes it . . . an attractive fable, where everybody is beautiful, everything is elegant, and all the children love father and mother and are loved

23

in return. . . . This philosophy is fundamental to everything I do' (Clark and Riddell, 1986, p.13). Berlusconi who, according to Federico Fellini, 'even packages women as if they were hamburgers' (*ibid.*), has already acquired television interests in France, Luxembourg and Spain, and is on record as having pan-European satellite ambitions which include Britain.

An economic corollary of pro-family ideology is public expenditure cuts, in social and welfare provision, leisure facilities and in public information and advice services (Golding and Murdock, 1986). As the home increasingly becomes the site for these activities, exploitation of the new communication technologies opens up ever more possibilities for the development of home-based commercial operations, from leisure (home video, pay-TV), to information and professional services (banking, shopping), to work itself (teleworking). The pressures which such developments will create, particularly on women, have barely been recognised. On the one hand, the isolation presently experienced by women within the privatised sphere of the home is likely to increase. On the other, the expansion of the home into a work-station and a leisure centre will surely make additional demands on women as they cater to the requirements of other home-based family members.

Japan's current scheme to develop a 'Teletopia' rests on the concept of an 'information society' organised around video and computer-based systems and services (videotex news, teleshopping and banking, teleschool and teleworking, even telemedicine). While perhaps revolutionary in a technological sense, such communication developments ensure that 'woman's place is still in the home, to which she is now tied not only by the invisible bonds [of social pressures] but also by ultra-modern optical fibres' (Crombers and Sangregoria, 1981). Not surprisingly, more than 60 per cent of Japanese housewives are opposed to the idea of their husbands 'teleworking' from home (Hartley, 1986). However, as we shall see, such findings are likely to be outweighed by the presumed industrial and economic rewards to be reaped from technological development.

Cost and design of the new communications media

If the range of choice – in entertainment, information and services – on offer from the new media is theoretically almost limitless, it is in practice circumscribed by one major prerequisite: the ability to pay. Information is becoming a commodity, and an expensive one. For example, the sophisticated interactive cable systems with which Japan has been experimenting are said to require a monthly subscription fee at least ten times above the cost of the standard broadcast licence (Ito, 1984). Incentives are thus necessary to create a 'market' for the new services. In Britain, operators of the new broadband cable systems generally use a 'tiered' price structure to attract subscribers: for example Windsor TV began transmissions in December 1985 with a four-tier service, of which the basic package (comprising Sky Channel, Home Video Channel, Lifestyle and Music Box) cost £7.50 a month. Windsor claims that 55 per cent of 'basic' subscribers subsequently upgrade to one of the 'premium' tiers. To receive all eleven channels offered by Windsor the subscriber has to pay £20.95 monthly – over four times the cost of access to traditional broadcast programming (Matthias, 1986).

Given the costs involved, the new video technologies and television-based information services appeal primarily to the socio-economic elite in Britain (Golding and Murdock, 1986). In Spain, Taiwan and the United States, research shows that the typical user is young, well-educated, affluent, white and, of course, male (Alonso, 1986; Wang, 1986; Dozier and Rice, 1984). The economic differential between the two sexes, however, only partly explains why men are the main users of the new communication technologies. Design is another reason. The new media reflect a predominantly male view of the world, in terms of content priorities and audience disposition.

The computer-based video technologies are patently oriented towards male-dominated areas of life. Video games, initially marketed as a way of introducing children to computing, have been closely linked with the promotion of militarism. In the United States, the Pentagon has spent $2–3 million developing games for use in recruitment and training for the armed forces (see Mosco, 1982, pp.100–101). Video game content – largely violent action – is thus designed by males for males (Rice and Williams, 1984, pp.66–8). Videotex too, originally seen as a technology which 'would allow all points of view to be brought to all' (Mosco, op. cit., p.76), has inevitably developed into a male-controlled system. Male 'information providers' supply services which are primarily of interest to other men. In France there has been one attempt to establish a service specifically for women: Ellétel, launched in 1984 by Agence Femmes Information (AFI). It originally included items not provided by other French videotex (Minitel) services, and which AFI felt would appeal directly to women: information on women's rights and health, a baby-sitting service, consumer data, a swap-shop. All these have been subsequently dropped. The basic problem is that, although Ellétel does attract more women than other videotex services, the majority of users (at least 60 per cent) are still men. To survive commercially, Ellétel has had to concentrate on items which its predominantly male subscribers will pay for.

Design and commercial factors also work against women's interests in the new satellite and cable television systems. One of the largest-ever experiments in the use of satellite communication was launched in India in 1975. The Satellite Instructional Television Experiment (SITE) lasted for one year, bringing entertainment, information and educational messages to 2,340 remote villages but research indicates that, in various ways, SITE had privileged men (Gore, 1983). Programmes were scheduled at times when most women were unable to watch, either because they were too busy, or because their families would not permit them. Programme content reflected a male view of reality: for example, the agricultural programmes were addressed almost exclusively to men, ignoring the fact that women were heavily involved in agricultural work. Programmes intended specifically for women were of poor quality in terms of content and presentation, revealing 'a great poverty of thought' which contrasted sharply with 'the giant strides made in space technology' through SITE (Kalwachwala, 1986, p.89).

The SITE experiment illustrated two fundamental obstacles to the development of communications technology along lines which might benefit women. The first is the way in which beliefs about the nature and composition of the female audience lead to a programme schedule which helps to 'prove' that women-oriented material is of marginal interest and popularity. According to Gary Davey, head of television services at Sky Channel, 'family structures and lifestyle patterns within them vary little from country to country' (Davey, 1985, p.46). Since Sky transmits to countries as different as Sweden (where for example, women are 46 per cent of the paid labour force) and the Netherlands (where only 30 per cent of the labour force is female), this is an extraordinary statement. Yet it is on this kind of assumption that Sky bases its policy of programme 'stripping' (i.e. offering an episode of the same programme at the same time daily). So Sky schedules programmes for 'women' between 1 pm and 2 pm but not, for example, between 10.30 pm and 11.30 pm when it assumes that 'adult men' will be watching (and presumably that 'women', whether adult or not, will be in bed). Audience categorisation along these lines is also incorporated into the programme schedules of the new British cable systems. Windsor TV transmits Lifestyle (the 'women's channel') in the mornings, despite research showing that 'many [viewers] confessed they were never at home' at that time (Matthias, 1986, p.41). Predictably, the research also found Lifestyle least 'popular' among the channels offered by Windsor TV.

The second problem is the tendency to concentrate on technological development rather than women's needs: a recurrent feature of the communications revolution. For example, current Japanese ambitions to develop 'New Media Communities' and 'Teletopia' (Hartley, 1986) were preceded by two now-famous experimental projects, Tama CCIS (Community Cable Interactive System) and Hi-OVIS (Highly Interactive Visual Information Service). The daytime audience for both projects consisted on the one hand of women and children at home, and on the other of local government offices and businesses. For the women, a most popular aspect was the television camera installed in each household. This helped break down the isolation they felt, allowing them to see and speak to their neighbours through the television set, and even to make new friends. That finding, although surprising, was considered unimportant by the (male) researchers and designers involved. They were interested in, and continued to provide, specialised information services which were favoured by the local business community (and which allowed the development of national telecommunications, computer and electronics industries) but which the women found of much less value (Crombers and Sangregoria, 1981).

Production and editorial control in the new media

If overall planning and design of the new media systems is largely outside women's control, what of programme content? In the traditional television industries, women fill only a tiny minority of senior production and editorial positions (Gallagher, 1984). It is often argued that new communication technologies – particularly cable television with its supposed local, community dimension – will offer women better jobs and more influence than the long-established systems. But there is no evidence that this is happening. On the contrary, the first – and so far only – state-by-state survey of employment in the US cable industry found women in only 15 per cent of posts in the top four job categories in cable, compared with 21 per cent of such jobs in broadcast television (Engsberg, 1982).

Recent cable developments in Britain promise little likelihood of access for women, or for local and community groups in general. British multi-channel cable operators must carry the national broadcast services but are under no obligation 'to make any other particular programme services available to their customers' (Home Office, 1983, para.233). Although 'the range and diversity of the services proposed' (*ibid.*, para.65) is one of the criteria used by the Cable Authority in granting franchises, the government's assertion that diversity and quality of service will 'best be encouraged' by leaving such matters to the market (Hollins, 1984, p.284) diminishes the prospect of anything beyond minimal investment in basic technical facilities for locally originated material. For example, in its first year of operation the single concession of Windsor TV to 'local programming' was to provide, alongside its eleven 'entertainment' channels, a single text channel giving details of local events. The introduction of a local news programme was a 'possibility' for 1987, although Windsor's head of sales was 'dogmatic' that this would 'only be done on a shoestring basis' (Matthias, 1986, p.44).

If cable developments promise women little hope of increased access to television production and editorial control, satellite prospects look even worse. It is doubtful whether even the 'public service' applications of satellite technology will offer women scope to develop programming which challenges established definitions of reality.

The Washington-based Women's Institute for Freedom of the Press did successfully organise international teleconferences by satellite during two of the Conferences of the United Nations Decade for Women: in 1980 between Copenhagen and six US cities, using facilities of the US Corporation for Public

Broadcasting; in 1985 between Nairobi and three US cities, using facilities provided under INTELSAT's Project Share. Both exercises, while important technical achievements, were limited by lack of access to full broadcast services: in order to participate, women had to assemble at local public television stations. Moreover, the content of the teleconferences was surprisingly muted, sticking to areas such as health, education and training, and avoiding the highly charged political issues which dominated the Conferences themselves.

Reluctance to become embroiled in controversial questions may have stemmed from an earlier, unsuccessful attempt to gain satellite access. In 1977, the National Aeronautics and Space Administration (NASA) granted official 'experimenter' status to the National Women's Agenda, a coalition of over one hundred US women's organisations, which was seeking to establish a satellite communications network for women. An agreement was reached between the Agenda, NASA and the Public Service Satellite Consortium (PSSC) to provide a demonstration of the possibilities offered by satellite communication at the Agenda's annual conference in March 1978, using the Canadian/American Communications Technology Satellite (CTS). The Agenda's subsequent treatment by both NASA and PSSC, and its 'discovery of the depth of contempt for and disinterest in women, of the extent of fear and misunderstanding of the rights of our constituencies, and of the wanton abuse of position' in both agencies (*Media Report to Women*, 1978, p.7) makes salutary reading. Finally, a month before the planned demonstration, the Agenda was forced off the satellite when NASA made it clear that discussion of abortion and lesbianism would be unacceptable. The experience was 'an invaluable educational tool for the Agenda', which concluded it 'could never seriously contemplate the successful completion of a full-fledged experiment [in satellite communication] without major changes in the institutions with which we must deal' (*op. cit.*, p.4).

In terms of commercial satellite systems, entry costs are prohibitive. The consortium selected to launch and operate the UK DBS system will have to find an estimated £250–£450 million annually. The 'new' actors in satellite television systems and programme services will be, in fact, the existing media moguls – major publishers, electronics manufacturers, advertising interests, film companies and the telecommunications industry. The five consortia bidding for the UK DBS franchise in 1986 contained many familiar names: Rupert Murdoch, Tiny Rowland, the Pearson Group, the Virgin Group, Saatchi, Columbia Pictures, as well as Australian businessmen Robert Holmes à Court and Alan Bond. The 'expansion' of new media opportunities is actually being appropriated by an exclusive club, 'with excessively high entry fees, exceedingly few members and exceptionally large benefits' (Ferguson, 1986, p.58). Judged on past performance, none of the club's members can be expected to use their new programming opportunities with the interests of women in mind.

Content developments in the new communication media

There is little doubt that the current profit-oriented exploitation of the new and existing media, financed by private capital, is changing the nature of European television. Patrick Cox, managing director of Sky Channel, certainly thinks so. 'Typically, European television has been public-service television with commercials in it. What's happening is the emergence of proper commercial television with a commercial television ethic' (Schrage and Vise, 1986, p.17). The 'commercial television ethic' provides two basic alternatives: new programme services must be either supported by advertising, or paid for by the viewers. Each alternative inevitably has implications for the kind of television content we can expect.

Modern developments in cable and satellite broadcasting will drastically expand the possibilities of reaching, and selling to, new and more distant audiences, across national borders, at all times of day and night. Among the interests represented by the UK DBS bidders, it is informative to see the appearance of Saatchi & Saatchi, Britain's biggest advertising agency and the eighth largest in the world. Their bid for a stake in satellite television illustrates clearly the type of relationship between content and advertising we may expect in the new programme services. The media have forged a link between advertising and women since the end of the last century, when J. Walter Thompson decided that women's magazines were the most efficient and effective means of reaching a vast market. In the 1930s, following publication of Christine Frederick's book *Selling Mrs Consumer*, in which the concept of the 'consumer society' first emerged, radio soap operas assumed the two-fold function, later adapted by television, of selling household products while confirming the housewife in her household tasks by offering emotional distraction. The new media, in their turn, 'sell' women (particularly 'up-scale' women) to advertisers of consumer goods. For example, potential advertisers on the US satellite service Daytime (now the Leisure Channel), can be assured that 'The Daytime woman is a family woman in the active buying years. . . . She spends 31 per cent more on grocery/household items than the national average' (Hollins, 1984, p.160).

The new media offer, indeed 'sell', new ways of delivering the advertising message. The 1984 Cable and Wireless Act opened the door to sponsored programmes for the first time in British broadcasting history. This encourages a quite different advertising approach from that possible through the 30-second spot commercial. Advertisers can sponsor or produce programmes 'tailor-made' to sell their products as they do in the US. Bristol Myers, for example, produce *Alive and Well*, a two-hour daily health and fitness programme relayed by USA Cable Network, in which they place advertisements and information about their health and beauty products. On the Morning Satellite Network, a 'consumer information' service aimed at women, an advertiser can pay to be the guest on a half-hour chat show. Recent Japanese research identifies the same trend, since the early 1980s, towards morning 'news shows' – aimed at women – which are actually vehicles for the advertisement of goods and services. 'The control of TV by commercial interests has camouflaged advertising under the guise of information. Many women have not been aware of this gradual change in advertising strategy' (Suzuki, 1985, p.37).

The entry of newspaper and magazine publishers into the new media marketplace is a critical factor in the development of the 'commercial television ethic', based on specific appeal to women. Since 1980 the largest US publishing house, Hearst, has been buying its way into cable systems and channels. For The Leisure Channel (which it part-owns) Hearst produces segments from *Cosmopolitan* and *Good Housekeeping* (which it also owns), using some personnel from the magazines' staffs. Similarly CBS, also a major cable investor, owns *Woman's Day* (the largest circulation women's magazine in the US), which has a regular video equivalent on USA Network. Significantly D.C. Thompson,

31

which has the second largest share of the women's magazine market in Britain, is investing heavily in cable and satellite. A shareholder in Cablevision Scotland, Thompson owns a third of the Children's Channel and has shares in Sky Channel and Lifestyle (the 'women's channel'). Another important shareholder in Lifestyle is W.H. Smith, Britain's largest newsagent/retailer, which also has shares in The Arts Channel and an 80 per cent stake in Screen Sport.

The importance of these ventures is not simply that already huge organisations are able to use cable to develop new markets for their products, but that the interconnections between their interests across different media may lead to market domination and control. W.H. Smith, for example, is heavily involved in yet another new technology development – teleshopping – which has women as a key target. Several videotex-based home shopping experiments have already been carried out in Britain. All of them have been designed to turn 'an uncommitted public into frequent users' (*InterMedia*, 1985, p.7). In the United States, teleshopping has gone much further. Home shopping shows on cable television are run by 'perky hosts who breathlessly present marked-down goods' (Bearak, 1986). The viewer then dials a toll-free number to order by credit card. In 1985 Home Shopping Network became the first home shopping show to broadcast nationwide, reaching eight million homes, 24 hours a day. The company says daily sales exceed $500,000. The shows are directed mainly at women. 'Remember when your mother had a pot-bellied radio and she kept it going all day while she did housework?' asks the chairperson of Home Shopping Network. 'Well, this is the new pot-bellied radio' (*ibid.*).

These developments, basically revolving around advertising and the sale of consumer goods, illustrate clearly the economic interests which are driving the expansion of the new communication technologies. The same interests may also be served more directly, if people are prepared to pay for new programme services. Experiences of pay-TV, which has so far developed in a major way only in the United States, Canada and, more recently, France, show that the services which 'make money' are of two kinds: recent feature films, and pornography (Mascioni, 1986; Wiggins, 1985; Michaud, 1986).

Since the early 1980s, the new media have been the vehicles

for a startling expansion, both quantitative and qualitative, in the domestic availability of pornography. On the whole, these developments are threatening to women. The VCR, for example, not only permits viewing of (possibly violent) pornographic material but complete individual control over that material. The combined principles of 'deregulation' and 'market forces' which are guiding new media developments have produced an outpouring of pornographic content, from the apparently innocuous to the visibly degrading. In France, for example, La Cinq – the private television channel awarded in 1986 to a consortium headed by Silvio Berlusconi and Jérôme Seydoux – was quickly nicknamed 'Gros Lots et Gros Lolos' ('Big Money and Big Boobs'), because in its endless game shows both the prizes and the hostesses were extremely well-endowed. In one show, *Cherchez la Femme*, the prize was an important part in a Franco-Italian pornographic film. Canal Plus, the national pay-TV channel, within a year of its 1984 launch began to show hardcore pornographic films in a successful bid to attract the several thousand extra subscribers needed to make a profit. Add to this the proliferation of new 'adults only' pay-services offered through the Minitel and by telephone (similar to, but more explicit than, the 'porn lines' which were introduced in Britain during 1986), and by mid-1986 pornographic media were big business in France. Finally the rape of a young woman, who had been contacted by her attacker through one of the Minitel 'adult message' services, led to the establishment of a state-level working party to investigate the situation (Rind and Vial, 1986). Similar investigations were carried out in 1985–86 in the United States and Canada.

This is clearly a difficult and ambiguous area for women. The spirit of the 'moral majority' which often underlies such enquiries and their recommendations, may be utterly at odds with a feminist critique of pornography as an instance of violence and an instrument of control. It is an ambiguity of which the media and business interests involved in pornography are well aware, and ready to exploit. The annual profits from pornography (estimates vary from \$2–\$10 billion), remind us of the scale of the economic interests involved in every aspect of 'the communications revolution'. It is also an indication of the extent to which 'choice' is limited by, and for, male-defined imperatives. The conservatism of these, in terms of both culture and politics, is likely to reinforce a world view in which women's place is firmly circumscribed, and which is hostile to any social transformation – for example, of the sexual division of labour – based on a feminist perspective.

Public debate on the communications revolution

Given the implications of the changes taking place in British information and communications policy since the beginning of the 1980s, public debate on the issues and alternatives has been extraordinarily muted. For women in particular there is a difficulty in taking up the issues involved. If the public in general is distanced by the apparent opacity of technological development, this will be felt especially keenly by women who, through education and socialisation, are likely to believe themselves technically inept and ill-equipped to enter any discussion on the subject. An additional problem is the way in which debate, where it does exist, is structured so as to create an artificial distinction between, for example, 'communication issues' and 'women's issues'. European-level bodies such as the Council of Europe and the Commission of the European Communities, which have taken an increasing interest in developments in new communication technologies, have made no attempt to integrate these discussions with others, focusing on the status of women, already in progress under their own aegis. This sectionalisation is partly a bureaucratic drive to provide and maintain organisational 'spheres of influence'. But it also arises from, and reinforces, a mainstream perspective which locks the questions to be asked – and thus the answers found – within a self-defeating straitjacket.

This chapter has tried to outline some of the fundamental relationships which do exist between the position of women in society and the development and application of new communication technologies. Some of these interconnections are more obvious than others. To grasp their implications, and anticipate their impact in specific national or local settings, it is important that women locate new communication trends within a framework which acknowledges the increasingly global economic and political interests which are in play.

The question of whose interests are being served by new media developments is generally answered in economic terms. The merging and integration of different media institutions –

newspapers, cable and local television companies – already obvious in several European countries, makes this clear. In West Germany, one of the most ambitious satellite programme services is SAT-1, launched in 1985 and run by a consortium of publishers. Its news service is provided by APF, an association of 165 newspapers, whose programming is intended to balance what the publishers see as a left-wing bias in the public service TV news (Gallagher, 1985). With conservative governments in power in most European countries (including West Germany) in the mid-1980s, it is likely that rightist politics, based on a conservative approach to women's rights, may be strengthened by the new communication technologies.

But we need not be swept along by the apparent internal dynamism of new communication technology. In 1986 the Campaign for Press and Broadcasting Freedom (CPBF) launched a 'Media Manifesto', signalling its intention to generate a new nationwide debate on the British media. Women are already an important constituent in the CPBF lobby. Established women's media groupings, such as the Women's Film, Television and Video Network (WFTVN) and Women in Media (now part of the Fawcett Society), can be activated around the issues arising from new media developments. The European dimension will be increasingly important in terms of policy development, and Members of the European Parliament, particularly those involved in its Women's Committee, can be drawn into the debate.

Finally, technological development is not simply about systems but about people. Unlike system components, people are both knowledgeable and often unpredictable. Youichi Ito offers an example which inspires optimism about the strength of human resistance to the more sinister aspects of the communications revolution. Recently, the Japanese Agency for Natural Resources and Energy suggested a bizarre, and some might think insensitive, idea. It announced that it would present a Hi-OVIS type CATV (Community Antenna Television) system to those communities which accepted the construction of a nuclear power plant. 'The combination is symbolic of our time: in either case, technology goes ahead but people do not follow as expected' (Ito, 1984, p.156).

References

Alonso, M. (1986), 'Les Espagnols face aux nouvelles technologies', *Agora*, no.13, p.20.

Bardoel, J. (1985), 'When dykes are useless', *InterMedia*, vol.13, nos.4/5, pp.64–8.

Bearak, B. (1986), 'Discount shopping shows are spreading on US TV', *International Herald Tribune*, 22 July, p.3.

Brants, K. (1985), 'Broadcasting and politics in the Netherlands: from pillar to post', in R. Kuhn (ed.), *Broadcasting and Politics in Western Europe*, London, Frank Cass, pp.104–21.

Brants, K. and Jankowski, N. (1985), 'Cable television in the Low Countries', in R.M. Negrine (ed.), *Cable Television and the Future of Broadcasting*, London, Croom Helm, pp.74–102.

Clark, N. and Riddell, E. (1986), 'Commit now and get a bigger bathtub', *Airwaves*, no.8, pp.12–3.

Crombers, T. and Sangregoria, I. (1981), 'More of the same: the impact of information technology on domestic life in Japan', *Development Dialogue*, no.2.

Davey, G. (1985), 'Programming for loyalty', *InterMedia*, vol.13, nos.4/5, pp.46–9.

Dozier, D.M. and Rice, R.E. (1984), 'Rival theories of electronic newsreading', in R.E. Rice *et al.* (eds), *The New Media*, Beverly Hills, Sage Publications, pp.103–27.

Engsberg, J. (1982), 'Cable system employment 1980–1981: a report on the status of minorities and women', unpublished report, United Church of Christ, New York.

Ferguson, M. (1986), 'The challenge of neo-technological determinism for communication systems, industry and cultures', in M. Ferguson (ed.), *New Communication Technologies and the Public Interest*, London, Sage Publications, pp.52–70.

Gallagher, M. (1981), *Unequal Opportunities: The Case of Women and the Media*, Paris, UNESCO Press.

Gallagher, M. (1984), *Employment and Positive Action for Women in the Television Organisations of EEC Member States*, Brussels, Commission of the European Communities (V/2025/84).

Gallagher, R. (1985), 'Publishers and new media programming', *InterMedia*, vol.13, nos.4/5, pp.60–3.

Golding, P. and Murdock, G. (1986), 'Unequal information: access and exclusion in the new communications market place', in M. Ferguson (ed.), *New Communication Technologies and the Public Interest*, London, Sage Publications, pp.71–83.

Gore, M.S. (1983), *The SITE Experience*, Reports and Papers on Mass Communication, no.91, Paris, UNESCO.

Hacker, S. (1979), 'Sex stratification, technology and organizational change: a longitudinal case study of AT & T', *Social Problems*, vol.26, no.5, pp.539–57.

Hartley, J. (1986), 'The Japanese approach to the development of new residential communications services', in M. Ferguson (ed.), *New Communication Technologies and the Public Interest*, London, Sage Publications, pp.164–79.

Hollins, T. (1984), *Beyond Broadcasting: Into the Cable Age*, London, British Film Institute.

Home Office (1983), *The Development of Cable Systems and Services*, Cmnd 8866, London, Her Majesty's Stationery Office.

InterMedia (1985), 'Videotex: take-off at last?', vol.13, no.6, pp.6–7.

Ito, Y. (1984), 'Japan', in Peter M. Lewis (ed.), *Media for People in Cities: a Study of Community Media in the Urban Context*, Paris, UNESCO, pp.141–58.

Kalwachwala, D. (1986), 'Portrayal of women in India – a viewpoint', in B.C. Agrawal and A.K. Sinha (eds), *SITE to INSAT*, New Delhi, Concept Publishing Company, pp.89–97.

Kramarae, C. and Treichler, P.A. (1985), *A Feminist Dictionary*, Boston, Pandora Press.

Mascioni, M. (1986), 'Paying your money, taking your choice', *TV World*, May, pp.76–80.

Matthias, G. (1986), 'In the shadow of the castle', *Cable and Satellite Europe*, September, pp.40–3.

Media Report to Women (1978), 'A chronology; why women did not get their promised satellite demonstration', vol.6, no.7, pp.4–10.

Michaud, P. (1986), 'Sex and the second channel', *TV World*, June–July, p.20.

Mies, Maria (1986), *Patriarchy and Accumulation on a World Scale: Women in the International Division of Labour*, London, Zed Books.

Mosco, V. (1982), *Pushbutton Fantasies: Critical Perspectives on Videotex and Information Technology*, Norwood, Ablex Publishing Corporation.

Rice, R.E. and Williams, F. (1984), 'Theories old and new: the study of new media', in R.E. Rice *et al.* (eds), *The New Media*, Beverly Hills, Sage Publications, pp.55–80.

Rind, A. and Vial, C. (1986), 'Minitel's "special" services alarm French jurists', *The Guardian Weekly*, 19 October, p.14.

Samuelson, R.J. (1986), 'Public "Family Policy" isn't the answer', *International Herald Tribune*, 25 August, p.4.

Schrage, Michael and Vise, David A. (1986), 'Murdoch and Turner: first global broadcasters', *International Herald Tribune*, 5 September, pp.13,17.

Scott, H. (1984), *Working Your Way to the Bottom: The Feminization of Poverty*, London, Pandora Press.

Smith, A. (1973), *The Shadow in the Cave*, London, George Allen & Unwin Ltd.

Suzuki, M. (1985), 'Women and informationalized television in Japan', *Newsletter: Sex-Roles Within Mass Media* (Stockholm: School of Journalism/Sveriges Radio), no.6, pp.36–8.

Wang, G. (1986), 'Video boom in Taiwan: blessing or curse?', *The Third Channel*, vol.2, no.1, pp.365–79.

Wiggins, A. (1985), *Sex Role Stereotyping: A Content Analysis of Radio and Television Programs and Advertisements*, Vancouver, National Watch on Images of Women in the Media.

Williams, F. (1982), *The Communications Revolution*, Beverly Hills, Sage Publications.

3 Behind closed doors:
video recorders in the home

Ann Gray

The video cassette recorder is arguably the major innovation in home entertainment in Britain since television. When we address questions of how women watch television and video we inevitably raise a complex set of issues which relate to women and their everyday lives. In talking to women about home video cassette recorders (VCR) and television use, I have identified some of the determining factors surrounding these activities which take place within the domestic environment.[1] With the development of VCRs and other products such as home computers and cable services, the 1980s is seeing an ever increasing trend towards home-centred leisure and entertainment. New technology in the home has to be understood within a context of structures of power and authority relationships between household members, with gender emerging as one of the most significant differentiations. This far from neutral environment influences the ways in which women use popular texts in general and television and video in particular, and the pleasures and meanings which these have for them.

The video revolution

Although it is a relatively recent phenomenon, home video arrived as long ago as 1972 with Philips VCR and Sony U-matic. But it wasn't until Sony Betamax and VHS (video home system), both of which use 19 mm tape, brought the cost down significantly, that the stage was set for a consumer boom. In 1983 15 per cent of households in the United Kingdom had access to a VCR, by 1986 the figure had reached 40 per cent. An important factor in the British VCR experience is that the distribution of recorders operates through the already existing television rental networks, thereby making it possible to rent a VCR on a monthly basis, without the necessity for large capital investment. This results in video recorders being made available to a much wider range of socio-economic groups than might at first be imagined. We are not, in the British case, considering a 'luxury' item which graces the affluent household, rather, a widely available home entertainment facility which has rapidly become an accepted and essential part of everyday life, cutting across economic and class boundaries.

The development and marketing of entertainment consumer hardware can often outpace the provision of 'software' or 'content'. Raymond Williams points out that when domestic radio receivers were first marketed there was very little to receive in terms of programming content, 'It is not only that the supply of broadcasting facilities preceded the demand; it is that the means of communication preceded their content' (Williams, 1974, p.25).

There are two major uses for VCRs: time-shift, which involves recording off-broadcast television in order to view at a different time, and the playing of pre-recorded tapes.[2] These can be purchased, though the majority are hired through video rental 'libraries'. Although off-air recording is an attractive proposition, it has become obvious to a few entrepreneurs that there is a large potential market for the hiring of pre-recorded tape. In Britain during the early 1980s one feature of almost every high street was a new phenomenon known as the 'video library'. These were often hastily converted small shops offering tapes, mainly of movies, for hire. In these early days, in order to finance their purchase of new material, the libraries demanded a membership fee, often as high as £40, as well as a nightly fee for the hiring of tapes. Nowadays it is possible to join a video library free of charge, with a nightly rental fee of £1.00–£1.50 per tape. There are now upwards of 6,500 movies[3] available for hire on video tape and at a rough estimate four million tapes are hired a week. Indeed, 97 per cent of film watching is now done outside the cinema, mainly on broadcast television, but the hiring of films accounts for a significant proportion of this viewership (Howkins, 1983).

The video library industry – and I use this term to describe the distributors and retailers of pre-recorded tapes for purchase or hire – has experienced major change. Many of the smaller retail outlets have gone by the board, forced out by the larger and well-established distributors who moved in once the market had been tested. The industry has established its own quasi-professional organisations in order to protect itself against 'video piracy' and to professionalise and improve its image, which has not been good. The 'moral panic' which resulted in the Video Recordings Bill of 1984, providing for every film on hire to be censored for home viewing, had a devastating effect on the public image of the video libraries. This was fuelled enthusiastically by the popular press (Petley, 1984; Kuhn, 1984a; Barker, 1984). On 1 September 1982 the *Sun* carried the headline 'Fury over video nasties' and referred to the video distributors and retailers as 'the merchants of menace' who were threatening the well-being of our children. This kind of response to a new development in mass cultural production is similar to those precipitated by the novel in the nineteenth century, cinema in the 1920s and television in the 1950s. The moral reformers were then, as now, fearful for the effects of these new mass-produced cultural forms on those 'weaker' members of society – women, children and the 'lower orders' in general – whom they sought to protect.

Video and family life

Although there are many aspects of the video phenomenon which are worthy of study, my research initially focuses on the potential choice which the VCR offers for viewing within the domestic and family context. The major reason for this is that, until recently, attention to the context of viewing seems to have been largely neglected in media and cultural studies.[4] The relationship between the viewer and television, the reader and text, is often a relationship which has to be negotiated, struggled for, won or lost, in the dynamic and often chaotic processes of family life. As video recorders offer, above all, extended choice of content and time management for viewing within the home, research into its use has to be focused within that very context. The context of 'the family' is, for my purposes, conceived of as a site of constant social negotiation within a highly routinised framework of material dependency and normative constraint,[5] and all these elements enter into the negotiations which surround viewing decisions. This family setting, with its power relationships and authority structures across gender, is an extremely important factor in thinking more generally of 'leisure' and, specifically, home-based leisure. The home has increasingly become the site for entertainment, and we can see VCRs as yet one more commodity which reduces the necessity for household members to seek entertainment outside the home, a situation reinforced by the present economic climate in Britain:

> JS: Well, we can't really afford to go out to the pictures, not any more. If we all go and have ice-creams, you're talking about eight or nine pounds. It's a lot of money.

What is especially important for women is that the domestic sphere is increasingly becoming defined as their only leisure space. Many married women are in paid work outside the home, but women are still largely responsible for the domestic labour in the home. Childcare, food provision, laundry, shopping and cleaning the living space, are ultimately women's responsibility even if their male partners help. While men in paid employment come home to a non-work environment, women who either work in the home all day or go out to paid employment still have to work at home in the evenings and at weekends:

> AS: Him? Oh, he sits on his backside all night, from coming in from work to going to bed.

Indeed, many women do not consider themselves as having any leisure at all. (Deem, 1984). And many certainly would not allow themselves the luxury of sitting down to watch television until the children are fed and put to bed and the household chores have been completed:

> JK: I'd feel guilty, I'd feel I was cheating. It's my job and if I'm sat, I'm not doing my job.

This is a context which, at the most basic and practical level, positions women in relation to the whole area of leisure, but particularly in relation to television and video viewing:

> AS: Like, if he comes in and he's rented a video, straight after tea he wants to put it on. I say 'well let me finish the washing-up first'. I mean, I just wouldn't enjoy it if I knew it was all to do.

Video as technology

Women and men have differential access to technology in general and to domestic technology in particular. The relations between domestic technology and gender are relatively unexplored,[6] though there is more work on gender and technology in the workplace where, as Jan Zimmerman notes, new technology is entering existing and traditional sets of relations. Old values in this way become encoded in new technologies (Zimmerman, 1981; Cockburn, 1983, 1985). It is interesting to note that American researchers discovered that in the early 1970s the full-time housewife was spending as much time on housework as her grandmother had done fifty years earlier. Domestic technology may be labour-saving, replacing the drudgery of household work, but it is time-consuming in that each piece of equipment requires work if it is to fulfil its advertised potential. Rothschild argues that far from liberating women from housework, new technology, embedded as it is in ideological assumptions about the sexual division of labour, has further entrenched women in the home and in the role of housewife (Rothschild, 1983).

When a new piece of technology is purchased or rented, it is often already inscribed with gender expectations. The gender specificity of pieces of domestic technology is deeply implanted in the 'commonsense' of households, operating almost at an unconscious level. As such it is difficult for the researcher to unearth. One strategy I have employed which throws the gender of domestic technology into high relief is to ask the women to imagine pieces of equipment as coloured either pink or blue.[7] This produces almost uniformly pink irons and blue electric drills, with many interesting mixtures along the spectrum. The washing machine, for example, is most usually pink on the outside, but the motor is almost always blue. VCRs and, indeed, all home entertainment technology would seem to be a potentially lilac area, but my research has shown that we must break down the VCR into its different modes in our colour-coding. The 'record', 'rewind' and 'play' modes are usually lilac, but the timer switch is nearly always blue, with women having to depend on their male partners or their children to set the timer for them. The blueness of the timer is exceeded only by the deep indigo of the remote control switch which in all cases is held by the man:

SW: Oh, yes, that's definitely blue in our house. He flicks from channel to channel, I never know what I'm watching – it drives me mad.

It does appear that the male of the household is generally assumed to have knowledge of this kind of technology when it enters the household, or at least he will quickly gain the knowledge. And certain knowledges can, of course, be withheld and used to maintain authority and control:

AS: Well, at first he was the only one who knew how to record things, but then me and my young son sat down one day and worked it out. That meant we didn't have to keep asking him to record something for us.

Although women routinely operate extremely sophisticated pieces of domestic technology, often requiring, in the first instance, the study and application of a manual of instructions, they often feel alienated from operating the VCR. The reasons for this are manifold and have been brought about by positioning within the family, the education system and the institutionalised sexism with regard to the division of appropriate activities and knowledges in terms of gender. Or there may be, as I discovered, 'calculated ignorance':

CH: If I learnt how to do the video it would become my job just like everything else.

If women do not feel confident or easy in approaching and operating the recorders, let alone in setting the timer for advance recording, they are at an immediate and real disadvantage in terms of exercising the apparent choices which the VCR offers. This, combined with constraints in the hiring of video tapes, either financial or simply normative, means that for women the idea of increased freedom and choice of viewing may well be spurious.

Genre and gender

If women are 'positioned' within the context of consumption, it seems that they are also positioned, or even structured in absence, by the video industry itself in terms of the kind of audience it seems to be addressing. To enter a video library is to be visually bombarded by 'covers' depicting scenes of horror, action adventure, war, westerns and 'soft' pornography, traditionally considered to be 'male' genres.[8] Is it therefore mainly men who are hiring video tapes, and if so, what do women feel about the kinds of tapes they are watching at home? Do women ever hire tapes themselves, or do they feel alienated from both the outlets and what they have to offer? In other words, what are the circumstances surrounding the use of video libraries and what is the sexual division of labour associated with the hiring and viewing of tapes? I have already made reference to the so-called 'male' genres which imply that certain kinds of films address themselves to and are enjoyed by a male audience and the same, of course, could be said for 'female' genres. But why do certain kinds of texts or genres appeal to women and not to men and *vice versa* and how should we conceive of the audience for these texts made up of women and men?

The 'gendered audience' has a theoretical history which, as Annette Kuhn usefully points out, has developed within two different perspectives, one emerging from media studies and the other from film theory (Kuhn, 1984b). This has resulted in two quite different notions of the gendered audience. The sociological emphasis of media studies has tended to conceive of a 'social audience', that is, an audience made up of already constituted male and female persons who bring (among other things) maleness or femaleness to a text, and who decode the text within that particular frame of reference. Film theory on the other hand, has conceived of a 'psychological audience', a collection of individual spectators who do not read the text, but rather the text 'reads' them. In other words, the film offers a masculine or feminine subject position and the spectator occupies that position. Of course, this is not automatic and there is nothing to prevent, for example, a female spectator taking up a masculine subject position. However, the construction of masculinity and femininity across the institutions within society is so powerfully aligned to the social categories 'male' and 'female' that the two usually coincide apparently seamlessly. But, as Kuhn points out, what is suggested by these two perspectives is a distinction between femaleness as a social gender and femininity as a subject position. The problem here is that neither of these two perspectives is sufficient in themselves to gain a full understanding of what happens when men and women watch films. In the former case, context is emphasised over text and in the latter text over context. The spectator-text relationship suggested by the psychoanalytic models used in film theory tend to disregard those important factors of social context involved in film and TV watching. Also, they find it difficult to allow for the subject constituted outside the text, across other discourses, such as class, race, age and general social environment. The social audience approach, conversely, sees the response to texts as a socially predetermined one, and in this way does not allow for consideration of how the texts themselves work on the viewers/readers.

There have been some attempts to link text with context by examining the particular features of 'women's genres'. Soap operas, for example, have been looked at in terms of their distinctive narrative pattern, which is open-ended and continuous; their concern with so-called 'female' skills; their scheduling on television which fits into the rhythm of women's work at home, all of which can be seen as specifically addressing a social audience of women (Brunsdon, 1981; Modleski, 1982). However, this would still seem to stress context over text and in this area the film theory perspective has certainly been limited by its implicit assumption of an intense and concentrated relationship between spectator and text in a darkened cinema. For television this relationship is more likely to be characterised by distinction and diversion. As Kuhn points out:

> This would suggest that each medium constructs sexual difference through spectatorship in rather different ways: cinema through the look and spectacle, and TV – perhaps less evidently – through a capacity to insert its flow, its characteristic modes of address and the textual operations of different kinds of programmes into the rhythms and routines of domestic activities and sexual divisions of labour in the household at various times of day. (Kuhn, 1984b, p.25)

This distinction is important and useful, but when thinking about the use of VCRs the two media are viewed in the same context. Movies have long been a part of television's nightly 'flow' as well as part of daytime viewing. But in video recording movies off television for watching at a later date, and in hiring movies, we have a discrete 'event' which disrupts the flow of television and its insertive scheduling:

AC: Oh yes, we all sit down and watch – 'we've got a video, let's sit down' – TV's different, that's just on.

Concepts of the psychological audience and the social audience are not sufficient in themselves to explore the whole complexity of text, subject and context and the ways in which they intersect. But both are necessary, representing as they do different instances within the process of consumption of popular texts. While the psychological model posits an unacceptably homogeneous and 'universal' audience, it does allow us to consider the importance of how texts work, not only in terms of subject positioning and interpellation, but also in terms of pleasure and desire. The social model demands that the audience is heterogeneous and requires us to explore those other differences and contexts which, to a greater or lesser extent, determine the ways in which women and men read those texts. It seems clear that the problem of the relationship between text and gendered audience cannot be resolved at the theoretical level, but rather must be kept in play and, if possible, problematised throughout the research enterprise.

Viewing contexts

It would seem that women do have certain preconceptions about what constitutes a 'film for men' as against a 'film for women', and furthermore, a typology of viewing contexts is beginning to emerge, along with appropriate associated texts (see Table 3.1).

I wish to focus mainly on Context (Female alone), but before I do it is worth mentioning the difference between the negotiations around Contexts (Male alone) and (Female alone). For the latter to exist, the male partner must normally be out of the house, either at work or at leisure, whereas, Context (Male alone) would be likely to exist when both male and female were in the house together. The women simply wouldn't watch:

BA: If he's watching something I'm not enjoying, I'll either knit or read.

JS: Well, I can read when the telly's on if it's something I don't like.

DS: I usually go to bed with a book, or sometimes I'll watch the portable in the kitchen, but it's damned uncomfortable in there.

CH: Well, when he's in, Father has priority over what's on. Yes, he does, but I can go in the other room if I don't want to watch it.

Table 3.1 Typology of viewing contexts[9]

Context	Film	TV
1 Family together	*Superman* Walt Disney *Jaws* Comedy	Children's TV Quiz shows Comedy *EastEnders*
2 Male and female partners together	*An Officer and a Gentleman* *Kramer v. Kramer* The Rockys Any Clint Eastwood	*Aufweidersehen Pet* *Minder* Shows *Coronation Street* *EastEnders*
3 Male alone	War Action adventure* Horror* Adults*	Sport News Documentaries
4 Female alone	*Who Will Love My Children?* *Evergreen* Romance	*Coronation Street* *Crossroads* *Dallas* *Dynasty* *A Woman of Substance* *Princess Daisy*

* These are the category headings used by many video libraries

Women only

For women who are at home all day, either with very small children or children of school age, and whose husbands are out at work, there are obvious opportunities for them to view alone. However, most of the women I have talked to are constrained by guilt, often referring to daytime viewing as some kind of drug:

SW: No, I've got too many things to do during the daytime, I couldn't do it to myself, I'd be a total addict.

JK: Well, I watch *Falcon Crest* – it's a treat, when I've done my work, then I sit down and it's my treat. But I'm not one to get videos during the day because I think you can get really addicted, then everything else suffers.

The second woman quoted indicates what is a fairly common

strategy – that of using daytime television programmes to establish some time for herself as a reward to which completion of household tasks will lead. This assuages the guilt to a certain extent and the pleasure afforded by this particular viewing context seems to go far beyond the pleasures of the text itself. What it represents is a breathing space when the busy mother can resist the demands of her children and domestic labour for a brief period of time. One of the most popular daytime programmes cited was *Sons & Daughters*, an Australian imported soap opera, transmitted three afternoons a week in the Yorkshire region. Most of the women preferred to watch this alone, some taking the telephone off the hook to ensure uninterrupted concentration, but they would watch it with a friend if they happened to be in each other's houses at the time. Janice Radway in her study of women and romantic fiction talks with regret of the isolated context within which popular romances are consumed by women (Radway, 1984). The next viewing context I wish to discuss reveals a more optimistic state of affairs for women.

This context is again female only, but is one in which several women get together to watch a video which they have hired jointly. This would normally happen during the day when their children are at school. Far from being instrumental in isolating women, it would seem that there is a tendency to communal use of hired videos, mainly on economic grounds, but also on the grounds that the women can watch what they want together without the guilt or the distraction of children:

BS: There are three of us, and we hire two or three films a week and watch them together, usually at Joyce's house when the kids are at school. We can choose what we want then.

JK: Yes, if there's something we want to see we wait 'til the kids have gone back to school so's we can sit and watch it without them coming in saying 'can I have . . . can I have . . . ' it makes it difficult.

The idea of viewing together during the day for this particular network of women living on the same street came when one of them found herself continually returning the video tapes which her husband had hired the night before. She discovered that there were films which she would like to watch but which her husband never hired. A good relationship was established with the woman who worked in the video library who would look out for good films:

> BS: She comes into the shop where I work and I go 'have any new videos come out?' She tells me. She knows what we like.

One favoured form for this viewing network is that of the long family saga, often running to two or three tapes:

> JK: We like something in two or three parts; something with a really good story to it so's you can get involved.

> BS: Mm . . . the other week we had a Clint Eastwood and Burt Reynolds film because she [MD] likes Clint Eastwood but we talked all the way through that, didn't we?

When the group views sagas which extend over two or three tapes there is obvious pleasure in anticipating both the outcome of the narrative and the viewing of the following tape. A considerable amount of discussion and speculation ensues and a day for the next viewing is fixed:

> MD:We like to spread them out – every other day, it helps to break the week up. Sometimes we have them on an evening, if our husbands are away or out. We'll have a bottle of wine then, then we don't even have to get up to make a cup of tea.

These women are also devotees of the American soap operas and operate a 'failsafe' network of video recording for each other, refusing to discuss each episode until they have all seen it. These popular texts form an important part of their friendship and association in their everyday lives and give a focus to an almost separate female culture which they can share together within the constraints of their positions as wives and mothers. Furthermore, they are able to take up the feminine subject positions offered by these texts comfortably and pleasurably. In contrast, the films which their husbands hire for viewing Context (Male & female partners together) mainly offer a masculine subject position which the women seem to take up through their male partners, who in turn give their approval to such texts.

The major impetus for a viewing group like this is that films which women enjoy watching are rarely, if ever, hired by their male partners for viewing together because they consider such films to be 'trivial' and 'silly' and women are laughed at for enjoying them:

> BA: I sit there with tears running down my face and he comes in and says 'you daft thing.'

This derision also applies to soap operas, and is reproduced in male children:

> JK: Oh, my son thinks I'm stupid because I won't miss
> *Dallas* – perhaps I am.

It is the most powerful member within the household who defines this hierarchy of 'serious' and 'silly', 'important' and 'trivial'. This leaves women and their pleasures in films downgraded, objects and subjects of fun and derision, having to consume them almost in secret. But the kinds of films and television soap operas which women enjoy watching alone deal with things of importance to them, highlighting so-called 'female' concerns – care of children, concern for members of one's own family, consideration for one's own sexual partner, selflessness in characters – all of which are the skills of competence, the thought and caring which husbands and children expect of women and assume as a matter of natural course.[10] This is a deeply contradictory position for women, lying between the realities of their day to day lives and the pleasures and gratifications that they seek to find in texts that their partners and very often their children, look upon as so much rubbish:

> JS: I think a lot of storylines in soap operas are very weak and I think a man needs something to keep his interest more than a woman. That makes a man sound more intelligent, but that's not what I mean. It's got to be something worth watching before he'll sit down and actually watch it, but I'd watch anything. I think he thinks it's unmanly to watch them.

> SW: All the soap operas are rubbish for men, fantasy for women.

> *AG: Do you think men need fantasy?*
> SW: They need fantasy in a different way, detectives and wars, that's their fantasy world, and science fiction, a tough, strong world. Not sloppy, who's fallen in love with who, who's shot JR – it's rubbish. Men know it's rubbish, that's the difference.

Here are two women talking about a genre they love in relation to their male partners, giving us a sense of the 'power of definition' within the partnerships, but also the ways in which the women themselves think of their own pleasures.

Conclusion

Theories of the gendered audience as they have been developed are useful, but when women and men watch movies and television they become that hybrid, the *social spectator* (Kuhn, *ibid.*) and, in understanding the subject-text-context relationship, the social and the psychological have to be kept in play to a proportionately greater or lesser degree. This allows us to consider how texts and contexts (both the specific and the wider social context) combine together in producing the gendered reading subject. Charlotte Brunsdon, writing on *Crossroads*, has attempted to resolve this dualism and suggests that, 'The relation of the audience to the text will not be determined solely by that text, but also by positionalities in relation to a whole range of other discourses – discourses of motherhood, romance and sexuality for example' (Brunsdon, 1981, p.32).

This enables us to think of the subject in the social context occupying different positions in relation to different discourses which change across time. As particular discourses become central issues, they will affect the ways in which the social subject occupies, or resists, the subject position constructed by a text.

The viewing and reading of texts takes place, for the majority of people, within the domestic context. However, this is a context which is not singular and unchanging, but plural and open to different permutations, dependent upon the negotiations between members of the household and the particular texts involved. The VCR offers the potential for extended choice of viewing in terms of text and context. But in order to explore how this potential is being used the particular conditions of its consumption must be addressed. The viewing contexts and their associated texts which I have outlined here have emerged from my discussions with women who occupy different social positions and there are remarkable similarities in the ways in which all the women have spoken about their domestic viewing practices. However, it is simply not sufficient to have identified these similarities, and my analysis of the interview 'texts' continues in an attempt to make visible the important differences between the women's accounts of these practices. These differences must be seen in relation to their particular social positioning and the various specific discourses which they inhabit. The interview material I have gathered demands a framework of analysis which uses theories and concepts developed within different disciplines and will, I am sure, test their relative strengths and weaknesses in revealing the complexity of how women relate to television and video in their everyday lives.

Acknowledgments

I am grateful to Andrew Tudor for his thorough reading of an early draft of this article, and indebted to the women who gave me much more than their time.

Notes

1 This research was initially funded by the Economic and Social Research Council and has taken the form of long, open-ended discussions with women whose age, social position, employment and family circumstances differ (race is a variable which has not been introduced). Part of my strategy has been to encourage open discussion and allow the women themselves to introduce topics which are of importance to them. By keeping the discussions open they can take pleasure in having the opportunity to explore and express their own ideas and feelings on these matters. For discussions on feminist research methods see Roberts (ed.), 1981; Stanley and Wise, 1983; Bell and Roberts, 1984.

2 VCRs can also be used in conjunction with a video camera to produce home video tapes.

3 'Movies' in this context include films made specially for video distribution, films made for TV, both British and American, as well as 'feature' films which are produced primarily for the cinema.

4 There are notable exceptions (Hobson, 1981 and 1982; Morley, 1986; Collette, 1986).

5 I am grateful to Elizabeth Shove and Andrew Tudor for this working definition.

6 However a recent publication by W. Faulkner and E. Arnold (eds), *Smothered by Invention Technology in Women's Lives*, Pluto Press, 1985, does address issues of domestic technology and gender.

7 These were ideas discussed at a seminar given by Cynthia Cockburn at York University, June 1985. See also Cockburn, 1985.

8 It is interesting to note that video tapes are now being distributed which are specifically aimed at a female audience; IPC and Videospace combined magazine and video to market their *Woman's Own Selection*, along with their more recent label *Images of Love*, while Polygram Video are offering a label, *Women's Choice*. However, in the North of England certainly, these have a very limited distribution.

9 These are the names which the women themselves gave to the different texts and genres.

10 Charlotte Brunsdon has made this point in relation to *Crossroads*, but we can see that it can apply to other 'women's genres' (Brunsdon, 1981).

References

Barker, M. (ed.) (1984) *The Video Nasties*, London, Pluto Press.

Bell, C. and Roberts, H. (eds) (1984), *Social Researching*, London, Routledge & Kegan Paul.

Brunsdon, C. (1981), 'Crossroads: Notes on a soap opera', *Screen*, vol.22, no.4, pp.32–7.

Cockburn, C. (1983), *Brothers*, London, Pluto Press.

Cockburn, C. (1985), *Machinery of Dominance*, London, Pluto Press.

Collett, P. (1986), 'Watching the TV audience', paper presented to International Television Studies Conference 1986.

Deem, R. (1984), 'Paid work, leisure and non-employment: shifting boundaries and gender differences', paper presented to British Sociological Association Conference 1984.

Faulkner, W. and Arnold, E. (1985) (eds), *Smothered by Invention*, London, Pluto Press.

Hobson, D. (1981), 'Housewives and the mass media', in Hall, S. *et al.* (eds), *Culture, Media, Language*, London, Hutchinson.

Hobson, D. (1982), *'Crossroads': The Drama of a Soap Opera*, London, Methuen.

Howkins, J. (1983), 'Mr Baker: a challenge', *Sight & Sound*, autumn, pp.227–29.

Kuhn, A. (1984a), 'Reply to Julian Petley', *Screen*, vol.25, no.3, May/June, pp.116–17.

Kuhn, A. (1984b), 'Women's genres', *Screen*, vol.25, no.1, Jan/Feb, pp.18–28.

Modleski, T. (1982), *Loving With a Vengeance*, Hamden, Connecticut, Shoe String Press.

Morley, D. (1986), *Family Television: Cultural Power and Domestic Leisure*, London, Comedia.

Petley, J. (1984), 'A nasty story', *Screen*, vol.25, no.2, March/April, pp.68–74.

Radway, J.A. (1984), *Reading the Romance*, Chapel Hill, University of North Carolina Press.

Roberts, H. (ed.) (1981), *Doing Feminist Research*, London, Routledge & Kegan Paul.

Rothschild, J. (1983), *Machina ex Dea*, New York, Pergamon Press.

Stanley L. and Wise, S. (1983), *Breaking Out*, London, Routledge & Kegan Paul.

Williams, R. (1974), *Television Technology and Cultural Form*, London, Fontana.

Zimmerman, J. (1981), 'Technology and the future of women: haven't we met somewhere before?', *Women's Studies International Quarterly*, vol.4, no.3, p.355.

4 Campaigning for change

Loretta Loach

Since the beginning of the 1980s the British television industry has undergone immense upheaval. It has seen the advent of breakfast television and Channel 4, the growth of the independent sector, the promised expansion of satellite and cable television and, through the Peacock report, the reappraisal of public service broadcasting. The institutions of progress and change have been left shaken by the pace of these developments and by the political climate in which they have occurred. Trade unions have been weakened by legislation and the demoralising climate of unemployment. Yet, in spite of this adversity, the challenge of women in the television industry has been vigorous and consistent. Over the decade a strong but changing women's movement has influenced and involved women in television and suggested certain strategies for media reform. These changes have been reflected in my own area of activity with the Campaign for Press and Broadcasting Freedom.

When the Campaign was set up in 1979 it was predominantly a trade union-based organisation with a central campaigning focus on the industrial right of reply. This involved liaising with the media unions to help secure a right of reply for groups of people who were particularly abused or misrepresented by the media. Government restrictions on trade unions have undermined their collective strength and confidence. The introspection this crisis has provoked, however, could provide a renewed opportunity for a wider strategic programme for media reform with the specific needs of women at its core. There are many obstacles which stand in the way of women campaigning in and around television. A male dominated management is just one. A male dominated trade union movement is another. Women have been campaigning on two fronts: both within and against the trade unions, but also separately and apart from them. This has produced overlapping, but often different, results. This chapter attempts to assess the strengths and weaknesses of our political effort so far.

Positive energies

Positive action became an important and central campaigning strategy for feminists in the 1980s, mainly because laws against sex discrimination and unequal pay proved to be so ineffective:

> Our laws are negative in the sense that although they outlaw discrimination they do not require positive action to overcome the heritage of past discrimination and social stereotyping of women which discourages them from applying for 'male' jobs or seeking promotion. (Gill and Whitty, 1983, p.301)

The sex discrimination legislation of the mid 1970s did little to change the deep discrepancies in women's employment opportunities. The inequalities of the system had been internalised and few women pursued possibilities because of lack of confidence, fear of failure or simply a belief that only a man could do the job. Crudely, positive action aims to increase the numbers of women in jobs done predominantly by men. Positive action does not mean discrimination against men. It means that women should be given the opportunity to compete with men on an equal basis. In America the principle has long been accepted. In 1970 the US National Organisation for Women won an executive order which stipulated that employers were obliged to fulfil a specified quota of jobs with women (Coote and Campbell, 1982, p.131). Companies in breach of the order were prevented from getting government contracts. In Britain, the 1980 Trades Union Congress passed a resolution calling for 'positive action in favour of women' to help remove the gender basis of job segregation and to increase the level of women's pay. Positive action is different from positive discrimination, which is unlawful in this country and which is widely misconstrued by men as discrimination against them. (For a more detailed outline of positive action see Robarts, 1981.)

The sexual division of labour which exists in the workforce as a whole is also reflected in the film and television industry. In a report published by the Association of Cinematograph, Television and Allied Technicians (ACTT) in 1975, the same year as the Sex Discrimination Act was passed, it was found that women's employment opportunities in television were greatly circumscribed by the subjects girls were encouraged to do at school. Young women who entered the industry without science or technology qualifications were not deemed eligible for a technical training. Training and promotion opportunities were seen to operate more in men's favour, allowing them greater mobility across and between occupations. 'Men are more likely to work up from being post boys or enter directly as production assistants, researchers, assistant editors, vision mixers, cameramen and sound recordists. Women are effectively denied entry into both these types' (Baehr, 1981). The report also showed that in over half the grades covered by union agreements in film and television production, not one woman was employed. The majority of women, 60 per cent, were employed in the secretarial grades as production assistants or typists. The ACTT report indicated that only 8 per cent of directors or producer/directors in independent television were women.

A report by the BBC two years earlier in 1973 described the Corporation's attitude to women as one of 'benign neglect'. It revealed widespread sex discrimination and few women in middle-management jobs and even fewer further up the scale. Women graduates expressed disappointment and resentment at the lack of promotion opportunities. The Association of Broadcasting Staff (ABS) who had pressed for the report argued, 'Even if a woman applied for a training course which could be the prelude to a production career, she would be unlikely to succeed because her present job would probably be of low status' (Gill and Whitty, 1983, p.149).

Developments within television in the early 1980s brought together the interest and involvement of a number of feminists, and positive action strategies were appropriately suggested. The new fourth channel, breakfast television and the re-allocation of the ITV franchises all became a focus for change, both in terms of women's employment in television and in our portrayal on the screen. Around this time London's largest ITV contractor, Thames Television, responded to a pilot positive action scheme initiated by the National Council for Civil Liberties (NCCL). Sadie Robarts, a barrister, undertook the initial research using information supplied by the company's Staff Relations Department. She conducted interviews with managers and supervisors and got the views and feelings of the women at Thames by holding 'women only' meetings. These provided the interest and impetus for the establishment of a women's committee which persuaded both the unions and management to co-operate and learn from the scheme. All the women Sadie Robarts interviewed were keen to improve their career prospects. The report's final proposals included a number of practical steps to remove some of the obstacles to women's advancement. They included improved training schemes, a code of practice on interviewing directed at managers, better childcare facilities and an equal opportunities committee to monitor the implementation and outcome of these proposals.

In December 1981 Thames accepted a number of the recommendations in the Robarts report. The company, however, was in no way obliged to implement any of the recommended policy changes. Nevertheless, Thames management did take a number of important initiatives. They seconded a personnel officer to the position of Women's Equality Officer. (Thames is still the only company to have a formal post with this title.) In 1983, the post was redefined as Equal Opportunities Advisor to take in a consideration of race as well as sex discrimination, although no extra resources were provided for this expanded brief. The company also adopted a code of practice on recruitment and selection and an equal opportunities appeals procedure to allow women who are unfairly treated because of their sex to seek redress. There was also a pledge to monitor the progress and effectiveness of the policy. A thirteen-week technical training course for women resulted in two women transferring from their secretarial and clerical jobs to work in camera and sound. Thames Television has gone further than any of the other ITV companies but the changes still have some way to go. In 1981 when the pilot study was carried out, there were no women in senior management posts and in 1985 there were still none. According to the ACTT Equality Officer (a post established in 1980), Thames are not exemplary employers in spite of their written policy:

> If you look at their employment figures now and compare them to the rest of the ITV companies, there is still very little to show for the Equal Opportunities project. There's been no substantial change in

attitude from management and no real change in policy. (personal interview, 1986)

Christine Kerr, the Equal Opportunities Advisor at Thames, disagrees. She says:

> There has been some progress, though obviously it's not as dramatic as people first expected. Women have moved into supervisory areas and technical jobs and this is directly attributable to our training programmes. The next step forward for women is into management positions but one of the main problems is the general low turnover of staff so opportunities are limited to technical and programme areas. (personal interview, 1986)

A similar situation continues to exist in the BBC. The 1973 report produced a policy document which outlined actions to be taken to improve women's employment and promotion opportunities. No action was taken which is why the Sims inquiry in 1985 found only six women compared to 159 men in the top BBC grades, representing no increase for over a decade. In BBC Current Affairs, no deputy editor posts are advertised: they are filled without competition. Head-hunting goes on for senior posts and inevitably those heads are male. Employment hierarchies are also reflected in the social relationships of the workplace where jobs and technical know-how are informally passed on. One woman in the report expressed it thus: 'Men and women function in different ways; men are "clubby" and stay on drinking in the club after a programme whereas women have to do the shopping and prepare a meal' (Sims, 1985). Christina Driver, an officer at BETA (Broadcasting, Entertainment Trade Alliance), the union with chief negotiating rights at the BBC, suspects that the Sims report was simply a holding operation. 'Our immediate concern was whether the BBC would commit itself to negotiations on the eventual recommendations, or whether the fact of rediscovering the problems would be deemed enough to show the BBC was a caring employer' (*BETA Journal*, July/August 1985). The recommendations of the report were regarded by BETA as weak, particularly in the two crucial areas of recruitment and training, which were outside the brief of the Sims inquiry. According to Christina Driver, the suggestions in the report are inadequate as a basis for improving employment opportunities, and radical action is needed to take the Corporation forward as a respectable and lawful equal opportunities employer. Monica Sims says that her report was only one of many initiatives and that she is heartened by the response it has created within the BBC where the report has, in her view, 'acted as a catalyst which has led to some action by the management and by the women employees themselves. My discussions with male colleagues in the BBC suggest that the text of the report has caused some of them to question their own attitudes and assumptions' (personal interview, 1986).

The BBC Equality Network was set up in January 1986 in the wake of the Sims report. Women working at the BBC felt that the report was useful but that its recommendations had not gone far enough. An Equality Officer had been appointed on the strength of the Sims report but only as a two year secondment from another post. In an organisation of 30,000 employees, more than half of whom were women, a temporary Equality Officer with no clear brief appeared inadequate. One woman told me, 'Structural changes need to be made at every level and there needs to be a commitment to positive action to make sure women are recruited and trained in proper numbers.' She added that in a large bureaucratic organisation like the BBC, changes that are pursued vertically through the personnel department are very slow. 'It's such a traditional organisation, you meet so much resistance and inertia when it comes to implementing these sorts of changes; that's why it's useful to have moves from the top' (personal interview, 1986).

The Equality Network is optimistic because they see a friend in the Director of Programmes at the BBC, Michael Grade. He has spent time in the American broadcasting system, where they are more open to equal opportunities policies, and he has responded sympathetically to the views of the Network. Over the past years, women's initiatives inside the BBC have been given a very poor response by senior management. So his response is regarded as an encouraging sign. Grade's acknowledgment of women's position inside the Corporation has done more to change attitudes than all the years of campaigning put together. 'Changes can come very quickly from the top,' one women from the Network told me, 'now it is legitimate to recognise women's unequal position perhaps something more immediate will be done about it'.

Putting on the pressure

Positive action is regarded as important to feminist politics because it focuses on the systematic nature of male dominance and points an accusing finger at men. Their power is the apparent obstacle which stands in the way of women achieving equality. Positive action programmes implicate men and makes them bear the responsibility for accelerating the process of change. Positive action is a useful device for raising awareness (Coote and Campbell, 1982, p.131). Yet its fundamental weakness as a strategy is precisely that it does depend entirely upon men's goodwill for its success. Sadie Robarts, who produced the proposal for Thames, had taken the idea from the United States where legislation not only outlaws sex discrimination but also requires companies to take 'affirmative action' against it. Women and black people are legally encouraged to enter the sanctuary of white male concerns. Fiscal sanctions are also used to discourage discrimination. These operate through a system of 'contract compliance' where companies must meet certain targets or quotas before they become eligible to receive government contracts. No similar incentives exist in the United Kingdom, although contractual conditions could be institutionalised by the Board of Governors of the BBC and the Independent Broadcasting Authority (IBA). However as the situation currently stands, proposals for positive action rely on the consent and commitment of a male management and a male trade union movement, each threatened by changes which might squeeze them out or make them question practices they have cherished for centuries.

Positive action is obviously one way of resolving the imbalance of power and the issues of representation in broadcasting but it in no way amounts to any structural transformation of it. A political weakness of this strategy lies in the emphasis it places upon individual career development. This can easily mean opening up the hierarchy to women which, though important, still leaves the lines of power and authority in broadcasting unaltered and possibly even more legitimised. Individual women can be helped by positive action to compete successfully in a man's world. But this can serve to isolate many women, allowing their identity and experience to become submerged in the male-defined world of work: 'There is a value which middle-class men place on their work that is derived from the power it gives them. It is a value so intense that it can often mean more to them than life itself' (Cockburn and Loach, 1986, p.24).

Women working in television are particularly vulnerable because the industry is so competitive: 'The potential for feminist solidarity is impeded by these conditions. The identity of women becomes fragmented and turned inwards or turns into competition with other women and with men' (*ibid.*).

In this scenario, the values and habits of an organisation will continue to thrive unchallenged. To be effective and far-reaching, the dimensions of any positive action strategy need to go beyond simply supporting women's career aspirations. They need to include a challenge to the values, procedures and practices of the broadcasting institutions. Initiatives that do try to operate different working methods are inevitably beset by contradictions (see Chapter 8).

Finally, central to the design of any positive action programme must be some provision for childcare. Of course not all women have children, but assumptions about women's careers, ambitions and capabilities are negatively based around the perceptions of women as child-rearers. Thames Television did recommend the extension of childcare facilities but the Sims report on the BBC made no equivalent recommendations, in spite of the fact that numerous women interviewed complained of the pressure of combining childcare responsibilities with demanding BBC work (Sims, 1985). The Corporation has a long history of resistance to the idea of providing crèche facilities. No one quite remembers when it all began, but the BBC Crèche Campaign emerged in the 1970s, faded and has re-emerged again at different times. In 1986, it was re-activated to claim a workplace nursery in the new building to be constructed at Television Centre in London. Five years earlier the BBC had agreed, in principle, to provide crèche facilities, but nothing happened. The new site provides the opportunity for the matter to be raised again and ensure that the Corporation fulfils its promise. The BBC Equality Network was responsible for the 1986 crèche campaign. BETA organised lunchtime meetings and leafleted the workplace. But a woman official from BETA still expects the BBC to say that feasibility plans were made for crèche facilities but no money can be made available. Another concern she expressed referred to some of the unspoken assumptions about those who would be eligible to use crèche facilities should they eventually appear. Secretarial, clerical or catering staff might be unable to benefit from the new facilities. Such a development reflects the implicit narrowness of a strategy which makes a genuine attempt to be broad. Potentially this problem exists in a strategy which has been designed and developed by a relatively privileged group of women. Unwittingly, their efforts can sometimes fail to encompass others less fortunate than themselves. Historically, the activities of an elite group of women can often do more to move things forward than those of others less powerful in the broadcasting institutions. For example, it was the efforts of a successful pressure group called the Women's Broadcasting and Film Lobby (WBFL), which prompted Thames to take part in the positive action project. This group was set up in 1979 and comprised a number of professional women who were frustrated by the poor career prospects available to them in the industry.

WBFL approached the IBA in 1980 with a number of suggestions for how the new fourth channel could meet the needs of women. They proposed that the Broadcasting Bill should include specific provision for women's training, that a senior officer should be appointed to the channel to oversee positive action and that there should be a weekly current affairs programme made by women. WBFL's strategy was to gain access and influence over senior management and decision-makers inside and outside television. They lobbied a broad range of establishment figures and received support from the Liberal Party Peer, Baroness Seear, for their proposed amendment to the Broadcasting Bill. They exchanged regular correspondence and held meetings with officers from the IBA. But still WBFL did not achieve total success. They did not secure a provision for women's training in the Broadcasting Bill and their request for a Channel 4 Positive Action Officer was ignored. But the Lobby's high-level approach did bring a number of achievements and advantages. Before the time came for the re-allocation of the ITV franchises in 1982, the ITV companies came under small but significant pressure to improve their record on equal opportunities. The then Chairman (*sic*) of the IBA, Lady Plowden, sent a supplementary question about the number of women employees to all companies intending to bid for a franchise.

Like the BBC Equality Network, WBFL's aim was to go straight to the top. In an institution as hierarchical as broadcasting, any change initiated from the highest level is bound to have an immediate impact on the rest of the organisation. If a liberal-minded individual in senior management can be prevailed upon to introduce small changes in favour of women, then the rest of senior personnel can be expected to fall into line. However, the demands which WBFL were making were limited to their most immediate concerns. Inevitably, these were far removed from the needs and anxieties of women engaged in the less glamorous end of broadcasting. But this is not to invalidate their efforts. The changes WBFL were pressing for had implications well beyond the individual career frustrations of the group. Their efforts brought the position of women in the industry, and our representation on the screen, much more sharply into the public eye.

Union moves

WBFL chose to operate outside, although with the support of the unions. The strategies developed by women inside the two main broadcasting unions, BETA and ACTT, centre on the immediate needs and the potential aspirations of their female membership. The emphasis on training has been a particularly important initiative in overcoming some of the historical obstacles to women's employment. In an industry which is based on technology and engineering, not many women have the educational background and confidence to apply for jobs. A recent training initiative called Jobfit aims to reduce the barrier to women's technical inexperience, Jobfit is an imaginative scheme originated by the ACTT in 1984. The union pushed and negotiated for two years with the film employers' organisation to interest them in the scheme. Eventually they agreed to support it and member companies are now required to pay a levy to help finance the project. The money pays for the training of fifty young people, and the important provision of Jobfit is that 50 per cent of its intake has to come from the ethnic minorities.

> Up until now there has been no proper training in the film industry. You got in either because you were somebody's son or because you had been to college. Now, because employers have to pay money into Jobfit, they are less likely to take someone's son – they take someone

from the scheme they are paying for. (ACTT Equality Officer interview)

Jobfit involves one year of general training and one year of specialised work. The scheme is deliberately pitched at non-graduates, 'It tries to aim for the young people who did not have a nice middle-class education. They may not have had formal qualifications either, though obviously they have an aptitude and interest in technical things' (*ibid.*).

Women in BETA also identify training as the weakest area of the BBC's employment policies. Commenting on the Sims inquiry, Christina Driver says:

> From the start of the BBC career structure, including traineeships and at every level of responsibility, there is a scarcity of women. Although women enter the job market in roughly similar proportions to men, as to numbers and abilities, the BBC fails to recruit them in the same proportions into the crucial trainee posts. (*BETA Journal*, July/August 1986)

Sims reported that, in the case of management training courses, there had been no increase in the proportion of women attending. She suggested that career guidance and selection methods were not encouraging enough women who deserved promotion. She added that training attachment schemes were under-resourced and managers unwilling to let people go on attachment if there was no money available for replacement staff. Women, specifically, suffered when there was less available training. The union has suggested that the BBC adopt a policy of quotas on traineeships and that appropriate courses be designed for secretarial and clerical staff who wish to move on in their careers. Out of a total of 589 women secretaries and clerks who stayed in the BBC for five years only sixteen moved to higher grades. These findings led Sims to conclude, 'If more women are to be encouraged to leap across [jobs] the time may have come to consider effective training courses designed solely for women' (Sims, 1985). Most of BETA's female members are concentrated in the traditionally segregated areas of clerical, cleaning and catering jobs, thus reflecting the sexual division of labour which exists in the workforce as a whole. The majority of these jobs are low-paid. Catering staff, for example, often receive less than the Low Pay Unit's minimum of £3 per hour (*BETA Journal*

July/August 1986). Pay agreements are therefore important immediate concerns. The needs of this layer of workers have become more acute since the election of the Conservative Government in 1979. The Peacock Committee, set up in May 1985, inquired into new ways of funding the BBC. When it reported in July 1986 it fell short of recommending advertising, except to suggest its partial introduction on radio. Many consider this to be the thin end of the wedge of privatisation. In 1985, the BBC announced 4,000 redundancies and the targeted areas were cleaning and catering, with an additional 10 per cent reduction in secretarial jobs. BETA launched an effective publicity campaign to resist privatisation and redundancies. But a strategic weakness of this campaign was its almost exclusive focus on the bread and butter issues. The campaign was traditionally defensive and the important issue of pay became isolated from the wider, more long-term political priorities of recruitment, training and child-care provision. One official from BETA told me:

> Our priority is to defend jobs and conditions. One of the things which annoys me about the left's view of the broadcasting unions is that they say we do not storm the barricades for the issues of access and accountability etc. But you have to start from the baseline and that is, most people go out to work to earn their living. They are not excited about the product. The priority of the trade union movement is to get members (personal interview, 1986)

The problem however is that women trade unionists do not have an equal share of the benefits of trade union membership because the history and outlook of the unions have been shaped by men. The majority of union agreements fail to prioritise women's different needs properly. Active feminists, inside and outside the unions, have been struggling to change this. In public service organisations, such as the Health Service, women have pointed to the need for trade unions to change their organisational forms and concerns to attract women members. Why should women lend their active support to defend an organisation whose practices often embody and institutionalise their oppression? Any campaign to protect broadcasting also needs to take into account the particular nature of the role of women in that institution.

Many trade unionists now accept that effective opposition requires more than a defence of what we have; we need some strategic thinking for how we can improve it. There are three to four million women trade unionists and the unions have to some extent widened their concerns to meet the needs of this growing membership. Job-sharing and improved maternity agreements have been established and procedures around issues such as sexual harassment have been secured. But it seems that the political and economic constraints of the mid 1980s are threatening to undermine the influence of feminism and reduce the possibilities of emerging new strategies. The issue of improving, rather than defending, public service broadcasting has unwittingly become a campaigning luxury.

Women in hiding

Historically the labour movement has always allowed the specific needs of women to become eclipsed in times of economic crisis. In this current 'historic watershed in the evolution of the British media' (Curran and Seaton, 1985, p.90) it is vital that the political concerns of women do not get left behind. The need to defend public service broadcasting, maintain jobs and services and protect editorial independence need not be counterposed to the long-term feminist strategies which are still required to bring about changes in the position of women in television.

Appropriate to these changes at a theoretical level, is a perspective which has the principles and values of feminism at its centre. As yet, no such framework exists. The intellectual history of television studies has involved a consistent 'genderisation' of ideas. In the 1970s, theoreticians of the left focused on the political means by which a certain class ruled and the ideological means by which that class encouraged us all to make sense of the world (Curran and Seaton, 1985, pp.251–315). In particular they explained the ways in which the media reflect and naturalise power relationships, identifying these inequalities primarily in terms of class. The Glasgow University Media Group's work also focuses on the media in class society. The framework of their analysis is the political and economic interests at work in television. Journalists and editors, they say, are 'one part of a society which takes private ownership, social hierarchies and profit for granted as the natural way of organising economic production and social relationships' (Glasgow Group, 1982, p.128). The other 'natural way' of organising things is through gender inequalities. While the needs of women are not isolated, they are nevertheless different. It is this difference which has not been adequately theorised in media studies. This theoretical inadequacy underpins many of the campaigning weaknesses of mixed organisations for media reform. The questions of democracy and accountability raised by the women's liberation movement have been crucial to the politics of organisations. It is also worth remembering that the democratic changes we are seeking in television remain to a large extent contingent upon a more political, feminised trade union movement.

Positive action as a strategy evolved during the 1970s and correctly focused on the patriarchal style and structure of broadcasting. But because the power relations within these institutions are not always gender-specific, the particular needs of working-class women were under-represented in these campaigns. An essential requirement of any positive action programme is that it should cater for the different discrimination faced by particular groups of women, such as working-class and black women. It should also enable us to challenge the structures of the television industry rather than just work for equal participation within them. The owners of our cultural industries are offering us an apparently freer and more diversified media through new technology. However, their pledges conceal and mystify the real ways in which that technology is changing our lives. Feminists are trying to uncover the process of this transformation by going beyond observable facts to piece together what lies behind them:

> To understand the different relation the sexes have to new technology
> today we need to recognise the relevance of technology to
> power. . . . In technology the exclusion of women secures men as a
> sex a very tangible form of authority and power. (Cockburn, 1986)

New technology in broadcasting is influencing the politics of representation as well as restructuring employment. As a consequence, society's sexual division of labour is deepening and television images are creating a different sense of ourselves. Positive action is therefore an essential unifying element in the wider strategic objective for a more open, representative media. We are struggling in a cold climate but there is always the possibility of something better. Our recent history has shown that at different moments, and with different energies, we always return to the possibilities and our long continuous efforts to realise them.

References

Baehr, H. (1981), 'Women's employment in British television: programming the future?', *Media, Culture and Society*, vol.3, pp.125–34.

Cockburn, C. (1986), *Machinery of Dominance*, London, Pluto Press.

Cockburn, C. and Loach, L. (1986), 'In whose image', in J. Curran *et al.* (eds), *Bending Reality*, London, Pluto Press.

Coote, A. and Campbell, B. (1982), *Sweet Freedom*, London, Picador.

Curran, J. and Seaton, J. (1985), 'Theories of the media', *Power Without Responsibility*, London, Methuen.

Gill, T. and Whitty, L. (1983), *Women's Rights in The Workplace*, London, Penguin.

Glasgow University Media Group (1982), *Really Bad News*, London, Writers & Readers.

Robarts, S. with Coote, A. and Ball, E. (1981), *Positive Action for Women*, London, NCCL.

Sims, M. (1985), *Women In BBC Management*, BBC Report.

PART TWO
Programming Strategies

5 'Programmes for women' in 1950s British television

Joy Leman

'Programmes for women' has been a constant theme of daytime programming from the earliest period of broadcasting up to the present day. These programmes were constituted at a watershed point in the establishment of television in Britain. Television was legitimised both as an industrial and cultural institution in the 1950s during a crucial period of economic and social change spanning the swing from postwar austerity to conditions of economic boom. A consideration of economic, organisational and political determinants on programmes designated for women at that time offers a useful dimension to current debates on 'progressive' television programmes for women. The analysis presented here takes as its starting point a number of key questions. What purpose was served in the overall economic and ideological project of the institutions of television by a genre of 'women's programmes'? What assumptions of class, gender and the family were inscribed in this area of broadcasting at a time when television was becoming established with a wider, working-class audience? How did 'women's programmes' change when other areas of television were becoming 'liberalised' for a time in the 1960s?

From 'woman at war' to 'invisible worker'

The first television programmes – in the 1930s – had been restricted to a privileged middle-class audience in the southeast of England, largely because of the high cost of receivers and transmission limitations. After the complete closure of television during the Second World War, a similar small-scale service began again in 1946. With the economic boom of the 1950s, a consequent reduction in the cost of television sets and an expanded transmission system, figures on the ownership of receivers indicated for the first time a primarily working-class audience (Briggs, 1979, pp.240,265). The focus of expenditure and output of programmes was on hearth and home and the target audience was the family, with women defined largely in relation to the home. It took the blood, bombs and bullets of the Second World War to force British broadcasting for a brief period to recognise women workers as audience. The need to mobilise women for the war effort and sustain morale pushed the BBC into a direct address to working-class women. Women's magazine editors and programme producers had stumbled on a largely untapped market. In wartime the market was defined as workers. In peacetime it was defined as housewives. In either case, broadcasters had accepted the usefulness of a 'women's programmes' genre, but not without a debate which forced the acceptance of a very different perspective of women's interests (Leman, 1983).

Janet Quigley, a radio talks producer who started work at the BBC during the 1930s and went on to produce *Woman's Hour* in the 1950s, argued for more programmes directed towards working women since the 'war effort' required their compulsory mobilisation.[1] The hierarchy of the BBC was sceptical but eventually agreed to expand the appeal of series such as *Women at War* to include women working in factories as well as in the services. The 'national interest' here required that 'women's interests' should include domestic issues but it was agreed that war work in the factories and services be put temporarily at the forefront of importance.

The ending of the war was the cue for a re-adjustment of the dominant ideology with regard to women's role in society, with wife and mother first on the agenda and the worker rendered invisible once again. Programme-makers reverted back to a mode of address and programme topics which were home- and child-centred (Leman, *op. cit.*). A major shift of emphasis took place in which the ideology of domesticity was brought to the foreground and the exemplary model of manners and cultural assumptions were again middle-class. The BBC radio series *Woman's Hour*, which started in 1946, is the most well-known example of this trend. A pronounced redefinition of 'women's interests' was taking place with pressure from every direction to accept the new emphasis. Exhortations came from academics and social policy-makers, concerned at declining population levels, to focus on home and children with a new professional status offered to the housewife and mother.[2] For many women the luxury of a choice between work or homemaking did not exist. The problem of a forcible ejection from the wartime workplace to make jobs for the men was matched by the need to get employment in industries where women were accepted. The price to be paid was poor rates of pay with bad conditions and minimal trade union organisation (Boston, 1980).

The labour shortage of the late 1940s, and the fact that many women simply changed jobs but did not give up paid employment, were hardly manifested in the 'women's media' of the time.[3] The continued employment of women, in traditional women's industries and often on the twilight shift, did not feature in the postwar address to women from broadcast programmes or from women's print magazines. Suddenly the only representations of women at work were of white-collar jobs (Leman, *op. cit.*). Even the Equal Pay Campaign of the 1940s and 50s received relatively little coverage on radio and television.[4] This was in sharp contrast to government appeals encouraging more women to go out to work, even part-time, to earn the extra cash which eventually made possible the purchase of TV sets and other consumer goods. Postwar reconstruction shifted to the 1950s launchpad of economic boom with expansion (largely into arms expenditure) and consumer spending fed into an actual improvement in living standards for many people (Kidron, 1970; Boston, *op. cit.*). Women's interests were still defined as practical/domestic, neatly excluding the other half of the double job routine experienced by women as workers and trade unionists.

Designing 'women's interests'

Initially, daytime television programmes for women were broadcast by the BBC on only one afternoon monthly. This increased gradually to one afternoon fortnightly and later to four days a week, usually under the umbrella programme title of *Mainly for Women*. Often surviving on shoestring budgets, daytime programming was seen by executives as a useful way of 'taking up the slack'. Equipment and staff which would otherwise be 'lying idle' could be used to produce cheap programmes to fill the screen during daytime transmission hours.[5] Magazine programmes for women became established as a genre in daytime schedules in the late 1940s and 50s, but not without constant lobbying by the producers and editors of the programmes for additional resources and an increase in the frequency of broadcasts.

The first television series for women began in October 1947 and was entitled *Designed for Women*. The focus on fashion, cookery and childcare was not new but a formula developed in pre-war print magazines and to some extent in radio programmes. The affinity of interests between those involved in media production aimed at women was a key factor in the consolidation of a narrowly defined assumption of women's interests. Broadcasters seemed to think that the print magazines had discovered the right formula for the female audience and tried to develop firstly the radio equivalent to this and later the television version.

Designed for Women was planned as the first 'Women's Hour Programme' and was initially entitled *Television Tea Party*. *Picture Post* described it as 'television's experiment in offering a show aimed at one section only of its audience' (17 April 1948). The aim was 'to produce an afternoon gathering of women in the news, at which viewers were invited to attend'. This was the celebrity chat show in embryo, with the addition of the practical inputs thought by some to characterise 'women's interests'. The original plans for this series described it as 'a magazine programme of special interest to women'. The initiator and first producer of the programme was Mary Adams. She had worked in radio in the 1930s and with the Ministry of Information during wartime. A Cambridge graduate, she later became head of Television Talks. In suggesting the title *Women's Page* for the new series, Mary Adams acknowledged the values and forms inscribed in well-established print models for women. The programme proposals which she submitted for approval by the Director of Television Programmes were organised under the following headings: children; house and home; personal appearance; cookery and shopping; films ('We've tracked down at least half a dozen ten-minute films which could find a place here, e.g. *Care of your Children's eyes, teeth, ears, etc., Nursery Schools, Women in India*, etc.'); leisure activities ('e.g. choosing a library list [by some critic of repute], music, current picture shows, a poem – also here might come some news items, e.g. Parliamentary report [women's interests]').

Figure 5.1 *Designed for Women* BBC TV programme. In it are children's welfare expert, Myra Curtis (left) interviewed by editor-hostess Jeanne Heal, and (right) Lady Douglas Hamilton who gives health exercises.

Figure 5.2 *Designed for Women* BBC TV programme. Marguerite Patten (l.) demonstrates cookery, assisted by pianist Geraldine Peppin. On right is studio manager Roland Price.

In a simple and direct way Mary Adams here established the basic format for the magazine programme. She explained her approach pragmatically in terms of sustaining programme categories within the bureaucratic structure of the BBC, 'The emphasis in my list is on the practical aspects of women's interests – justified by the fact that other interests are provided for in ordinary evening transmissions.'[6] Mary Adams here both explained and acknowledged the 'absences' in women's programmes, but more importantly defined the rationale which would attract the organisational recognition of staffing, resources, power and control of 'women's programmes' within the structure of the BBC. Later, when it came to pressures exerted from below to establish an editor for Women's Programmes and to form an independent section separate from the Talks Department, one of the crucial issues focused on the dividing line between established empires and areas of control. Thus anything produced within 'women's programmes' which dealt with politics or current affairs would require approval by the Talks Department. This provided a strong incentive to deal only with subjects which would be perceived as sufficiently different from 'talks' to justify the maintenance of a separate section.

The formula adopted for this first series for women became the norm, even though at the time the audience was few in number and mainly middle-class. Viewer response to the first broadcast was 'extremely favourable'.[7] Mary Adams commented that 'it is obvious that we have a ready-made audience of women who for one reason or another are tied to the home'. The key role of 'presenter' as mediator was also recognised by Mary Adams in her plan to 'continue building up a relationship with viewers through Jeanne Heal'.[8] The work of establishing the 'television personality' who would provide a familiar and 'friendly' contact point for viewers was already taking place. That privileged contact of 'direct address' allowed to the television presenter has particular significance in relation to media oriented towards women. Print magazines have traded on the intimacy of direct address to women readers in which a discourse of friendliness and confidentiality is brought into play. The class nature of the communication had to be disguised in the magazines in order to sell the produce (Leman, 1980). In broadcasting, upper-class accents and presentation could not so easily be rendered neutral.[9] Scripts offer some indication that a 'friendly', informal style was aimed at, even though this was delivered in the tones of 'BBC English' of the southeast of England. Jeanne Heal, for example, assumes direct access to viewers of *Designed for Women*, pulling the viewer into the magic circle of intimacy, patronising and thanking us for sending in recipes – providing the raw material for the programme at no cost to the BBC – 'Your ideas are so good we hope to get one of you along each time to demonstrate'.[10]

Women in vision: taboo and token

While the issue of class was hardly discussed at the BBC, the presence of women both in vision and behind the scenes was (and still is) a contentious question. In spite of the fact that the first Heads of Talks in radio and later in television were women (Hilda Matheson and Mary Adams), a recurrent debate has focused on the inherent unsuitability of women to the medium of radio and later to major areas of television. An interview with Grace Wyndham Goldie, who became Head of BBC Television Talks and Current Affairs in the 1960s, offers a revealing insight from one of the few women to have achieved a position of power in broadcasting:

> Good women interviewers are extremely rare. . . . Women's diction, for some reason, produces a more class-conscious connotation.
> Listening to a woman on TV, one can almost put her into one class or another, but this doesn't apply to men for some reason. It's my theory anyway. But we do have some excellent women producers. (*Sunday Times*, 20 January 1963)

There were in fact very few women producers or interviewers. A style of professionalism and authority had been adopted by male presenters and interviewers in television, which was linked to the male dominance established by the ruling class in society as a whole. A key factor in the style was the inadmissibility of the class nature of the address and the maintenance of the ideology of neutrality so important to the ruling institutions in society. Women, even with the required class credentials, were often considered, in both production and presentation, less credible authority figures than men by the BBC hierarchy.[11] This may have been partly due to the fact that with less experience at generating a style of objectivity, women presenters inadvertently revealed the class basis of the broadcasting enterprise, thus undermining its credibility as a whole. Generally, the question of women on and in television was seen not as an issue of class but became a problem of gender and a debate about the suitability of women as such to appear on television. The style of the upper-class woman was condemned as the style of all women in connection with television.

The presence (or absence) of men, both as producers and as presenters in women's programmes, has a significance which derives from that continuing debate. Significantly, one of the first experimental television broadcasts in May 1946 was a hat show, presented by a man.[12] The experiment concerned mixing and cutting between cameras in the studio. The visual subject was the female face and the use of headwear to emphasise or conceal particular features according to the dominant aesthetic and fashion selling point. The script indicates the male presenter in control, moving the 'expert' (female) along from model to model – the female face framed by the camera as an object of pleasure and voyeurism – the male presenter 'standing in' for the male viewer, distancing himself from the 'feminine mystique' on display. This approach became established in later fashion shows broadcast in the evening and aimed at both women and men in the audience. Many of the earliest television programmes for women were produced by a man – S.E. Reynolds – including a short-lived series of interviews with 'celebrity' women broadcast in 1950 and entitled *Women of Today*.[13] In 1951 David Bryson produced a series entitled *Women's Viewpoint* which again featured celebrity women and was intended to deal with a range of controversial issues including divorce, equal pay, and married women at work.[14] Bryson was worried about how women viewers would react to 'women-only' programmes. He foresaw criticisms of his approach as a 'ghettoisation' of women in television, and anticipated that 'some feminists, who are more concerned to break down the male grip on general discussion programmes may suspect a sinister plot to restrict women to a sort of radio "purdah"'. He seemed to be looking for a distinctively 'feminine' style of television to counter 'the intensity and all-in wrestling' of men in TV debate. Interestingly, Bryson saw the visual signification of these apparent gender differences as important to the *mise en scène* of the series, commenting that, 'They will be

Figure 5.3 *About the Home* Eileen Fowler teaching keep fit 'to keep muscles toned up with daily exercise and lighten the housework'.

provided with a setting appropriate to women. Sofa and easy chairs will replace the uncompromising battle-stations and name cards of the successful *In the News* forum'. Breakfast television in Britain in the 1980s lost a lot of viewers before learning this hard lesson, but then went on to incorporate many other aspects of women's programmes into the 'informality' of the early morning format.

A genteel approach in an informal domestic setting, with 'celebrity' spokespersons offering established opinion to viewers was classified as 'women's viewpoint' – the closest approach to a discussion programme on 'serious' issues. A long-running series called *About the Home*, which started in 1952, indicates both in content and style the class-specific nature of the practical homecare programme. *About the Home* spanned the period of take off for television in the mid-1950s when the sale of TV sets in Britain rapidly expanded, the audience became primarily working-class instead of primarily middle-class – and the BBC had to face competition from ITV. But relatively little change is apparent in the series over that time. Each programme contained at least one item presented by a man, ranging from gardening to cobweb knitting. Recurrent topics, clearly popular with the producer (S.E. Reynolds) and editor, concerned dogs, flower-arranging, cookery, shopping, health and keep-fit (see Figure 5.3). As in the case of television news construction, the selection and treatment of material was determined by ideological factors, some of which were transparently crude in their class arrogance. A typical example can be found in the presentation of a 'health' item in a programme which dealt with hygiene factors in the preparation of food. The device of drama documentary was used to indicate the 'wrong' way to prepare food. The didactic tone of the drama was extended to the depiction of a stereotypical working-class family. References to flies, dirty washing-up cloths, meat warmed up in the oven, cats and 'grubby boy's dirty fingers' all pointed to the conclusion that 'their' dirty habits were the reason for outbreaks of food poisoning. That separation between the 'innocent' viewer (assumed to be middle-class) and the 'guilty' subject of the programme (presented as working-class) was neatly reinforced by the narrator's comment – 'Now most of you will have very few flies in your kitchen, but . . . '[15]

A separate department and a strategy to counter ITV

The establishment of 'Editor Women's Programmes', with similar control of resources and money as that of Head of Department, marked BBC acknowledgment of the importance of programmes for women in the run up to the start of ITV in September 1955. Women's programmes, initially on radio and later on television, had arisen out of the Talks Department and in both cases there was strong resistance to the possibility of a separate section. Whether this was due to reasons of misogyny or to a tendency to preserve the status quo is not clear. The inherent conservatism of bureaucratic structures when presented with change was certainly a factor in the situation. Briggs comments on the sensitivity of organisational issues at the BBC at the time, 'Finding the right procedures for organising television seemed just as important in 1954 and 1955 as new ideas' (Briggs, 1979, p.987). The key changes started at the beginning of 1954 when Mary Adams became a special assistant to Television Programmes' Controller – Cecil McGivern. In a memo explaining the plan to the Head of Talks Department, McGivern stressed the 'natural development' of the move. Television as a separate section inside the BBC with its own cluster of Heads of Departments had only been set up in 1951. The new head of Television Talks, fresh from radio, was clearly not keen on the idea of losing control over part of his department. An equally lukewarm response came from the Assistant Head of Talks, Grace Wyndham Goldie, who saw the split as 'premature'. A separate department for Women's Programmes was eventually approved by the Director of Television Broadcasting in 1955, on condition that the editor consulted the Head of Talks on any items concerned with political and current affairs speakers. This was both a vote of confidence for the recently appointed editor of Women's Programmes, Doreen Stephens (who had become 'fully operational' in the job on 1 April 1954), and a strategy for containment of the serious matter of politics and current affairs in their 'rightful' place in Talks Department, well away from 'women's issues'.

Doreen Stephens was to have a major influence on the direction of women's television programmes during the 1950s and 1960s. Her social and political interests, therefore, offer a useful insight into the programme policies which she pursued. She stood as a Liberal in four national and two borough council elections and at one stage was President of the Women's Liberal Federation (*Television Annual*, 1955, p.149). She was Secretary of the Red Cross Overseas Department, a welfare adviser to the London County Council, and 'Chairman' of the Council of Married Women. In the period leading up to the start of ITV, Doreen Stephens attended a series of fourteen meetings around Britain with 'representatives from Women's Organisations . . . and Women's Institutes' to ascertain the needs of women viewers. The contact list for women's programmes consisted of largely middle-class, statutory organisations such as the National Townswomen's Guilds, the Electrical Association for Women and the Women's Voluntary Services. The only trade union contact was the TUC Women's Officer. The result of these meetings was a request, never properly met, for a home magazine programme in the evenings and approval for the existing emphasis on 'practical' programmes: 'Majority demand is for a practical down to earth programme with a few items done in a thoroughly straightforward manner.'[16]

Family Affairs was a 'practical' series 'for mothers with young children' which began in 1955, arising partly out of Doreen Stephens's meetings with viewers. Experts on 'the family' were a key element in the programme. A typical panel considered qualified to answer 'general family problems' consisted of a doctor, a JP and a clergyman. The careful selection of 'experts' was crucial to the ideological reinforcement of family norms and in this respect representatives of the law, religion and professional medicine were seen as the acceptable authorities on family life. While a neutrality of approach is implied in the stress on the 'practical' and the presence of the 'expert', the norms of family life and the standards of good practice adhered to were middle-class, as were the criteria for making judgments.

Another major series during the first half of the 1950s was *Leisure and Pleasure*, considered less 'practical' in its orientation, and subject to intense criticism from the Controller of Programmes, Cecil McGivern. The series devoted roughly 25 per cent of its output to items concerning childcare, education, and the condition of the family, all with appropriate 'experts' provided. Typical content in the remainder of the programme included flower-arranging, embroidery, antiques, Welsh tweeds, and 'celebrity' guests adding a cultural dimension from music, literature, theatre and fashion. In the BBC strategy for countering ITV a range of other programmes featured in the *Mainly for Women* slot, targeted at different sections of the female viewing audience. Launched with a 'tea dance' broadcast from BBC TV Centre, the package of new programmes included *Twice Twenty*, 'a magazine programme for older women', *Your own Time* and *Around and About*, 'for the younger married woman'. *Pennywise* and *Look and Choose* were consumer advice programmes, chaired by Lady Isobel Barnett. Conspicuously absent were programmes dealing with the immediate problems faced by the majority of women at the time – bad housing, inadequate nursery provision, low wages, poor conditions of work, etc. It seems hardly surprising that, according to a 1955 BBC Viewer Research Report, of the potential audience of women 'available to view' in the afternoons, only 12 to 15 per cent were even 'fairly regular viewers'.[17] The choice between official pronouncements on family life and the cultural preoccupations of a home counties elite, may have rendered women's television programmes irrelevant to the concerns of the majority of the 'potential audience'. Women's Programmes Organiser, Robin Whitworth, constructed a list of probing questions in response to these findings, including the following:

> Bearing in mind that over fifty per cent of the actual and potential viewers of Women's Programmes left school at the age of fourteen or less, do the programmes show signs of any class-consciousness or bias in either direction? With regard to social class and income group, are the programmes appropriately tuned to the audience?[18]

Unfortunately, Robin Whitworth's questions were never properly answered, and the implications of the audience research apparently ignored.

Women's programmes as advertising magazines

Women's programmes were a small but essential part of the fanfare opening of commercial television, which professed both an informality and an excitement unknown to the BBC.[19] The 'new ITV age' was committed, for the first few months at least, to the recognition of a wider audience of women and to programme content not yet exclusively advertising-oriented. Initially, the presence of men in the programmes was emphasised. The *Daily Herald* announced, 'Men will run women's world on rival TV', suggesting, 'Men will be the main attraction of the morning programmes for women' (*Daily Herald*, 19 May 1955). The first commercial television programmes for women were produced, directed, and in some cases introduced by men. The prejudice noted earlier by David Bryson against women as broadcasters was not restricted to the BBC and neither was the related assumption that a male presence adds authority/sexual interest to women's programmes.

The timing of transmissions was clearly geared to connect with an audience of women at home, many of whom might not be viewers of BBC afternoon programmes. *Morning Magazine* was broadcast by Associated-Rediffusion Ltd every weekday morning, 11.00–11.30, and combined the traditional interpretation of 'women's interests' with the populist emphasis of the commercial companies on genres thought to constitute 'entertainment'. In this case, the entertainment item came first with fifteen minutes of *Sixpenny Corner*, probably the first TV soap opera in Britain. The second part of the programme alternated between the three traditional pivots of 'women's interests' as established by the BBC – 'practical' home-making, childcare and female physical appearance.

Although the morning programme was explicitly directed towards women viewers, a range of magazine programmes at other times, particularly at weekends, seemed to be targeted at 'the family', with a particular address to women. *Weekend*, which went out on Saturday mornings, 9.30–10.30, was 'an informal magazine for the family' introduced by Daphne Anderson and including items on 'how to look and what to cook' as well as entertainment for 'the younger members of the family'. *Home with Joy Shelton* for twenty minutes on Saturday afternoons presented itself as 'an informal, entertaining guide to shopping, with advice on cookery . . . labour-saving gadgets, beauty hints by Steiner, and a wide variety of items of interest to the whole family'. *Sunday Afternoon* offered an even broader base of 'family interest', encompassing current affairs issues with the theme, 'Nothing interests people so much as other people'. Profiles of 'remarkable personalities' were presented by Tom Driberg, Ludovic Kennedy and Anthony Wedgewood Benn, while Jill Craigie gave a 'film report on some of the things women do' (*TV Times*, 20 September 1955). High culture was included with poetry reading from Dame Edith Sitwell and 'handmime' from Chin Yu. *Sunday Afternoon* was described by Sendall as 'intelligent, ambitious, highly praised and overcrowded' (Sendall, 1982, p.322).

Single topic, short programmes on domestic subjects were already oriented towards advertising. The *TV Times* pre-Christmas edition for 1955 featured a double page spread on *Going Shopping*. The reader was taken on a 'shopping spree' with five of the regular women presenters of the programme through three major named stores. The style of both the article and the 'candid' photographs would have fitted well into the pages of *Woman* or *Woman's Own* with the headline '*TV Times* takes these Shopping Girls shopping'. The seasonal focus was used to bind together the printed article and the programme with a common selling point. The lighter, 'friendlier' tone of the print magazines for women is characteristic of the *TV Times*' presentation at this stage, and arguably of the programmes themselves. This contrasts with the more didactic approach of the BBC, which in the *Radio Times* had connotations of the Health Visitor on Family issues, the Women's Institute on homecraft, and a sub-Vogue approach to fashion.

The commercial basis of ITV programmes for women was sharply revealed within a few months when drastic cuts were made to save money and morning television was wound up. The logic of commercial television transformed women's programmes into advertising magazines. By 1957, the only trace of even the traditional women's interest areas in ITV was in the brief but nightly advertising magazine. *Television Beauty Salon* was presented by Honor Blackman and typical items included fashion journalist Iris Ashley talking about autumn hats and an advertising feature by Ponds. *Slater's Bazaar, Jim's Inn, For Pete's Sake* and *Open House* were all variations on the theme of displaying and selling goods for the home. 'Women's interests' had been officially restored to the marketplace – for the time being at least.

'Women's programmes' become 'family programmes' at the BBC

Programmes for women in BBC television were, throughout the 1950s, subject to constant criticism and attack within the institution while all appeared smiling amiability to the public. Controller of Programmes, Cecil McGivern, sent the editor of Women's Programmes detailed and often acerbic critical analysis after each broadcast:

> I realise more and more as I watch women's programmes that there is almost a complete lack of imagination and sparkle in the presentation. (7 February 1955)

He attacked the programmes for their lack of 'professional' presentation, making snide comments on personalities and presenters, but offered no alternative concept of women's programmes – only a glossier, slicker version of the same.[20] Cecil McGivern wanted more fashion and cookery programmes in evening transmissions to counter the output of the commercial channel, while Doreen Stephens favoured expansion of daytime programmes to five afternoons a week. In 1957, cuts were made in women's programmes due to 'excess of permitted transmission hours', and the following year McGivern proposed a review of 'the whole question of Women's Programmes'. Nevertheless, Doreen Stephens and the Women's Programmes team survived and went on making programmes up until the mid 1960s.

The different ideological climate of the 1960s, combined with organisational changes at the BBC (including the start of BBC 2) led to the demise of women's programmes. The Women's Programmes Unit was replaced by the Family Programmes Department, headed by Doreen Stephens, whose staff combined those of the Women's Programmes and the Children's Departments. In explaining the new structure internally, the following explanation was given: 'There are no longer, as you know, any programmes purely aimed at a women's audience in the afternoons or at any other time. The programmes mainly now transmitted can be defined as features or documentaries of social interest.'[21] The memo also referred to confusion regarding the new departmental structures – 'in view of the brevity of the original promulgation about the formation of Family Programmes'. The editors of radio's *Woman's Hour* and of television programmes for women had both fiercely defended their respective areas when at different times there had been attempts to make cuts. It is certain that when instructions came to axe Women's Programmes a debate must have ensued. The fact that the record of this debate seems to have disappeared suggests that the discussion became acrimonious at the personal level, or that issues were debated which the BBC would not want made public.

The cocktail party set

Alternative proposals for programmes directed towards women were made by staff in the BBC's Family Programmes Department. A weekly magazine programme entitled *Gilt and Gingerbread* was intended as an evening programme 'for women which men will want to watch'.[22] The idea for the series originated by Lorna Pegram, a producer with experience in both radio and television programmes for women, did not gain official approval for broadcasting but the discussion it provoked indicates a different phase in the attitudes towards programmes for women. An experimental approach was suggested, with ideas for moving away from the anchorman (or woman!) formula, and from the 'jaded alternatives of a cosy sitting room or a studio with lights and cameras. . . . The set for *The Cocktail Party*, neutral, elegant, stylised but patently not a studio, might be one possibility'.[23] The programme was to be a mixture of serious and frivolous elements, and was to include news comment. The influence of both political satire programmes and colour supplements is apparent in the suggested contents list: 'consumer grievance, the Queen's new hairstyle, the sale of *Les Grandes baigneuses*, intra-uterine contraceptive devices, egg marketing board subsidies, sale of chastity belts, the Beatles' biography, Sandie Shaw's cold feet, [and] Parliamentary debate on health clinics.'[24] Unfortunately, what was seen as an attempt to 'allow pace, variety and an astringent tone of voice' simply had a trivialising effect on the serious subjects by placing them next to the 'frivolous' topics – somehow making safe all items in the list, like the standard comic/sentimental ending to a news report. The content remains the same: only the packaging has changed. The explanation given for 'shelving' the plan for the series was limited resources and transmission hours for BBC2 although Michael Peacock, Chief of BBC2 Programmes, had 'doubts about it on programme grounds'.[25] However, one unsigned comment on the proposal offers a significant and unpleasant insight into the sexist attitudes of some broadcasting executives:

> If in its basic programme attitude and content *Gilt and Gingerbread* wants to appeal to men, I would suggest that it drops the suffragette approach, which was outdated by 1917. The equality of the sexes doesn't interest men . . . in the sexual opposition of male and female, nothing is more subtly powerful than feminine charm, guile, beauty, and other sides of female nature that women know so much better than [men-deleted] I do. Women analyse what makes them desirable, package that desirability, and sell it quite brilliantly. (After all, at the lowest level, it's always the woman who is the prostitute, never the man.) I feel certain that the superiority of the feminist is the approach which appeals to the men – they are bored by the struggle for equality, children's clothes and the tax on eggs.[26]

The writer was clearly more concerned with the male response to the programme than with the female viewing audience, positioning women not only as objects of display in the programme but in the other traditional stereotype of seductress and femme fatale. Even the three 'resident personalities' planned by Doreen Stephens to present the programme would have been drawn from a list largely consisting of 'celebrity' men.

Important changes were taking place in BBC television at this time. A 'new broom' had arrived in 1959, with Hugh Greene as Director General, and a range of new appointments was intended to reshape BBC output and to 'take on' ITV in the battle for audience support. That situation in itself produced the possibility of innovation, development of new areas of programming and a sense of populism in broadcasting which locked into the political climate of the sixties. The CND movement, the angry response to the Suez events, and a general commitment to measures of social reform expressed through the election of a Labour government in 1964, were all part of that climate in which a key determinant was the economic boom. Expansion and a low level of unemployment had helped to shape a more confident and optimistic working class. Young working-class men and women were spending their regular wage packets on consumer goods, clothes, records etc., thus creating and extending the 'leisure industries'. At the level of representation, social class was a saleable commodity – the Beatles and other media celebrity material appeared from areas outside the traditional home counties enclave of the women's programmes personalities and presenters. Fast-paced and socially challenging documentaries, stark and disturbing drama, political satire: all made women's programmes appear an anachronism, at least in the traditional form set out by the old school of broadcasters.

Why then was a new format not considered? If the traditional aura of upper middle-class gentility which surrounded women's programmes was finally considered unacceptable to the 1960s executives of the BBC, then why wasn't a more hard hitting approach developed? If 'progressive' innovations were being made elsewhere in television, why not in programmes for women? New approaches could have been attempted, addressed to the working-class audience of women, and could even have encompassed evening viewing. Unfortunately many broadcasters, then as now, perceived programmes which focused on women as a group as 'soft', with the Women's Institute as the only image they had of women's collective strength. That image was then predominant in the wider society, even in left-wing political organisations. It is therefore, perhaps, not surprising that among the new school of young broadcasters, who saw themselves as more 'attuned' to the needs of the viewing public, women as workers or trade unionists should be ignored. Since the elitism of the established formula and presentation of women's programmes was anathema to the populist orientation of BBC television in the 1960s and no viable alternative was acceptable, the whole project of programmes for women was closed down.

The politics of television: women's programmes no exception

What conclusions can be drawn from this consideration of women's television programmes which might benefit us today – as viewers, trade unionists, workers, media practitioners, students and teachers? It can be demonstrated that even in this apparently marginal area of television, economic, political and bureaucratic demands play a major part in shaping programmes. This is particularly obvious at key moments of change such as the start of ITV or the 'liberal' era of the 1960s at the BBC. Women's programmes were economically and organisationally beneficial to the broadcasting institutions because they utilised daytime resources of studios and personnel which otherwise would have been lying idle. Schedules were filled and the wheels were oiled and ready for evening output. There was a certain flexibility offered by this type of programming, like the resource pool of labour constituted by women workers: daytime programmes for women could be expanded or contracted to meet the needs of the overall system. The programmes positioned women in the family because that is where most broadcasting executives and practitioners unquestioningly believed women should be – except, of course, for a tiny elite of 'specially talented' career women who were allowed to organise programmes for women. The ideological operation of the programmes arose from society's hegemonic definitions of the family, children and domestic labour, and of the desirable attributes and behaviour of women and men. The field of wage labour, determinants of class with regard to the material quality of life, notions of struggle or collective organisation geared to social change: all are significant absences in the discourse of the programmes.

The content and mode of address of women's programmes was upper-class even when the audience was considered to be mainly working-class. The concept of 'women's interests' was used by both BBC and ITV to justify a focus on 'domestic' issues in a way which was supposedly natural and 'neutral' but which was in fact class-specific and rooted in the dominant cultural and socio-economic assumptions of the time. There is no evidence to suggest that the economic, political and ideological concerns of broadcasting institutions in the present day are different in any fundamental respect. Changes in the structure and content of television programmes directed towards women continue to be determined by the commercial and political needs of broadcasting organisations which are in themselves shaped by the wider economic and political context. In the 1980s watershed of broadcasting, the expression of those needs may look and sound different, or more 'progressive', and may even at times appear to connect with the experiences and concerns of many women. It is important to remember, therefore, that at a fundamental and all-pervasive level the class interests and control mechanisms of broadcasting organisations are, as always, irredeemably determined by the State and the dominant class in capitalist society. All broadcast programmes are shaped in this way and women's programmes are no exception to the rule. Nevertheless, attempts should continue to challenge and expose the dominant assumptions of the organisations of broadcasting, while recognising that it is unlikely that major shifts will be made in television programmes, with respect to class and gender, until there is a fundamental transformation of the social, economic and political structures in which we live.

Acknowledgments

I wish to thank the staff of the BBC Written Archives Centre for their help in researching this material. Thanks are also due to Stuart Hood, Rosalind Coward and Mike Healy for reading and commenting on early drafts of this article.

Notes

1 Janet Quigley argued the case for more wartime programmes for working women in an extended series of memos and reports sent to the Director of

BBC (Radio) Talks during 1942. This material and most of the historical data which refers to the BBC is in the form of memos and letters preserved in the files of the BBC Written Archives Centre. This is an invaluable resource for broadcasting researchers, staffed by an extremely helpful team of archivists.

2 This was also a concern in the *Beveridge Report* and the *Royal Commission Report on Population*, 1949. Theories of 'maternal deprivation' developed by John Bowlby also fed the fire of this argument. A comprehensive and useful account of this can be found in 'feminism as femininity in the 1950s' by the Birmingham Feminist History Group (1979), *Feminist Review*, vol.3.

3 The official tables on women in employment in the postwar period suggest a shift from heavy industry to traditional areas of women's employment.

4 *BBC Written Archives*. A memo from Norman Collins of Nest Bradney on the *Woman's Hour* coverage of an Equal Pay Conference (9 December 1946), warns her to make certain that 'this is an objective report of the Conference rather than an argument for equal pay'. This is despite another memo from Collins in the same period pleading for more 'serious, including controversial, talks and discussions in *Woman's Hour*'.

5 In the postwar period the general trend of investment in studios and cameras led to the need to make programmes suited to studio conditions. Broadcasters and writers who have stressed the importance of technical and organisational determinants in shaping programmes include Stuart Hood (1980), Philip Schlesinger (1978), Tom Burns (1977).

6 *BBC Written Archives*, memo from Mary Adams to the Director of TV Programmes, 8 August 1947.

7 The 'flavour' of that first programme in the series *Designed for Women* can be found in a synopsis held in the BBC archive. The set is described as 'fireplace with pleasant chairs, and low table for tea' with 'no attempt at dramatic setting'. The planned speakers or 'guests' were 'Jeanne Heal, Dr Edith Summerskill (Under-Secretary, Ministry of Food), Marguerite Patten (Cookery), Mrs Hervey (Millinery), Mary Wykeham (Ascher Scarves), Olga Katzin (Sagittarius).' The culmination of the programme and the tea party came when the guests were to sign a historic tablecloth containing the signatures of suffragettes.

8 *BBC Written Archives*, memo from Mary Adams to Director of Television Service, 19 November 1947.

9 *BBC Sound Archives*. I listened to a range of talks recorded for *Woman's Hour* covering the years 1947–51. The voices were notable for their upper-class accents and mode of address, even at a time when the BBC had intended to speak with a more populist voice.

10 *BBC Written Archives*, *Designed for Women* (script outline), Christmas edition, December 1947.

11 The many biographies of ex-BBC executives and employees map out assumptions of broadcasting as a male preserve. BBC policy has tended to reinforce this from the official marriage bar of the 1930s through to present day attitudes.

12 *BBC Written Archives*, provisional running order for *Hat Show*, experimental session 16 May and 8 June 1946.

13 S.E. Reynolds produced many other magazine programme series for women,

including *About the Home, Leisure and Pleasure* and *Family Affairs*.

14 David Bryson's line-up of 'distinguished' women for the series included Dame Vera Laughton Matthews (ex-Head of WRNS), Lady Violet Bonham Carter (Liberal MP), Margery Fry (expert on penal reform) and Jill Craigie (film director).

15 *BBC Written Archives, About the Home* script – Safe Food No.1, 20 March 1952.

16 *BBC Written Archives*, notes on visit by editor, Women's Programmes, to Regions.

17 *BBC Written Archives*, an enquiry about afternoon TV programmes for women, BBC Audience Research Department, 7 November 1955.

18 *BBC Written Archives*, memo from Women's Programmes Organiser Robin Whitworth to Mrs Mary Adams (November 1955).

19 *TV Times* No.1, 20 September 1955, p.14 and No.2, 30 September 1955, p.22, bear similarities in layout and presentation to women's magazines. The informal, 'friendly' tone is exemplified by an article in the first issue of *TV Times* which carried the chatty headline, 'And now it's television in the morning – by Mary Hill, editor of *Morning Magazine*'. Most of the historical data which I have used concerning commercial television is available at the library of the Independent Broadcasting Authority. The library contains a useful collection of mainly published sources but little internal documentation of the television companies for this period.

20 *BBC Written Archives*, memo from Family Programmes Organiser, 20 October 1964.

21 *BBC Written Archives*, memo from Family Programmes Organiser, 20 October 1964.

22 The producer, Lorna Pegram, had already tried out the new formula she was proposing in *Wednesday Magazine* in 1963. Doreen Stephens complained that Donald Baverstock, the new Chief of BBC1, had encouraged the early work on the idea only to reject it later. She was writing as editor of Women's Television Programmes, in a memo to the Chief of Programmes, BBC2, 4 July 1963.

23 *BBC Written Archives*, a memo headed *Gilt and Gingerbread*, signed JHB, 30 November 1964.

24 *Ibid.*

25 *BBC Written Archives*, Chief of Programmes BBC2 (Michael Peacock), in a memo to Head of Family Programmes TV, 12 January 1965.

26 *BBC Written Archives*, *Gilt and Gingerbread*, unsigned memo.

References

Birmingham Feminist History Group (1979), 'Feminism as femininity in the 1950s?', *Feminist Review*, vol.3.

Boston, S. (1980), *Women Workers and the Trade Unions*, London, Davis-Poynter Ltd.

Briggs, A. (1979), The History of Broadcasting in the United Kingdom, vol.4, *Sound and Vision*, Oxford University Press.

Burns, T. (1977), *The BBC: Public Institution and Private World*, London, Macmillan.

Hood, S. (1980), *On Television*, London, Pluto Press.

Kidron, M. (1970), *Western Capitalism since the War*, Penguin.

Leman, J. (1980), '"The advice of a real friend". Codes of intimacy and oppression in women's magazines 1937–55', in H. Baehr (ed.), *Women's Studies International Quarterly*, vol.3, Oxford, Pergamon Press.

Leman, J. (1983), 'Capitalism and the mass media: a case study of women's magazines and radio programmes 1935–55', unpublished MPhil thesis, University of Kent.

Schlesinger, P. (1978), *Putting 'reality' together*, G.B. Constable & Co Ltd.

Sendall, B. (1982), *Independent Television in Britain*, vol.1, Macmillan.

6 Women's programmes: why not?

Rosalind Coward

The year 1986 marked the fortieth anniversary of *Woman's Hour* on BBC Radio. It was a much applauded occasion. After all, it is a remarkably long time for a programme to survive, especially given the radical changes which have affected women through those four decades. Few women, whether feminists or not, question *Woman's Hour* right to exist. It is pretty well a national institution and by no means the cosily domestic institution that it is sometimes thought to be. Cosy it may be, but it has also been able to take on board feminism in a way that suggests the programme's radical edge was revived, rather than invented, by feminism. But if few question the value of a topical women's magazine programme addressing women's interests on BBC Radio 4, the story on television is entirely different. At the moment of writing, there is not a single television programme which explicitly addresses women. Perhaps because television is so much more of a mass medium than the relatively limited reach of Radio 4, the issue of women's programmes seems more controversial. Indeed the whole subject of women's programming provides a terrible source of paranoia for television executives, as well as being an arena of disagreement among women. The questions of whether or not there are women's interests to be served, and whether or not a specific women's programme would be the best way to serve such interests, form a Protean monster which will not allow itself to be slain.

The question of whether or not to have separate women's programmes on television does have a long history, one which Joy Leman explores in Chapter 5. Drawing out points from her article which are relevant to my argument, it is interesting to note that the principle of 'women's interests' programmes was accepted when television first started regular transmission in Britain. This was almost certainly to do with the huge influence exercised on television by radio, where *Woman's Hour* was already successfully established. As Joy Leman points out, the women's magazine programmes on television in the 1950s and early 1960s generally defined women's interests as exclusively domestic and disregarded the fact that so many women at that period were working. These women's magazine programmes were discontinued in the 1960s, mainly because television executives saw them as stiflingly middle-class and backward-looking in defining women's interests as being exclusively in the home. Typical of libertarian thinking of that period, the policymakers' argument was that to segregate the audience was to assume inequality. It was in fact a disingenuous argument. From the late 1960s until the present day, programming has continued to make assumptions about the sexually differentiated audience; these assumptions just have not been made explicit. On the one hand, daytime television has, until very recently, assumed a predominantly female audience and catered for it with magazine programmes like *Pebble Mill at One* and recycled soap operas. On the other hand, programme-makers have never worried about making programmes when the interests served would be largely male. Football and snooker are obvious examples of this. And there can be little doubt that if a significant sector of the male population had taken up tiddlywinks in the 1970s, we would even now be watching the world tiddlywinks contest. Certainly on commercial television, advertisers have no such 'egalitarian' qualms and are sold spaces with appropriate viewers for their commodities – nappies at teatime and beer during the late match.

But if policymakers and libertarians had decided that women's interests were bad for women, feminism changed all that. The whole question of women's interests took on a new life with feminism, although the definition of women's interests was drastically changed. Feminism has insisted that social issues like housing, childcare, health, sexual and work experiences do affect men and women in different ways and that women's side of the story has been almost totally disregarded by the media. Perhaps more radically, feminism has argued that these different experiences in fact give women a very different perspective on issues and that there might just be, after all, a women's viewpoint. As regards the media, this re-assertion of women's interests has taken two main forms. One has been the call for more women to be involved in the production of programmes, newspapers and journals. The other has been for more articles and programmes which put a women's point of view or cover issues which have importance for women but which male editors and producers are likely to disregard. Certainly as regards newspapers, feminism has caused the tide to be turned on the idea of separate women's pages. If the fashion in newspapers, as in television, in the 1960s was to abandon the idea of women's pages, now they are widely recognised as the one place where women can read about issues which concern and affect them. The feminist perspective seems to have confused television policymakers, who seem to be locked into a new version of sixties libertarianism which thinks it is bad to 'ghettoise' women and sees the feminist view as a step backwards. The confusion is possibly not without its uses. It has the convenient effect of excluding the feminist viewpoint with its much more extensive critique of mainstream television.

The views of Roger Laughton, appointed in 1986 as the BBC's Head of Daytime Television, seem representative. He is engaged in shaking up daytime schedules and introducing a service which looks much more like local radio with regular news programmes and phone-ins. He is catering for an audience available for viewing, 60 per cent of which is known to be female. Yet, in spite of the fact that he commissioned one of the first all-women's programmes (*Revolting Women* in the 1970s), he does not feel there should now be separate daytime programmes for women:

> We've got *Woman's Hour* on the radio and I don't think that we need to recreate that on television. It's the same argument that applies to women's pages in newspapers. We shouldn't need them. I'd argue that we're in a post-revolutionary situation. Far more people are now affected by a feminine (as opposed to a woman's) viewpoint and this should be incorporated into the mainstream of TV. (personal interview, spring 1986)

Maybe such views will signal the incorporation of a more 'feminine' perspective into the news and other programmes. More probably, though, they signal the disappearance of any explicit concern with women as audience in the daytime. Increasingly, discussion of daytime television has concerned itself with the unemployed and retired people. Even on Channel 4, there seems to be an increasing readiness to 'cater for' these newly identified audiences and an increasing unwillingness to view daytime television as being an appropriate place for women's programming. Undoubtedly the issue of daytime scheduling is a complex one; no-one wants to reinforce the belief that women do not work outside the home. And there is increasing evidence that those women who do work in the home are simply unable to give television their undivided attention (Collett and Lamb, 1985). Nevertheless these arguments are strangely contradictory in their support for these new audiences and their antagonism to the old idea of daytime television for women. It is not clear, for example, why unemployed girls, women and elderly women might not also conceive of themselves as women and be pleased to have women's issues addressed. What is worrying about these shifts in conceptions of a daytime audience is that there is no parallel shift in evening scheduling.

Even on Channel 4, there seems to be a lack of enthusiasm for finding successful ways of addressing women. Carol Haslam, commissioning editor for the channel until 1986, is someone with a known sympathy for women's production groups and a commitment to feminist ideas. Yet, even so, she was dubious about the value of a separate slot for women:

> The issues affecting women should be there in the general output of television. Women shouldn't look at the *TV Times* and think 'Ah, there's my programme' but instead see the issues affecting her as a woman there in the mainstream. I think we've done that in making health programmes so important to our schedules. (personal interview, spring 1986)

The reason why feminists might find such views disappointing is not just because Channel 4's output so often looks like that of the other companies. It is also because Channel 4 contained in its original brief a commitment to experiment and innovate. Not unreasonably, many took this to mean that the channel would commission from groups habitually excluded from the media. Certainly in its early days, it seemed to respond to the feminist view that too much television reflected male pleasures and priorities. Indeed the beginning of Channel 4 looked and sounded good for women. Several women were appointed as commissioning editors (although no-one had special responsibility for women). But the early promise has not been fulfilled. It is certainly true that several women's production companies were commissioned, itself a radical departure from previous television practice, and the outcome has been varied and interesting. There have, for example, been different series about sex, sexuality and sexual attitudes made by all-women teams and the women's current affairs series *20/20 Vision* and *Broadside*. But all these very different programmes have one thing in common. They have all, in various ways, been allowed to fail and have been stored away in the channel's memory as 'interesting experiments'. This is not to suggest some sinister disregard for women, but instead a half-hearted approach to making women's programming successful. The most recent example of this half-heartedness could perhaps be seen in the fate of *Watch the Woman*, broadcast in 1985. The programme was designed by Channel 4 as an evening magazine programme for women and, as such, was crossing the crucial barrier of addressing women specifically at a time other than daytime. *Watch the Woman* was for many women a highly problematic cause to espouse. Certainly at the beginning of its run, its relation to feminism was ambiguous. It had a token male presenter as if women were not 'adequate' on their own, and it attempted to translate on to television all the more traditionally 'feminine' concerns of the women's magazine, such as fashion or problem pages. Even so, it did carry many items which were more in the tradition of *Woman's Hour*, that is, offering women's views on current issues and communicating information about issues currently affecting women.

Whatever the criticisms of the programme, the fact is that it joined other women's productions in having been given a remarkably short space of time in which to 'prove itself'. Any magazine programme will take time to find the right format and it will be a particularly tricky job for a women's programme which includes the highly critical feminist movement in its audience. Carol Sarler, producer of *Watch the Woman*, described how the programmes were beginning to change:

> We started with a glitzy Covent Garden image, a sort of television version of *Cosmopolitan*, with fashion inserts and so on. As we got more and more letters, we realised that there were masses of women out there who wanted more information and more discussion, who could really use a current and topical women's magazine programme in the evening. (personal interview)

It is very likely that the format and style of *Watch the Woman* was fundamentally miscalculated, but Channel 4 chose to disregard the evidence that there was a need for a women's programme and the series was allowed to end. The treatment of women's programmes is in curious contrast to other programmes where Channel 4 clearly has a more protective attitude. *Voices*, for example (or *Male Voices* as Anne Karpf once called it in the *New Statesman*), and *A Week in Politics* (hardly a radical perspective on current affairs), were both given far more time to develop and establish themselves. Carol Haslam explained that although the situation on Channel 4 was far from ideal, nevertheless women were generally seen as well-represented within the channel. She went on to say that with so many women working as commissioning editors and so many women working in the independent sector from which Channel 4 draws its programmes, there is not a need at the moment for a separate commissioning editor for Women or for a slot set aside for women's programmes:

> There are so many other constituencies in this country whose voice is *never* heard on TV – northern working class, rural communities, ethnic minorities – that women's programming doesn't seem the absolute highest priority at the moment. It's the old problem of what's more important: gender or class? (personal interview)

Both in these words and in Channel 4's response to the submission from the Women's Film and Television Network, arguing for more opportunities to be given to women, the impression given by the channel has been that the battle about feminism is over (WFTVN, 1986). Women, it seems, have had a high profile and are no longer one of the most important constituencies.

There are numerous problems with this view. First of all, it suggests that in diverting resources away from women they are actually being spent on drawing in other disenfranchised or powerless groups. This clearly is not the case. While it is true that far more than other media institutions, Channel 4 is making efforts to employ and appeal to ethnic minorities, there are also indications that programming for these groups is still approached with great caution. There is a far less equivocal attitude towards the more traditional (money-spinning) broadcasting areas, such as sports and youth programming. It is worth noticing, too, that the Commissioning Editor for Youth creates nothing of the unease that the idea of a Commissioning Editor for Women does. No-one seems to worry if 'youth' feels 'ghettoised' by being targeted as a specific audience in programmes like *The Tube*. The other major reservation about the idea of women's issues being somehow already on the agenda is that there is in fact no formal way in which the coverage of women's issues and the presentation of women's views can be monitored. As Carol Haslam said, 'We have only the general programmes review committee and the informal pressure which we can put on each other in the corridor for more women in programmes and more programmes about women' (personal interview). Women outside the channel are far from happy with the situation. The Women's Film and Television Network, mentioned earlier, have been critical of the lack of opportunity given to women programme-makers as well as the lack of true equality of employment within the channel. While this is undoubtedly justified, Channel 4 does have a very much better record of employing women and women's production groups than any other similar institution.

Concentrating on employment opportunities somehow plays along with the thinking that is already present among television executives, and it confuses adequate coverage of women's issues with the number of women working in television. It neglects perhaps the more important issues of the lack of commitment to women's issues or of introducing a women's perspective into existing entertainment structures. Anna Coote of *Diverse Productions* said that Channel 4 made the classic mistake of thinking that because it had women at the top, something must actually be happening in the programmes:

> It isn't. Very occasionally you get a woman's view of current affairs. It
> was tried on *Broadside* and by some of the journalists working on
> *20/20 Vision*. And although I'm sympathetic to the idea of integrating
> women's issues into the mainstream, I also don't think that it is
> actually happening. I think that unless you have someone or
> somebody pushing for those interests, they get forgotten. (personal
> interview)

Marion Bowman, a reporter who has worked on a number of different programmes for Channel 4, took this theme further:

> It's just not true that a women's viewpoint has been incorporated into
> the mainstream. *Channel 4 News* is meant to be doing news
> differently, for example they give far more time to the arts than the

other news programmes. But where is the coverage of women's issues? Where is there any evidence that there's a whole tradition of feminist journalism which might take a completely different perspective on news values? (personal interview)

There is certainly no evidence of any real transformation of television as a result of feminist criticism. There may be more documentaries about issues which are supposed to affect women – health, the body and childbirth – and there may be the occasional feminist appearing on interviews or in 'serious' chat shows. But as regards 'mainstream' entertainment, very little has changed. Peak-time entertainment still largely reflects the apparently correct, assumption that men's interests dominate choices about viewing; scenes of male violence, images of aggressive masculinity, and women placed in domestic sexual contexts, largely prevail. As Marion Bowman points out, not only are women's issues largely absent from news and current affairs but it is almost laughable to imagine that news priorities might have already been transformed by a women's perspective. There is not even a job description for a reporter to cover women's affairs in the way that there are specialised reporters for religious affairs. Children's programmes also reflect very traditional male and female stereotypes. Cartoons have central male characters with peripheral, highly feminine (and silly) female figures. American imports such as the *A-Team* and the *Dukes of Hazzard* are particularly culpable, promoting images of masculinity as violence. Yet, in spite of the overwhelming evidence that traditional views of masculinity and femininity prevail, the belief that feminist battles are over still dominates the thinking of many television executives.

And there is an odd way in which this predominant view of the liberal media – that feminism is now out of touch – is extremely demoralising for those women working on the edges or inside the institutions of the mass media. There can be little doubt that the effect of such an ideology has been to make feminism extremely uncertain about its own discourse. It is difficult enough to put feminist views over in situations which feel unsympathetic, but even more difficult if you are made to feel that what is being said is all 'old hat' and out of touch with the ordinary woman. Yet the simple fact is that, in spite of many superficial changes, what feminism has to say is still extremely relevant to the structures of contemporary entertainment. Feminists may now occasionally appear on television, but usually with health warnings, or in some context where 'extreme' views are in the nature of the entertainment; that is, in serious or intellectual talk shows. And the kind of feminism which is tolerated is revealing. It is the white, middle-class, articulate feminist, the nearest to the media's own brand of careerwoman. On these occasions, feminism has little chance to explain itself. Views have to be short and succinct – the more controversial the better. On the few occasions that feminism has been given the chance to define its own terms – in the programmes made by all-women production companies – the internalised sense of being a minority group has created tremendous problems in the mode of address. Because liberal ideology has convinced feminists that they are the out-of-touch minority, programme-makers are anxious about whether they are talking to ordinary women or to feminists. It is this which seems to have created the uneasy equivocation between obscurantism and pedantry which sometimes has marked women's productions. Yet it is important to note that *Woman's Hour*, with which this chapter started, suffers from no such insecurity. There may be problems in the way that the format levels all issues to equal importance (for example, rape and boils treated with complete equality). Nevertheless, there is an unquestioned assumption that feminists are also talking to ordinary women, that what constitutes feminism is precisely a movement which is trying to transform the quality of the ordinary woman's life.

On television, assumptions by policymakers about the ordinary viewer seem much more restrictive. Strangely, this comment seems applicable even to Channel 4, which claims to operate with no such sense of the ordinary British viewer – the ignorant, sexist philistine – that the other channels are so keen to woo. Channel 4 executives are highly articulate about the differentiated audience, the fact that British culture has no hegemonic identification and can be addressed as a series of disparate and differentiated 'minority' groups. Yet on all sorts of levels (and the woman question is one of them), this seems to break down. There appears to be a deep commitment to the existing aesthetics of television and a distrust of more experimental forms, which are criticised as too difficult and too disruptive for the average viewer. This attitude presents particular difficulties for at least one strand of feminism working within British television. For there is a strong argument that the existing, aesthetic conventions of television *need* to be disrupted on the grounds that they encourage a certain kind of passivity and acceptance of dominant ideologies which almost invariably militate against women.[1] The superficial 'progress' that has been made against crude stereotypes of women on television, and the conviction of television policymakers that the battle is over, suggest that feminism needs to rethink some of its criticism and demands made of television. It is clear, for example, that arguments conducted purely in terms either of stereotypes or of lack of opportunity will not advance our cause very far. More productive would be a full-scale critique of the way sexual difference is inscribed in television, both in the images with which we are presented and in terms of the assumptions made about viewers. Where the images are concerned, it is clear that the problem is by no means confined to the question of how women are represented, but is much more deeply concerned with how masculinity and femininity are presented and what the interaction between these is supposed to be.

Once feminism becomes critical in these terms, a far more radical critique of mainstream television will emerge. Programme-makers and executives might have to confront the fact that egalitarian arguments about not targeting broadcasts at specific sex groups do not hold water. It will become clear that mainstream television – news and current affairs and the majority of 'entertainment' programmes – inscribe priorities and pleasures which are, broadly speaking, male. It does not do to deny this by pointing out how many women enjoy television output in its current form. The lack of visible protest from the so-called average viewer surely in no way invalidates what feminists have said, and are now saying, about the implicit assumptions about masculinity and femininity which dominate broadcasting values. The paradox is that in order for women to have any effect on mainstream television, it is necessary first to articulate the fact that women, in contemporary society, do have interests, different interests and priorities from those of men. It is only with specific programmes for women, with specific policies to cover women's interests, and through encouraging women to put their point of view, that we will be able to prevent television from hiding the divisions between women and men. Pretending that differences do not exist between women and men, or making other social divisions seem more important than that between women and men, is an act of concealment in which all contemporary broadcasting is complicit. And it would be an act of no small political significance when feminists refuse this complicity and refuse to put the issue of women's programming to one side.

Update

At the time of writing Channel 4 is in the process of commissioning a new women's current affairs magazine programme due to begin transmission in late 1987.

Note

1 It is interesting to see that feminism has so often allied with 'the avant garde', both in film-making and in television production. In both areas, radical workers tend to agree that the dominant aesthetic, particularly of a sort of 'transparent realism', means that the viewer remains unaware and therefore uncritical of the process by which the apparently natural ideologies of television are actually constructed.

References

Collett, P. and Lamb, R. (1985), *Watching People Watching Television*, unpublished report, IBA.

Women's Film, Television and Video Network (1986), *Channel Four Television and Equal Opportunities*, WFTVN.

7 Women as TV audience: a marketing perspective

Sue Stoessl

As a relatively new activity in people's lives, television has only been a truly mass medium for the past twenty years. Older people have lived with it for only a small proportion of their lives and it is they who are the very heavy viewers. People over the age of 55 view, on average, over forty hours of television a week. There is evidence that future generations are likely to be lighter users of the medium and will be more selective. It has become apparent over the last ten years, through audience research conducted by JICTAR and BARB,[1] that viewers switch from channel to channel to programmes they particularly want to view. The very fact of positive selection has made the younger groups lighter viewers than their counterparts ten years ago. From this decline, and from the use of video recorders, it would seem that future generations may well have learnt to use the medium that they have grown up with more selectively.

Television companies are increasingly interested in factors such as patterns of viewing and audience profiles, as this allows them to produce, target and schedule programmes in a much more precise way and in an environment of increased competition. During the winter months the average adult watches some thirty hours of television a week, with women viewing substantially more than men: women watch for about thirty-five hours, men around twenty-seven, according to BARB. This very different pattern of viewing for men and women reflects the fact that women are more likely to be at home during daytime hours. Work carried out by the BBC on people's availability to view shows that the majority of people at home during the day are women and old people (*Availability to View Study*, Research Department, BBC, 1983). The increase in unemployment has put more men into the daytime audience of television, but this has not changed the

107

relative ratio of viewing between the sexes. Women still view more television than men during the daytime and the schedules on ITV have been constructed with the female audience in mind. BBC daytime television, which started transmission in October 1986, sees its potential audience of 25 million as including high numbers of old people, women and the less well-off (BBC Audience Research, 1986).

The differences in men and women's watching of television is fairly illustrated by Table 7.1.

Table 7.1
Average hours of viewing per week
Week ending 2 March 1986

	Age	[Channel 4]		[Total TV]	
		Hours	Mins	Hours	Mins
Men	16–24	1	: 47	15	: 48
	25–34	2	: 18	21	: 54
	35–44	2	: 10	22	: 17
	45–54	2	: 39	26	: 25
	55–64	3	: 24	33	: 42
	65+	3	: 34	39	: 00
Women	16–24	1	: 56	18	: 55
	25–34	2	: 57	32	: 23
	35–44	2	: 33	26	: 52
	45–54	3	: 02	31	: 05
	55–64	3	: 59	37	: 09
	65+	3	: 38	40	: 20

Source: BARB/Channel 4

Women normally view more television than men, but this is true more in terms of total TV than it is in Channel 4's case. Viewing tends to increase with age. The main exception to this is among women over 65 who have been the slowest to take up the habit of Channel 4 viewing. Analysis of afternoon viewing between midday and 4 pm on weekdays, during the same period indicated in

Table 7.1, shows that men watched just over eight hours of television on average a month, whereas women watched thirteen and a half hours. Men under the age of 55 watched about a third of the amount that women viewed, whereas those over the age of 55 narrowed the gap of viewing between the sexes. Against this background of substantially higher viewing among women than men, it is interesting to note that the viewing pattern ranges from *Saturday Sport* on BBC1, where 63 per cent of the audience are men, to *Dynasty*, which gets only 34 per cent of its audience from male viewers. Perhaps surprisingly, news programmes still have more women viewers than men, with a split of about 55 per cent to 45 per cent. The exception to this is *Channel 4 News*, which has 52 per cent men and 48 per cent women viewers (BARB).

Viewing statistics from the Broadcasters' Audience Research Board (BARB), carried out for the BBC and Independent Television companies by Audits of Great Britain (AGB), defines viewing as meaning 'present in the room when the set is switched on', rather than requiring full attention to be paid to what is shown. This is an important difference with regard to women's viewing in particular, as women tend to be less attentive to television (Morley, 1986). The qualitative difference in women's opportunity to be fully attentive in their viewing remains impossible to measure in the BARB system.

Information on who is present in the room when the television is on shows the size of the audience to programmes and is therefore of great interest to programme-makers and schedulers. It has assumed an importance to others because of the way it is used by the press. Each week a 'top ten' is produced, showing the programmes that have the highest audiences for each of the four channels. This in itself is misleading if taken in isolation, as the size of the audience is determined at least as much by the other programmes available to view at a particular time, as by the appeal of the programme in question. If a James Bond movie is on ITV, no competing programme, whatever its merits, can get the significant amount of viewing to figure in the 'top ten'. When BARB first came into existence it was agreed that no such list would be produced, because it was felt that if a programme did not get into the 'top ten' it would somehow be deemed a failure. This is far from being true, as the size of an audience for any particular programme reflects not only the appeal of that programme, but also the opposition from the other three channels, the time of day it is shown and even the weather at the time. The newspapers, however, decided that they wanted to publish such a list and started to produce one themselves, which meant it contained substantial errors. BARB reconsidered their decision and now produce a list which is compiled by each of the four channels individually.

Audience research shows that in most households the programme viewed has to be chosen by consensus (BMRB/ Channel 4). Given a particular set of programmes, and bearing in mind a third of households now have video recorders to increase their choice, the options are relatively wide. The process has two stages. The first is to decide 'Shall we watch television or do something else?'. The decision to watch television at all is only affected to a small degree by what is on the screen. Probably 90 per cent of viewing would happen regardless of what is shown. Only 10 per cent additional viewing comes from the audience appeal of particular programming. This can be shown when the total viewing by all the audience is considered. The difference between a high and a low viewing day is about 10 per cent. Peak-time audiences for all channels falls to between 40 and 50 per cent of potential audience throughout the year, but within one season it would only vary by about half that amount or 10 per cent viewing. These variations can only be accounted for by the programmes' availability at the time, as this is the only variable. Having made the decision to watch television, the second stage is to decide which programme will be viewed. This process will depend on the size and make-up of the family. In surveys carried out for Channel 4 by the British Market Research Bureau (BMRB), regular questions are asked about how people make decisions as to what they view. The decision-making process takes place within a context of family relationships and domestic space. Increasingly, young people say they move to a second set or video when they want to see programmes of their choice, whereas older people, and particularly women, claim to sit in the main sitting room and watch what is on.

The ways in which these kinds of decisions are taken give interesting insights as to how family relationships work. Who makes the decision to watch? Ann Gray's chapter in this volume (Chapter 3) and David Morley's work with South London families illustrate the role of men and women in decision-making and how alliances are formed and who has to give way. Is there a way for women to get more chances to make their own viewing decisions? One possible solution seemed to be the advent of the second television set. Over 40 per cent of households have two sets and these are predominantly in large households. Unfortunately, the majority of homes in the UK have only one sitting room. This contains the main family set which is very likely to be a colour set. It is a well-heated room, probably the only warm and comfortable room in the house. There is a strong disincentive for people to go and view elsewhere. So the choice is, 'Do I go into the uncomfortable room to watch a black and white set to view a programme that I really wish to see, or do I stay with the family?' In the United Kingdom it seems that there is very little use of the second set – less than 10 per cent of the viewing in multi-set households comes from the second set, which has an equal chance of having the same channel on as is on the main set. Where another programme is watched it is very likely to be by young people (BMRB research for Channel 4). Teenagers are more likely to want to go and watch their programmes – music, early evening movies, late night zany humour. Women are much less likely to go and watch their soap opera on the second set.

David Morley has focused on the effectiveness of gender as an influence on viewing behaviour (Morley, 1986). His research was carried out on twenty households in South London. The sample was atypical in so far as the households were 'nuclear families' – husband, wife and two children. This type of household accounts for less than 5 per cent of the population. Nevertheless, Morley's work does go some way towards explaining why women seldom have control of the set to view programmes of their own choice. He talks about women's feelings about watching television. A number explained that their greatest pleasure is to watch 'a nice weepie', or their favourite serial, when the rest of the family is not there. Only then do they feel free enough of their domestic responsibilities to 'indulge' themselves in the kind of attentive viewing which their husbands engage in routinely. Morley refers to the sense of guilt that many women feel about their own pleasures:

> Women are, on the whole, prepared to concede that the drama and
> soap opera that they like is 'silly' or 'badly acted' or
> inconsequential – that is, they accept the terms of a masculine
> hegemony which defines their own preferences as having a low status.

111

Having accepted these terms, they then find it hard to argue for their preference in a conflict (because, by definition, what their husband wants to watch is more prestigious). They then deal with this by watching their programmes, where possible, on their own, or only with their women friends, and will fit such arrangements into the crevices of their domestic timetables. (Morley, 1986)

Evidence suggests that the television is switched on for company. Voices and music in the background help fight the loneliness of the elderly, of people living alone and of those housebound with small children. Qualitative research carried out by Channel 4 shows that the music played on the test card, during hours when programmes were not shown, was used instead of radio because it was uninterrupted music. (Channel 4 gets a number of enquiries each day as to which piece of music is being played over the test card.) Programmes were also switched on, but not viewed, because people claimed to like to hear voices in the background. It might be thought that radio would be more appropriate to give background music, but in the living room TV has become a more natural source of sound.

The 1981 Broadcasting Act set up Channel 4 as complementary to ITV and one interpretation of this is that it should show programmes which have a different audience appeal. ITV programme schedules for weekday afternoon television recognise the predominance of females in the audience, as measured by BARB, and aim to cater for them with drama, quiz shows and cookery programmes. When Channel 4 started weekday afternoon programmes up to 5 pm in autumn 1984, it was decided to schedule television fare complementary to ITV and therefore show programmes of more male interest. Complementarity works in so far as on Mondays and Fridays ITV shows feature films in the afternoons and Channel 4 shows other programmes, while on Tuesdays, Wednesdays and Thursdays feature films are shown on Channel 4. This results in war films, documentary series repeats, *Mavis on 4*, programmes for the retired, and the introduction of mid-week horse-racing on Channel 4. Although the plan works reasonably well, the majority of the audience is still women, except for horse-racing where 70 per cent of the viewers are male.

Much of daytime television is viewed by people on their own or with friends rather than by families. It is when family viewing takes place that some of the difficulties of targeting programmes at particular people arise. Taking the simplest situation first – single person households account for 22 per cent of the total in the United Kingdom. Most of these are women over 55 years old (BARB Establishment Survey, 1986). Here the decision as to what to view is relatively easy. As long as these single people have information on the viewing choices available, they make their own decisions. Research shows that these are coloured by recommendations of friends and relatives, as people like to talk about what they have seen. A number of studies in the UK in the late 1970s showed that television is by far the most talked about subject among general topics of conversation (Advertising Association, 1979). Soap operas are popular in single person households. The characters become part of the family, and they are people who can be thought about and become topics of discussion with others (Hobson, 1982). People living on their own also view a considerable amount of Channel 4. They are likely to watch the special interest programmes such as gardening, history, documentary series, flower-arranging and old movies. Analysis of the BARB data shows that single person households contribute disproportionately to the audience for special interest programmes. It is easier to watch items of particular interest when you are on your own. There is a very good chance that other members of a household might not share the same special interests.

Two person households make up 35 per cent of the viewing population. Here the decision-making becomes more complex. Many women, especially those in the older age groups, do not watch programmes that would be of particular interest to them. They say things like, 'My husband does not like that so I cannot watch it,' or, 'My husband always watches the news so I cannot see that programme' (Morley, 1986). Because women are less active viewers, i.e. they do other things at the same time as viewing, they tend to be part of the audience for sport and documentary series that would normally be of little or no interest to them. Another side of the BARB service measures how interesting and/or enjoyable people find the progammes they view. Results of this continuous research show that sport and current affairs programmes are the only ones that women derive less interest or enjoyment from than men. In the documentaries area women enjoy nature programmes more than men, but factual and historical series rather less. The fact that women do other

113

things while the set is on might be one reason why they are less assertive in their viewing choice. They will have particular favourites which they insist on watching, but these are few and far between, the most popular type of programme being the soap opera.

Evidence of the use of the video recorder suggests that soaps are the most likely programmes to be recorded both in Britain and in the United States. This is because women are less likely to get a consensus of viewing for these programmes and therefore watch them at a later time (such as mornings) when they are in control of the set. The problem arises when women claim to have difficulties with programming video machines. They usually rely on males or children to do this for them. Questions asked on the regular BMRB surveys have shown that women do not regard themselves as reliable users of video machines for recording purposes and this is confirmed by Gray (see Chapter 3). When television was relatively new, women had a decided reluctance to fiddle around with television sets. This was discovered when interviewers went into households in the 1960s and asked housewives to change channels to see what the set could receive. The rate of refusal was high, as many women felt that they would be unable to come back to where the set had been tuned previously and therefore would not allow the interviewers to touch the television set (Television Audience Measurement – TAM – 1966). This problem seems to have disappeared, so there is hope that the fears and doubts that women have of operating the video machine will also diminish with usage.

Given an overview of women's role in deciding which channel to watch, it is perhaps not suprising that programming specifically aimed at women does not get large audiences outside the daytime hours. This does not mean that such programmes are not continuing to be made and shown, but it has to be recognised that their audiences are likely to come from people who live on their own or find themselves alone at home during the evening when the programme is shown. Channel 4 has made some efforts to show programmes that might be considered of specific interest to women during peak hours of viewing. In its first year of transmission, the two current affairs series from women's production teams – *Broadside* and *20/20 Vision* – failed to get significant viewing among women, in common with all current affairs programmes. This does not mean that they were unsuccessful in dealing with different subjects in a different way from other current affairs programmes, but they were not seen by the audience as being particularly for women, nor were they viewed by women. While these programmes were on air research was carried out, through BMRB together with Channel 4's regular work, to find out audience attitudes to the programmes. Women did not regard these series as being particularly aimed at them, nor as having specific appeal to them. It might now be argued that, together with many other programmes on Channel 4, time could have helped to solve this problem as many people had difficulty in finding things of particular interest to them at that stage in the channel's life.

Another of the channel's efforts to attract the women's audience was the women's magazine programme *Watch the Woman*, transmitted during 1985. The idea behind this series, which ran for ten weeks only, was to have something similar to a women's magazine format adapted to television. The audience was split 55 per cent women 45 per cent men. Viewers were spread across all age groups, but overall there was no particular age bias to this programme. Women did not begin to watch it and then switch away from it – they were not there to start with. There were two reasons for this. One was that at ten o'clock at night women have even less control over what is viewed on television than they do earlier in the evening. The second reason was that they were actively discouraged from watching by other members of the family who wanted to watch something else. Although some of the items were well-liked, and even useful, women found difficulties with the 'feminist' tone of the programmes that they had to watch in the company of others in their household. Channel 4's research on the series and the BARB Qualitative surveys showed that one of the main reasons many women did not watch was that other people in the household were in the room when the programme was being shown. They felt uncomfortable and expressed concern that the programmes appeared to be 'anti-men' rather than 'pro-women'.

It has been Channel 4's aim to cater for minority groups, but minority groups are not necessarily defined by the channel in terms of sex, age, colour, socio-economic groups or size of household. The aim is to provide programmes in areas of interest, so that people will have their own interest programmes that they can watch or record. Although Channel 4 has done a number of programmes in areas like knitting, health, consumer affairs, flower-arranging, home decorating and DIY, these programmes have to be enjoyable for men as well as for women in order for women to be allowed to watch them in the family situation. Minority groups must also be interest groups because broadcast material has to be accepted within a consensus of viewing arrived at in the family. Television viewing is not, as yet, an individual activity.

Notes

1 BARB was set up in 1980 (to replace JICTAR) by the BBC and the Independent Television companies to carry out a joint measurement system of television audiences. Viewing statistics establish who views which programmes, audience loyalty to programmes, the relative appeal of one programme to another, and the overall size of the audience. From ITV's point of view the system has to be able to measure the audience to television advertising. For this reason it continues to measure minute by minute audience. This is the unit considered most appropriate for the measurement of the relative size of audiences to advertisements.

The BARB data is collected by the meters in 3,500 panel households, and is read every night by computer through the telephone. Technically the size of audience to each programme is known next morning. However, it has been agreed that broadcasters only receive the data once a week. This is judged as sufficient time to take any action that might be considered necessary as a result of getting straight head counts.

References

Hobson, D. (1982), 'Crossroads': The Drama of a Soap Opera, London, Methuen.
Morley, D. (1986), Family Television: Cultural Power and Domestic Leisure, London, Comedia.

8 Firing a broadside:
a feminist intervention into mainstream TV

Helen Baehr
and Angela Spindler-Brown

In April 1982, Channel 4 announced that its weekly half-hour current affairs series would be produced by women. Liz Forgan, Senior Commissioning Editor for Actuality at the time, said this decision to hand over its current affairs to women had 'nothing to do with positive discrimination or social justice, it is a journalistic experiment' (Channel 4 press release, April 1982). In fact the Women's Broadcasting and Film Lobby (WBFL) had come up with the idea for the series two years earlier in 1980.[1] That was the year that women first made it onto the agenda of the Edinburgh International Television Festival, prompted by WBFL. Mary Holland addressed the EITF participants on the lack of a women's perspective in television news and current affairs.

> As for what one might call women's news – violence against women,
> blatant cases of sex discrimination, the condition of women
> prisoners – these do not get covered in the main news programmes
> unless there is some particularly sensational angle to them. Even in the
> comparative freedom of the ghetto areas we have yet to see a TV
> equivalent of *Spare Rib*. (EITF official programme, 1980, p.41)

In December 1980, Jeremy Isaacs, Chief Executive of Channel 4, publicly accepted the proposal for a women's current affairs series. In a *Guardian* interview with Liz Forgan (then editor of the women's page), he argued that women would show

117

'an interestingly different view of the world . . . I intend to give them the opportunity to demonstrate that' (1 December 1980). In those heady pre-transmission days the emphasis was on innovation. Isaacs was keen to include people from outside television, with a fresh outlook and new arguments, in his team. Indeed, twelve months later, after a different kind of interview with Liz Forgan, he appointed her Senior Commissioning Editor in charge of news and current affairs.

In the spring of 1982, Channel 4's weekly current affairs series was given to two new production companies: Gambles Milne, whose series *20/20 Vision* was headed by Claudia Milne and Lyn Gambles, and *Broadside*. Milne and Gambles were both experienced in television production but had never worked together before. *Broadside* had twelve members (shareholders) who had been working together as a television discussion and lobby group since 1979. When it became incorporated as a company in 1981, each member held one share, leaving the remaining eighty-eight shares unallocated. The group included experienced producers, directors, researchers and a camera operator as well as journalists and academics. All had played an active role in WBFL and in getting the idea of a women's current affairs slot accepted.[2] Unlike Gambles Milne, *Broadside* presented itself as a feminist production company. From the start these two very different companies – united only by the fact that they were women – were under enormous pressure. Like other television programmes produced by women, their slot came to stand for, and be judged as, representative of all women's work. *20/20 Vision* went on air in November 1982 and *Broadside*'s first programme, *Taking on the Bomb*, was transmitted in January 1983. By November 1983 the 'experiment' was over. Channel 4's weekly current affairs coverage was handed back to men's editorial control.[3]

Rosalind Coward in Chapter 6 of this volume offers one assessment of the demise of Channel 4's *20/20 Vision*, *Broadside* and subsequently *Watch the Woman*, 'All these very different programmes share one thing in common. They have all, in various ways, been allowed to fail and have been stored away in the channel's memory as "interesting experiments"'. It is not Channel 4 policy to give reasons for axeing a series. One commonly held interpretation of events is that the *Broadside* current affairs series 'self-destructed'. Yet today we know that during the spring and summer of 1983 Channel 4 was hastily re-evaluating its commissioning and progamming strategy in a drive for higher ratings, and had decided to limit its documentaries and increase its entertainment output. Jeremy Isaacs has since publicly admitted that this process may well have gone a bit too far, too quickly (Jeremy Isaacs's report presented at Channel 4's *Open Day*, 2 June 1986, held at the Royal Institution). Many of the difficulties and contradictions *Broadside* faced when making Channel 4's flagship current affairs series have since been encountered by other independent production companies. In this account, based on personal involvement, we focus on the influences and events which led up to the setting up of *Broadside* and examine its aims and objectives in the context of the pressures operating within the TV industry in general, and in its independent sector in particular.

Setting up the series

The twelve founding members of *Broadside* shared a basic feminist viewpoint. This ideological position and determination to make certain types of programmes necessitated a questioning of traditional ways of working in the industry. Television appeared as an impenetrable citadel. We had seen feminist enterprise flourish in the world of publishing, bringing with it ideologically new products and new ways of working. Women film-makers were attempting to create an alternative film language within a reconstructed context of distribution and exhibition. But for those women working within established broadcasting institutions, the possibilities of introducing alternative modes of production, distribution and consumption were severely limited. (That is not to underestimate the considerable difficulties involved in funding and exhibition of independent film projects.) In this sense, we felt we were engaging not so much in an 'experiment', as the channel had labelled us, but in a project to expand the frontiers of television coverage. The Broadcasting Act 1981 requires Channel 4 to transmit a suitable proportion of matter calculated to appeal to tastes and interests not generally catered for by ITV. This statutory obligation, in conjunction with Isaacs's and Forgan's earlier statements, were interpreted by the *Broadside* production team as a public admission that there was a lack of women and women's issues within television current affairs. The same Act encourages the channel to 'innovate and experiment' in the form and content of its programming. Together with many other independent producers, *Broadside* programme-makers saw this brief as an opportunity to shift – if not totally remove – conventional notions of 'balance' and 'impartiality'. We wanted to organise ourselves and make programmes informed by our feminism.

Most of us had tried to make these kinds of programmes within mainstream television. We were well versed in the stock responses from male colleagues in powerful positions who challenged 'women's interest' ideas as being 'minority' or – worse – of 'no interest' to a general audience. Our experience told us that only by holding editorial control might we collectively succeed where, as individuals, we had previously failed. Those who were experienced television researchers brought with them a history of many years stuck at researcher grade with little prospect of promotion. All the evidence points to the fact that the number of women employed in the television industry decreases as you move up the production ladder (ACTT, 1975; Gallagher, 1979; Baehr, 1981; Sims, 1985). In one survey of six BBC departments, including current affairs, general features and light entertainment, out of 79 researchers, 56 were women. At the next level – junior and senior director – the proportion of women took a sudden dive: 38 women compared to 64 men. Out of a total of 157 producers only 25 were women (Baehr, 1981). Those in *Broadside* who had reached producer/director level, or were camera operators, were keen to work with other women and share editorial control over the kinds of issues covered. We were all tired of the constraints imposed on us by the tried and tested ways of television. To use Mary Holland's phrase, we knew we were not victims of 'any particular wickedness of men within television' (Holland, 1980). We recognised that broadcasting is a practice carried on 'not by individual broadcasters, but by institutions' (Garnham, 1973). Our insistence on making pro- grammes which reflected women's position in society, their interests and views, was a reaction to a set of professional 'values' enshrined in the institutions of mainstream broadcasting rather than in its personnel. The only way to succeed in making the programmes we wanted to see would involve the construction and application of an alternative set of 'professional' values. It was in this context that the *Broadside* team was labelled by Diana Simmonds as 'feminist professionals' rather than 'professional feminists' (*Sunday Times*, 23 February 1983). At the same time, our aim was to make pleasurable and interesting programmes accessible to mainstream television audiences, not just to the feminist cognoscenti and metropolitan avant-garde.

In the run-up to *Broadside's* commission in April 1982, we held close to a hundred meetings in the evenings and at weekends. We endlessly rehearsed our editorial strategy and our production structure. We devised ways of reaching a consensus and paid enormous attention to the need to establish an atmosphere of support and collective effort which so many of us had found lacking in the working practices of the industry. We recognised a responsibility to employ women technicians and wanted to do our best to include them in the very early stages of production planning. We agreed that the practice within the BBC and ITV companies of putting a crew together at short notice might be cost effective, but did not necessarily make the best programmes or provide job satisfaction. Our discussions over *Broadside's* structure were hotly debated. All twelve founding members wanted to be involved and participate in the company's future. At the same time we recognised the need to delegate responsibility within the group. Discussions revolved around how, and whether, this could be achieved in a non-hierarchical but accountable way. The formal demands of union practices had to be considered in conjunction with our own need to provide opportunities within which we could develop new skills to take us higher up the production ladder. The question was: how to ensure all this within the context of a tight production schedule and fixed budget?

In the end, Channel 4 settled this issue for us. It demanded a traditional editorial structure with one editor at the top who would make all editorial decisions and liaise with the channel. It transpired, in our negotiations with the Commissioning Editor for Actuality, that this structure was to be the condition under which the commission for the series would be granted. We were asked to recruit a woman 'with top current affairs editorial experience' to act as our series editor, although both Liz Forgan and Jeremy Isaacs readily admitted that part of the reason for launching the series was precisely because of the dearth of experienced women in this field. If we were to have a conventional editorial structure imposed on us, we decided to elect one of the original *Broadside* members rather than appoint an outsider. We felt that since we had won the commission, we wanted to be in control of how and what we produced. Our feeling throughout this period was that, in comparison with other newly established companies, *Broadside*'s structure was being scrutinised and interfered with as if it were 'a special case'.

On balance, however, when we embarked on the first series we were pleased to be making the programmes of our choice, albeit with a chain of command that felt like an unnecessary intervention along the lines of the production practices we had been retreating from. Early on, the editor issued her own job description as follows: 'The editor should have final decision-making power on matters of staffing, editorial policy and budgets' (memo, 8 April 1982). Thus the debate around what would constitute non-traditional, new working practices and structures was cut short. The rest of us were in no position to protest under the terms of the commission. We decided to proceed in a spirit of mutual support and co-operation to get the job done. The editor was seen by the channel as the named contractual link and the person responsible for delivering the series. As she was there to take the brickbats for any failure she naturally became the one to receive any bouquets on offer. An industry which personalises every issue on the screen is not immune to this same tendency when dealing with its own affairs. In this sense, the editor 'became' the series.

The same memo hinted at an issue which was to plague us in the future – job security: 'Since we have only sixteen programmes at present the contracts will be essentially short-term and freelance; none should look to *Broadside* for security. Equally, I do not see jobs on the team as 'rewards' for the two years or more hard labour within *Broadside*.' In fact, out of the twelve founding members five were employed elsewhere in the industry and were not looking for jobs with *Broadside*. The remaining seven shareholders, including the series editor, had worked to make *Broadside* a going concern which would employ us, albeit on a freelance basis. We did not see our future employment in the company as a 'reward' for past efforts, but we certainly wanted the chance to be involved in a series of programmes which had only been made possible by years of our work. In retrospect this still seems a reasonable expectation. Certainly the appointment of an editor with the power to hire and fire changed the whole complexion of our enterprise. What followed was the gradual establishment of a traditional editorial structure. This development was most visible in the spatial organisation of the office. The editor established her office away from the open-plan production work area. As time passed, progressively her door shifted from the ajar towards the closed position. By the time we started on our second series of eight in May 1983, with no indication of any future commission, we all felt anxious about jobs and future prospects for the series and the company. As well as the current affairs series, we had other ideas in the pipeline, including film scripts and 'one-off' documentaries (several of which were subsequently produced by *Broadside* shareholders for different companies). By now, a struggle for control of the company was causing a split between ten of the original *Broadside* members and the editor. Her attempt to take control of the company failed. But, as editor of the series, she succeeded in effectively marginalising the majority of the company's shareholders, over half of whom were working as part of the current affairs production team. *Broadside* was only one of a number of companies kept uninformed right up to the last minute as to whether it would get a contract for another series. We were told in writing that no further series was to be commissioned from us only two weeks after our last transmission. The channel has since had to modify its terms of trade to include procedures for terminating long-standing series. In July 1983 a union dispute arose over alleged non-payment of monthly cheques. In reality, what was at issue was the future control and ownership of the company and its remaining shares.

The programmes[4]

We started our production schedule in the full glare of publicity and expectation. Liz Forgan readily admitted that the task ahead was to make 'this current affairs series a triumphant success in what we know will be the teeth of every kind of criticism, ridicule and carping from the world at large' (Blanchard and Morley, 1982). Economic considerations guided our productions very quickly into the tried and tested way of doing things: development, pre-production, perfectly planned shoots and fast post-production.

Given the constraints on budget (each programme was allocated a budget of half the cost of an edition of *TV Eye* or *World in Action*), people were employed for only as long as was absolutely necessary. Gone were all our ideas for pre-production meetings involving our technicians. Economic pressures produced an atmosphere in which we were reproducing established working practices. At all costs we wanted to do a 'professional' job and prevent carping from the world at large. This resulted in an economic and psychological lack of space for experiment.

If we were hampered in challenging the existing forms and practices of production, we were much more successful in breaking new ground in the kinds of topics we chose and the perspectives we adopted. With only sixteen programmes, we had to pick our subjects carefully. We launched the series with a film about women and the peace movement and followed this with a 'scoop' about the incidence of cancer resulting from British and Australian atom bomb tests in South Australia in the 1950s. Out of the sixteen programmes *Broadside* made, a surprisingly high number (four) dealt with the war and its aftermath. We were trying to get away from the *Boy's Own* approach to war, but by choosing to shoot conflict overseas we were also tackling the kind of story from which we, as women, had previously been barred. All our stories were thoroughly discussed at editorial meetings and subsequently within smaller production teams. As time went on, questions of resources and who got what job sometimes interfered with editorial judgment, but, on the whole, there was always agreement on which subjects should be included on our agenda. There were no arguments about 'women's interests' being of 'no interest'. As a production team of women, we were developing our own mode of representation. Our programme on alternative treatments for breast cancer was seen from the viewpoint of women who had the cancer and not from the point of view of the medical profession. When we covered the Irish referendum on abortion, we started from the premise that abortion and contraception are never just about notions of morality, they are a question of politics. Women witnesses were privileged and prioritised in our programmes and encouraged to talk without interruption. Experts, especially male experts, were not used to re-evaluate or explain what had already been said. We consciously avoided the use of 'experts' drawing conclusions and defining the issues. Wherever possible, we chose women as our accredited witnesses. We worked with all-women crews and this added greatly to the sensitivity and rapport between crew and subjects. As women film-makers we often had an advantage: we caught (male) subjects with their guard down. After all, to them, we were 'only women making a film'.

Although we had spent literally years discussing how we would produce feminist programmes, paradoxically there was no real opportunity to evaluate or assess our own transmitted programmes and learn from their successes and failures. Production teams were hired on short-term contracts and were often gone long before the delivery of the programme. This trend towards casualisation has been debated elsewhere:

> Researchers, journalists, production assistants and technical staff hired on short-term contracts from job to job have the worst of both worlds in Channel 4. They neither have the control, job satisfaction or autonomy of their employers, nor the compensatory wage-levels and job-security available in the ITV companies. (ACCT/NUJ Channel 4 Committee, 'An end to "lump" TV?', NUJ, 1984)

Whose 'wickedness' is it?

The question remains: was *Broadside* pushed or did it jump? Certainly Channel 4's record of 'allowing' its women's projects to fail and labelling them 'interesting experiments' has already been noted in Chapter 6. The general feeling at Channel 4 now seems to be that women are relatively well-represented both by commissioning editors and programme-makers, and that women's issues are constantly on the agenda. Should a situation ever arise again when 'women's programming' is actively encouraged by the television industry, a re-appraisal of *Broadside*'s experiences might be valuable. It is in this hope that we venture some analysis of our observations.

Broadside was formed out of a core of women who had initially come together to lobby for more opportunities for women in the industry. It subsequently changed from a campaigning group into a television production company. This unique history set it apart from other independent companies producing for Channel 4, which had been set up simply to produce programmes. These companies are run on the principle that 'small is beautiful' – at least in terms of their ownership structures. As it turned out, *Broadside's* size meant that not all of its members could be accommodated and satisfied within the limited number of opportunities available. In the two years that *Broadside* existed as a discussion and lobbying group, it had established an informal structure which made the difficulties it later faced as a production company very hard to manage. We had been used to meeting in each other's homes in our own time. We had become friends, exchanging stories about the industry's treatment of women and supporting each other in our careers and personal lives. Our individual experiences and professional aspirations, as well as the way we organised ourselves as a group, were informed by the women's movement. In this sense, we had combined the traditionally separate worlds of the 'public' and the 'private'. But our sense of 'solidarity' stood in direct contradiction to the professional values we had acquired through working in television. That world is notoriously competitive and does nothing to encourage a sense of co-operation over and above the line of duty (see Kumar, 1977; Alvarado and Buscombe, 1978; Hood, 1980).

The 'political unity' of *Broadside* was mixed up with individual and collective professional objectives which were in turn bound up with friendships. Once *Broadside* was operating as a fully fledged production company, sisterly intentions became undermined by highly charged personal ambitions and fears about job security. When conflicts arose they became bitter and, inevitably, highly personalised. The fight for the right to a job and the maintenance of friendships became irreconcilable. The imposed editorial structure did nothing to encourage collective effort. The editor's power to 'hire and fire' led to a classic situation of always trying to please the boss. As often happens in these situations, this was frequently given higher priority than programme production. There were clear structural reasons for dissent and dissatisfaction within the company. The lingering uncertainty about whether Channel 4 would commission another series produced feelings of anxiety and job insecurity for everyone. The fact that *Broadside* had been set up as a collective response to a set of individual frustrations faced by women working in the television industry increased the strain. *Broadside* appeared to offer the chance to show our skills unimpeded by male colleagues, many of whom have allergies to women and/or women's interests. However, the understandable ambitions of experienced researchers for promotion to producer/director level created a highly competitive working environment. We may not have had disagreements about programme content but it was difficult to contain the frustration and bitterness when people's professional ambitions were curbed – this time seemingly by 'sisters'.

Broadside was amongst the first batch of companies commissioned to produce a series for Channel 4. Since those early days new procedures have had to be introduced by the channel for re-commissioning and terminating series. Delays in re-commissioning and industrial disputes have been reported within other independent companies working for Channel 4 (reported intermittently in *Broadcast*; for specific cases see 25 April 1986). Nor are boardroom struggles an uncommon feature in the television industry. Witness the battles at London Weekend Television in the late 1960s and the near collapse of TV-am in 1983 (Tinker, 1980; Leapman, 1984). Put in this context, what happened to *Broadside* is hardly atypical or worthy of comment. But because it happened to a women's production company it refuses to be hidden by history. What *Broadside* did was to challenge the conventions of an industry which had hampered women's progress yet, by working in that industry, it internalised many of its professional practices and aspirations. Mary Howell, in her study of women and professionalism, offers this cautionary note: 'I believe that *none* of us survives socialisation as professionals without a profound compromise in the way we live out our feminism' (Howell, 1979). Within television, it seems, the contradiction that exists between professionalism and feminism remains unsolved and, possibly, insoluble.

Notes

1 The Women's Broadcasting and Film Lobby (WBFL) was set up in 1979 to improve the employment and training opportunities for women in the industry and challenge sexist images of women.
2 A more detailed history of this period (1982) is to be found in Blanchard and Morley (eds) (1982), *What's this Channel Fo(u)r? An Alternative Report*, Chapter 7, and Lambert (1982), *Channel Four: Television with a Difference?*
3 *20/20 Vision* was subsequently commissioned to produce a series of trilogies on topical issues. *Broadside* current affairs series ended but Broadside

Company Ltd went on to produce *Female Focus* (TX 1985) and *Five Women Photographers* (TX 1986).

4 List of *Broadside* programmes in order of transmission:

First series beginning 5 January 1983

Taking on the Bomb
The first television programme about the women peace campaigners of Greenham Common and their counterparts all over the world.

'No-one Suffered'
The first television account of what happened to British and Australian servicemen and Aborigines who were in Maralinga, South Australia during the British/Australian atom bomb tests in the late 1950s.

Fighting Back Cancer
The programme examined new alternative treatments for cancer which involve the mind as well as the body.

Khomeini's Other War
An examination of the war Iranian Kurds have been fighting against Iranian troops in their struggle for independence.

America's Silent War
A documentary about the CIA's silent war in Nicaragua.

The Hired Hands
A close look at the secretarial trap where women still play the role of 'office wife'.

Resist and Survive
A film about Asian and Afro-Caribbean women in Britain. A group in Manchester discussed their attitudes to work, health, education and the ways they confront racism.

Ireland – the Politics of Abortion
An examination of the issues and politics surrounding Ireland's 1983 constitutional referendum on abortion.

Second Series beginning 18 May 1983

Not Just a Statistic
A documentary about three servicemen's families and the after-effects of the Falklands War.

Different from Other Girls
An investigation into an epidemic of sexual abnormalities in Puerto Rican children caused by the indirect consumption of large doses of oestrogen either through the water supply or animal feed.

A Gentleman's Agreement
A look at the boom in so-called 'video nasties' and politicians' attempts to restrict their availability.

Whose Crime?
An investigation into the kinds of crimes committed by women and society's attitude to women offenders.

Message from Skinningrove
Skinningrove is a remote northern British coastal town with the highest unemployment rate in the UK. The film focused on a group of women who organised poetry writing as one way of fighting back.

Half a Loaf
A look at the government's cost-cutting proposals to change the thirty-year-old law governing the way Britain's bread is made.

Hidden Connections
A documentary about workers in three London agencies who dispute the widely held myths about drug addiction and argue the connection between drugs and social problems.

Women in Nicaragua
A film about the life of women in the Nicaraguan army.

References

Association of Cinematograph and Television Technicians (ACTT) (1975), *Patterns of Discrimination against Women in the Film and Television Industries*.

Alvarado, M. and Buscombe, E. (1978), *Hazell – the making of a TV series*, London, British Film Institute.

Baehr, H. (1981), 'Women's employment in British television: programming the future?', *Media, Culture and Society*, vol.3, pp.125–34.

Blanchard, S. and Morley, D. (eds) (1982), *What's this Channel Fo(u)r? An Alternative Report*, London, Comedia.

Gallagher, M. (1979), *The Portrayal and Participation of Women in the Media*, Paris, *UNESCO*.

Garnham, N. (1973), *Structures of Television*, Television Monograph 1, London, British Film Institute.

Holland, M. (1980), 'Out of the bedroom and onto the board?', *Edinburgh International Television Festival Official Programme*, London, Broadcast.

Hood, S. (1980), *On Television*, London, Pluto Press.

Howell, M. (1979), 'Can we be feminists and professionals?', *Women's Studies International Quarterly*, vol.2, pp.1–7.

Kumar, K. (1977), 'Holding the middle ground: the BBC, the public and the professional broadcaster', in J. Curran, *et al.* (eds), *Mass Communication and Society*, London, Open University Press.

Lambert, S. (1982), *Channel Four, Television with a Difference?*, London, British Film Institute.

Leapman, M. (1984), *Treachery? The Power Struggle at TV-am*, London, George Allen and Unwin.

Sims, M. (1985), *Women in BBC Management*, BBC Report.
Tinker, J. (1980), *The Television Barons*, London, Quartet.

PART THREE
On the Screen

9 When a woman reads the news

Patricia Holland

Angela Rippon's legs

> The paradox is that the harder they strive being serious in the solemn
> business of international news, the more delightfully coquettish and
> feminine they appear. By ignoring their femininity they heighten it.
> (*Evening Standard*, 6 June 1979, on what they describe as a
> 'newscasterette')

The *Evening Standard* is not alone in noting that the forms of
femininity and sexuality required of women are not readily
compatible with the solemn business of the news. Philip
Schlesinger's study of news production in the BBC was written
around the time of the introduction of women as regular
newsreaders, yet he describes his brief account of women in the
newsrooms as a 'digression' from his main discussion. He quotes
the senior official who, according to newsroom folklore, insisted
that 'a good reporter needs a pair of balls.' Women reporters give
rise to 'tampax problems' and can't get the right sort of story,
especially in situations like Belfast 'where you have to lean against
the bar with army officers and swill down pints' (Schlesinger,
1978, p.155). The imposed limits of femininity, it seems, cannot
easily be cast off, especially in the hard world of news reporting.
Women remain a digression, confined to the incidental, condemned never to break out of a circle in which they merely
heighten their femininity if they attempt to ignore or surpass it.
This is despite the fact that from the beginning of broadcasting in
this country there have been examples of women at all levels, in
front of and behind the cameras. Individual women have been
prominent in shaping broadcasting policy and style. In the postwar period Grace Wyndham Goldie became the chief architect of

BBC TV's prestigious Current Affairs department and before her Mary Adams was in charge of Television Talks. At ITN Barbara Mandell and Lynne Reid Banks were among the first news reporters. Yet Cheris Kramarae, in an account of the coverage of women's 'firsts' in broadcasting, points to press amnesia about those who have pioneered a field. (Kramarae, 1985, – from which I have drawn most of the newspaper quotations I have used here). Women who have intruded into the restricted area of hard news have had difficulty in holding on to the job and equal difficulty in being remembered. Lynne Reid Banks was 'taken off the road' in 1957 but merited an article in the *Lens*, ITN staff magazine, in August 1985, since she had achieved fame in a more suitable area as author of a best selling novel in the 1960s, *The L-shaped Room*.

From the early days women announcers and interviewers were occasionally heard on BBC Radio: Olive Schill in 1932, Sheila Borrett in 1933, Jean Gilbert and Thelma Carpenter in 1936, Olga Collett in 1937. Official reaction to them was summed up by Pauline Frederick, the prominent American broadcaster, in an account of the difficulties of her own early career, 'Chief objections raised were that women's voices carry no authority, that they don't transmit well, that women won't listen to women, and there's a tradition that men broadcasters should deal with news' (*The Times*, 1958). In 1960, six years after television newsreaders first appeared in vision, Nan Winton read for the BBC. She was to be sacked, then reinstated, three times. Other women, too, made brief appearances, 'Maureen Staffer and two other women have been barred from reading the news by an independent TV station – because they distract the attention of men viewers' (*Daily Herald*, 15 February 1963).

Yet when women newsreaders began to appear regularly on British television in the mid 1970s – Angela Rippon from 1975 and Anna Ford from 1978 – they were greeted as a total novelty by the press. They were seen as an opportunity for jokes, pictures and suggestive comments. Every detail of their dress and appearance was commented on, their styles were compared, their sexuality stressed:

Could I suggest that Miss Ford cuts out the frosty lipstick and shiny blush-on which makes my screen look wet and slippery? (*Daily Express*, 5 July 1978)

Angela, your lips are just smack on. (*Daily Mirror*, 29 December 1978)

Angela is forceful, even dominant. In how many secret viewers'
dreams does she deliver the *Nine O'clock News* in black leather. Anna
has a twinkle in her eye, a tease in her manner. Together they achieve
much for women's equality without loss of – indeed with
enhancement of – femininity. (*Sunday Telegraph*, 30 April 1978)

They were described as deadly rivals, like Joan Collins and Linda
Evans of *Dynasty*, unable to meet without exchanging a bitchy
word. Most of all there was a call to see their legs. Resistance to
this call itself became news:

Forget about legs, storms Anna. Television news girl Anna Ford is
fed up with people trying to compare her legs with Angela Rippon's.
Anna is also unhappy with 'show us your legs' cat-calls wherever she
goes. (*Sun*, 20 March 1979)

Angela Rippon decided to respond in the good-humoured way
expected of women. She did a high kicking dance routine on the
1976 Morecombe and Wise Christmas show. The reaction to her
performance included a worry that this sort of thing can trivialise
the solemn business of public affairs (*BBC TV News: The First 30
Years*, Prod. Gordon Carr, TX 5 July 1984). Angela Rippon and
Anna Ford were caught up in a familiar paradox. Women's very
presence invites comment. They are associated with the trivial,
forbidden the full seriousness of their job, but at the same time
they must take the blame for reducing the seriousness of that job,
for contaminating it with their own triviality. The public discourse
which accompanied the introduction of women newsreaders in
the 1970s – that chatter which circulated and continues to
circulate as gossip in the newspapers and the club rooms and bars
of the BBC and ITN – continually returned to a central problem.
Women are about sexuality, the news is not.

Despite the work done by the newspapers at that time, and
their efforts to discipline the women and remind them of their
place, nearly half of today's television newsreaders are women. At
the time of writing it is the convention to use a couple, one man
and one woman, in the main news broadcasts. The exceptions are
Channel Four News, which despite its extended length and wider
brief, is presented by a single man, and the BBC's weekend
round-up of news which is presented by two women. Sue Lawley
on the BBC's *Six O'Clock News* and Julia Somerville on the
BBC's *Nine O'Clock News* both 'lead' the broadcasts and both

have a substantial background in journalism. These women face us with confidence. They appear on our screens, a calm, head and shoulders image, presented in the unemphatic way we have long taken for granted in the image of a man. I want to argue that this apparently unremarkable image is a deeply challenging one and that the efforts to limit and control women's appearance have not been overcome but continue, shifted from overt comment and ridicule to more subtle forms of redefinition. There is a continuing effort to remind women of their inescapable position as women, as 'not-men'. This is the repeated process of subordination. If that process is accepted as normal and is acquiesced in, the fact that it can never fully succeed is of little importance. The fact that a few women, or even many women, can escape from its enforced limitations makes little difference to the positioning of women as a group.

The newsreaders' confidence derives partly from the fact that the way they look is less important than what they have to say. The image is subordinate to the speech. For men this is something we take for granted – it is only to be expected – but for women it is an unfamiliar situation. As the newspaper reactions to Angela Rippon and Anna Ford demonstrated, women's right to speak in public may easily be subverted by drawing attention to their visual appearance. The authoritative male newsreader is a well established presence on the screen. The image of a man, head and shoulders, in formal jacket and tie, is familiar across the media as a sign of assurance and power. It is used to introduce the company report, it appears on the business pages of the quality press, it presents politicians and statesmen. Characteristically it shows a middle-aged man of worldly experience and dignified presence, the lines on his face and his serious expression indicating the respect he commands. But it is an image which contains a problem. By refusing any hint of visual pleasure or sensuality, it attempts to deny its own image-presence. It suggests that this pictured man is not simply framed here to be looked at. His steady gaze, direct at the camera, appears to assert that he is the one doing the looking. He is the controller rather than the controlled, the active subject rather than the passive object. In its rigid formality his physical presence refuses to draw attention to itself, attempts to slide into invisibility. We take it for granted that, like the newsreader, what he has to say is more important than the way he looks. This paradoxical convention for men is in striking contrast to the familiar conventions for women, which contain a different set of problems and inconsistencies. We expect images of women to stress not head and shoulders, but faces and bodies. Women's faces, when they appear, are not normally poised for looking or for speech, but are painted, decorated, presented for beauty and the pleasure of the viewer (Berger, 1972). Laura Mulvey, and together with her a whole school of feminist critics, have argued that the very construction of sexual difference through the Oedipus and castration complexes makes women the objects of male scrutiny, their visual presence itself a symbol of sexuality standing in for male fears and losses (Mulvey, 1975 and 1984; Cook and Johnston, 1974; Cowie, 1978). Images of women are not images of *women* at all but images of men's impossible desires, of their fears for the full masculinity they can never achieve. The most striking examples of such fetishised imagery are among the most familiar ways in which women are shown as pin-ups, as the fragmented bodies of hundreds of advertisements, as the polished and streamlined limbs linked to the imagery of sado-masochism popularised in the work of Allen Jones (Mulvey, 1973). If this argument is accepted, it is not surprising that women have rarely been presented as Alastair Burnett, Robin Day and Leonard Parkin have long been seen, controlling and competent, grey-haired and unruffled.

On television the visual presentation of a head and shoulders image is always inadequate by itself. Something is missing; the image must be completed. In the case of a man it is unproblematically completed by what he has to say. In the case of a woman the commentators point to an absence of a different sort. For them what is missing is the woman's body. The *Sunday Telegraph* feels free to fantasise about Angela Rippon wearing the black leather of S/M, other newspapers discuss the absence metonymically as 'legs'. The head and shoulders of a man is completed by his speech, the head and shoulders of a woman only draws attention to the need to see her legs. As the *Evening Standard* said, 'By ignoring their femininity they heighten it'.

Women's speech, too, is beset by difficult problems, problems which, like those around the imagery of women, are linked to the very construction of femininity itself. Traditionally women's speech has been downgraded as mere gossip or babble (Spender, 1980). Some feminists want to reject this devaluation and lay claim to the 'neutral' language now appropriated by men. Others have embraced and celebrated a special 'women's language', a language that is more expressive and fluid, which is said to have sprung from a stage of development that was more creative, before the laying down of conventions and prohibitions (Daly, 1979). Yet the image of the woman newsreader has difficulty with both these options. Like the image of the man it claims to be completed not by 'legs' but by speech – a speech which is forbidden to be specifically feminine and must be taken seriously in the public world of the news. The tension between an image which may not forget its femininity and a speech which may not embrace the feminine is central to the challenge posed by women newsreaders.

The news and its place

The spaces on television that we describe as 'the news' must be understood both in continuity with and in opposition to the rest of the daily output. The audience is expected to understand and respond to 'news' in a way that is different from, say, sitcom, chat shows, or even its close relation 'current affairs' (Schlesinger, et al. 1983). One of the most striking characteristics of the news remains its dramatic under-representation of women. This absence – amounting, in the words of Gaye Tuchman, to a 'symbolic annihilation' – has been pointed out with increasing impatience by feminists in this country and elsewhere over the past fifteen years (Butcher et al., 1974; Tuchman et al., 1978; Eddings, 1980; Jensen, 1982). In news bulletins women still appear on the screen in smaller numbers and more limited roles than men, while opportunities for them to speak are even more restricted. A glance at almost any randomly selected news programme will confirm that women tend to be seen in the background rather than as the main subjects of a news item. They are passing in the street, shopping, working in a canteen or hospital. Certain well-known women, like Princess Diana and other Royals, actresses and performers, make regular non-speaking appearances as part of the public spectacle, but women rarely appear in their own right as actors in those fields which are the central concern of the news and they are rarely selected as experts to comment on or interpret the news. When they are invited to speak it tends to be either as an anonymous example of uninformed public opinion, as housewife, consumer, neighbour, or as mother, sister, wife of the man in the news, or as victim – of crime, disaster, political policy. Thus not only do they speak less frequently, but they tend to speak as passive reactors and witnesses to public events rather than as participants in those events (compare Goulden *et al.*, 1982, p.81). The use of women as regular newsreaders and to a lesser extent as reporters, has made a dramatic difference to the gender balance of news programmes.

The expulsion of women from the news can only be fully understood when it is seen in the context of the whole of the television output. John Ellis has argued that the television flow is typically divided not into programmes, but into 'segments' of around two to five minutes in length – an advertisement, a news item, a single scene in a soap opera (Ellis, 1982). Faced with this irregular sequence, members of the audience do not turn on for discrete uninterrupted cultural events as in the cinema or theatre, but they compose their viewing from fragments, dropping in and out, catching the end of one programme or the opening titles of another, perhaps turning their backs or watching with only half their attention. Recent studies of the television audience have shown that it is actually made up of many audiences, each reacting differently to different parts of the programme output. Women and men, in particular, tend to have radically different tastes. Thus the experience of watching together becomes itself a re-enactment of the relations of power between them. The man of the house tends to be in charge of the programme selector. It is left to the woman to react to the imposition of programmes she dislikes by leaving the room, busying herself with other tasks or mentally switching off (see Chapter 3 in this volume; Collett, 1986; Morley, 1986). When we look at the way women are represented in the news it is not surprising that this is one area of television that women in the audience feel is not for them; they pay little attention to it even though it is frequently on in their presence.

However, the news is only part of a stream of material. It flows inexorably out of and in to the quiz shows, the sports reports, the American cops series that surround it and the advertisements which, on ITV, interrupt it. This is the mass of material from which the disparate audiences can select their imagery and construct their impressions. The reduced visibility of women in the news is more emphatic, carries more significance, precisely because of its routine juxtaposition with their heightened visibility in the rest of the output. Those qualities that are absent from the news are inescapably present elsewhere. When we watch the serious face of the newsreader we are reminded that women's faces on television normally display emotion (in soaps, feature films, dramas), that women's bodies are part of the spectacle of television (in the ads, in game shows, as entertainers), that women are characteristically placed in a domestic setting (in sitcoms, family dramas) and that their sexuality is never forgotten. Standing in sharp opposition to the rest of this output the news is presented as a space where emotion is inappropriate, where domestic issues are defined as private and as subordinate to public conflict and the world of hard politics, and where women's sexuality is trivialising and a distraction.

There are important distinctions of style and content to be made within news programmes themselves, the most significant being between two types of realism which operate simultaneously (Ellis, 1982, pp.6–7). Each has a different implication for women. First there is the actuality of the filmed footage, the news items themselves. This is a realism of record. It seeks pictures from as close to an event as possible, transmitted to the audience as quickly as possible. Second there is a narrative realism provided by the studio and the presenters. A news programme takes place in the real time of the studio. Following the visual dazzle of the title sequence we are given a shot of the whole studio, an image of calm in its pale blues and greys, with the newsreaders relaxed yet prepared behind their sweeping desk. Firmly located in this secure and recognisible space, they greet us directly, then guide us through the programme. They act as narrators who can summon up other forms of input – stills, graphics, filmed reports – and weave them back into the overall shape of the programme. The actuality items are thus held together in a sequential narrative flow in which incoherences can be sorted out and contradictions contained. In the mid-1970s some BBC2 news broadcasts showed the reader in the busy news room, with sub-editors, secretaries and journalists at work in the background. Something of the process of producing the news was brought into vision. But this glimpse of news gathering and news selection has vanished in favour of a more finished surface. The uncertainties of production are now smoothed over by the calm professionalism of the presentation.

Thus a double thread runs through the news and its imagery, a search for excitement and a concern with the seriousness of status and power. Both themes depend on values that are recognised as masculine and both deal with areas from which women are excluded. The actuality material is a collection of disparate and fragmented short items – a collage of rapidly changing locations, characters and topics. Each item selects a high point from what could otherwise be seen as a complex of social and political relations. History is largely eradicated, depth of understanding sacrificed for the sense of immediacy, the effort to get as close as possible to the experience of an event. In the words of Kenneth Adam, a former Director of BBC TV, television is, 'the transmission of experience. News is no longer what it has always been, something heard or seen or reported on after it has happened. News is not then, it is now' (quoted in Schlesinger, 1978, p.129. See also Galtung and Ruge, 1973). This longing for instantaneity leads to a search for a particular type of imagery, an imagery that can convey the desired sense of involvement and immediacy, an imagery of conflict, of disaster, of war. We are shown crowds in action, running, shouting, throwing, struggling; men uniformed and armed for action; damaged buildings, distressed victims, flames. The excitement of gathering this type of news calls for the competitive spirit of reporters who have 'balls' – 'The target is to be first and best. There are no second prizes,' declared the IBA's *Guide to Independent Broadcasting*, 1985.

We would expect such material to evoke a strong emotional response from the audience – a special sort of pleasure. We watch with fascinated horror the flames of the inner city riot, the suspense-filled moments of the hijacked aircraft waiting on the tarmac: events whose outcome is still unknown. But the pleasurable excitement to which these images give rise is rapidly transformed by their management and presentation as 'news'. We are allowed only a brief glimpse into the troubled and chaotic world before we are returned to the security of the studio and handed over to the reassuring presence of the newsreaders. The continuity they provide literally contains the unstable material of the actuality footage, dealing with it and making it manageable. It is their task to replace the moment of action with the serious face of the expert commentator, be it politician, academic or special correspondent, who can return that moment back to the responsible world of public affairs. The 'talking heads', public figures speaking responsibly on matters of import, form the main visual mode of the seriousness of the news. It is they who moderate the moments of excitement and it is they who deal with those other major topics of the news, what Chris Dunkley once described as the 'depressing agenda' of politics, industry, economics and defence (Dunkley, 1981). The high seriousness of these subjects and of those who are called on to present them temper and control the illicit pleasures of the actuality dramas with which they interleave.

This area of seriousness and responsibility excludes women in its own way. Women are vastly outnumbered by men in positions of social and political power, by those whose views are most likely to be reported on or whose opinions sought. They include prominent politicians, police chiefs, union leaders, judges and bishops. Stuart Hall and his colleagues describe them as 'primary definers' of the issues of the day (Hall et al., 1978). They are individuals who are likely to have built up relationships with those who make the news through both formal and informal channels. Women are not prominent among them. Women are expelled from the imagery of the news just as they are expelled from those areas of public life from which the news is derived.

Here I must add the reminder that I am discussing the main national news programmes and not the local and regional programmes. Local news deals in a completely different range of topics and imagery and includes many items on social problems and everyday life. Indeed, where the national news discusses policy and interviews policymakers, the local news of necessity looks at the effects of policies and speaks to those who must carry them out and those who suffer them, often predominantly women.

In the national news, the area where women now play an increasingly visible part is that of presentation – as reporters who speak over and appear in the actuality footage and as newsreaders in the studio. It is in the studio, where they have become part of the narrative continuity of the news, that their presence has made the most noticeable change. Is there some quality expected of newsreaders which, despite the apparent contradictions, is turning this into a suitable role for women to play? The readers sit between the audience and the news, not quite belonging to either, but offering themselves as a point of identification through which the news can be understood. They mediate between the audience and the rawness of the actuality items, distancing viewers from potential involvement, placing them as willing observers, as people who are eager to be informed but never to be involved, as witnesses rather than participants in the reported events. Is this role of mediation and management one that can be reconciled with the forms of femininity that have been constructed out of power relations between women and men? To understand what is happening when a woman reads the news we must look more closely at the ways in which newsreaders' speech has evolved.

mediating ordinariness

The voice of authority versus sectional interests

Newsreaders belong to that group of performers on television who may look directly into the camera and hence directly at the viewer. This privilege is largely reserved for those whose presence and whose speech is sanctioned by the institution itself. By contrast, interviewees must direct their eyes slightly to one side of the camera where the interviewer sits and acts as mediator for their address. Yet for the newsreaders the intimacy of their direct gaze is in striking contrast to the formality of their speech. Apart from the relaxed moments at the beginning and end of each programme – 'That's all from us, we'll be back with you tomorrow' – they may not speak on their own behalf.

News is a form of knowledge. The newsreaders appear as those who know and whose job it is to pass their knowledge on. The professionals of the news are at pains to stress that this knowledge that constitutes news must not be partial. It cannot vary according to the knower and therein lies its jealously guarded objectivity. The newsreader, as the voice of that objectivity, may not present a point of view and may not speak from any recognised standpoint. To do so would be to admit to a 'sectional interest'. The newsreader must be the very voice of objective knowledge, must lay claim to a form of speech that can legitimately offer an account of the world and inhabit a position that will have universal validity. Yet the impartiality and objectivity of that voice is guaranteed from within the institution itself. Grace Wyndham Goldie describes the news as 'an anonymous statement of facts given with all the authority of a famous newspaper like *The Times* or a great organisation like the BBC' (Goldie, 1977). In her

143

account factuality and objectivity are linked not to universal assent but to the authority vested in prestigious institutions. 'Every time an announcer says "I" he ceases to become the voice of the BBC' (Controller of Programmes, April 1971, quoted in Cardiff and Scannell, 1981).

The voice of objective knowledge merges almost imperceptibly into the voice of authority, the claim to accuracy and truth of the one masking the power relations implied in the other. Clearly these claims present a problem for women, who neither see themselves or their interests represented in the subject matter of the news, nor tend to be among those who can shape institutional authority. Yet this voice of objectivity also makes a claim to universality. The news institutions have appropriated the right to speak for all people, and the powerful institution feels it must defend itself against those who cry that it does not, in fact, speak for them. Grace Wyndham Goldie begins her memoirs with a warning against 'groups with sectional interests,' who see television as 'an instrument which can be used to promote those interests, whether financial, social or political' (Goldie, 1977), and who put illegitimate pressures on broadcasters. Independence for broadcasters is achieved through the linked ideologies of objectivity, professionalism and, above all, balance. When Grace Wyndham Goldie goes on to justify the need for neutrality, her description is of a pragmatic balancing act between those powerful groups, in particular political parties, who could potentially exercise control over the BBC itself. Those outside this balance of power, women among them, must remain as a sectional interest. However, the claim of the BBC to speak with a single, authoritative voice is not natural or inevitable. It was fought for and achieved in the early days of sound broadcasting.

The establishment of news in the BBC occurred within the context of a struggle for seriousness under the forceful and patriarchal leadership of John Reith. Paddy Scannell and David Cardiff describe how the diversity and fragmentation of the loosely linked radio stations which made up the original British Broadcasting Comapny, established in 1922, were moulded into a centralised and prestigious national institution with close links to the established social and political order. This institution sought to evolve a single national standard of broadcasting whose technical competence was underpinned by cultural and moral judgments. Informality and diversity were squeezed out and production 'standards' were maintained through the establishment of a rigid hierarchy. Public service broadcasting aimed to satisfy the tastes of the educated classes and to elevate the tastes of the rest (Scannell and Cardiff, 1982).

At first news bulletins were severely limited because of an agreement not to compete with the daily press. But the potential of broadcast news became clear when that press was temporarily removed during the general strike of 1926 (Burns, 1977; Scannell, 1979). During the strike, with the aid of its news and public affairs broadcasts, the British Broadcasting Company gained the confidence of the government by making it clear that the virtues of moral and political responsibility it was pursuing were so closely linked to the interests of state power as to be all but indistinguishable from them. One year later the same government issued a licence to the British Broadcasting Corporation with John Reith as its Director General. The licence forbade the new public body to editorialise or express its own opinions and laid on it the duty to be objective and balanced (Burns, 1977). Krishan Kumar, in his study of the role of presenters in the BBC, has described how in the pre-war years Reith and his senior staff deliberately used the announcers to create the 'public image' of the BBC:

> The decision to make announcers anonymous followed from this policy as did the sedulous cultivation of their formality. Both were intended to create a particular style by which the BBC could be identified in the public mind and which more than any other device was used to establish its claim to a special moral and cultural authoritativeness. (Kumar, 1977, p.23)

If the announcers all sounded the same, wrote the Announcement Editor in 1936, it was a tribute to their training (*ibid.*, p.240). Women announcers were tried but they did not stay for long. Cheris Kramarae writes:

> In the 1920s and 1930s women applied for announcing jobs . . . and women's groups asked the BBC to consider the women's applications. But the BBC gave a variety of reasons why the women were not hired, including the argument that the job would be too strenuous for women, since announcers often have to rush from one studio to another. (Kramarae, 1985)

The Second World War consolidated the BBC's claim to speak

145

with a universal voice. The wartime Corporation saw itself as speaking for the nation as well as to the nation, expressing a united sense of purpose. Now it was able to speak directly to a working class no longer seen as challenging the public order but as united behind the war effort, while at the same time retaining a suitable sense of deference. 'The men want to be talked to by a gentleman, at any rate when the talker is speaking for a national body like the Corporation,' wrote A.R. Ryan, investigating the listening habits of the British Expeditionary Force in 1940 (quoted in Cardiff and Scannell, 1981). In a convenient paradox the objectivity of BBC news became part of a partial and self-congratulatory British self-image.

With the coming of television there was concern that vision in itself would distract from the Olympian detachment achieved by the voices of the newsreaders. Indeed, right up until 1954 news bulletins were read by an unseen announcer late at night over a picture of the BBC symbol. In her memoirs Grace Wyndham Goldie describes the feeling of the time:

> 'News was fact, comment was opinion. If a newsreader were seen while giving the news, any change in his visual manner, a smile or a lift of an eyebrow might, however little this was intended, be interpreted as comment. The sacred dividing line between fact and comment would be blurred.' (Goldie, 1977).

It was in anticipation of the coming of ITV that the BBC introduced newsreaders in vision in 1954. When ITN began in 1955 it rejected the stuffy British tradition and went to North America for its models. Not only were its newsreaders visible, but it scorned anonymity and built them up as personalities. News bulletins were combined with interviews, illustrative material and filmed reports and were broadcast at peak viewing times. The 'human interest' story was introduced, in which a raised eyebrow or a smile was positively welcomed. The coming of ITV, together with ITN, was widely hailed as a move towards the democratis-ation of the medium, appealing to a broader audience without the patronising tones of the BBC (compare Davis, 1976). Indeed the BBC itself began to change its style in response to the challenge. Presenters and newsreaders were no longer simply the voice of the organisation, their more relaxed and populist style seemed to speak partly for the audience, too. But there remained no sense of the diversity and plurality of that audience, no acknowledgment that individuals were embedded in social relations of power.

By the 1970s the confident assumptions of universality and neutrality shared by ITN and BBC news were challenged from many sides. Their claims to be balanced and objective were shown not to apply in major areas such as class and industrial relations (Glasgow Media Group, 1976), race and 'law and order' (Hall *et al.*, 1978) and Northern Ireland (Curtis, 1984). The fact that there has been no similar study of discrimination against women in the news has not been due to the inactivity of feminist critics, but rather that, unlike the areas quoted above, the news organisations have never claimed to balance the concerns of women against those of men nor to maintain objectivity between a male and a female point of view. During the 1970s the argument put by people like the Glasgow Media Group that the news organisations did not achieve balance and objectivity, was parallelled by another argument that balance and objectivity themselves – at least in the forms evolved by the BBC and ITN – were neither possible nor desirable. Many groups stood outside the recognised balance of power and were now demanding that their voices should be heard. Groups like the Women's Broadcasting and Film Lobby joined the campaign to establish 'a form of institutional control wedded to a different doctrine from existing broadcasting authorities, to a doctrine of *openness* rather than to balance, to expression rather than to neutralisation' (Anthony Smith, writing in 1974, quoted in Blanchard and Morley, 1982). When Channel 4 was set up in 1982 it was only a partial victory for those campaigns. The main news programme went to ITN with no change in their long-established values and style of presentation.

The notion that we now live in a complex and plural society has become part of the received wisdom of the programmers of the 1970s and 1980s and the news institutions have reacted defensively. The *BBC Year Book* for 1985 describes a 'polarised audience who sometimes find it difficult to accept the BBC's neutrality'. Krishan Kumar writing in 1979 saw the changing role of professional broadcasters – that is of the presenters, interviewers and newsreaders who speak on behalf of the organisation – as a kind of adaptive response to the fluctuating pressures on the BBC. The stress is now on professionalism and a certain kind of popular appeal rather than on the moral and cultural conviction of earlier days. It is in this context of a challenge to the claims to universality and an adaptable reassertion of those claims that women have become cautiously established as newsreaders.

When a woman reads the news

Women have become established as newsreaders, but they have not moved alongside men in the same way as those prestigious professional broadcasters, like Robin Day or David Dimbleby, whose popular presence is balanced by the political respect they command. Instead they are caught within the conflicting definitions of femininity and of 'the news' – themselves trivialised, they can be blamed for trivialising. Women represent the antithesis of news values. They are the very sign of dissent and disruption. Yet the job of the newsreader is to smooth over dissent, to provide the studio calm which receives and moderates the chaos from outside. Women newsreaders are called on to speak from a carefully constructed position, with the mythical neutrality of the universal voice, and yet, as women, they are defined as outside both the political consensus and the masculine structure of language. They cannot escape their femininity, yet the possibility of making a contribution that is specifically on behalf of women is ruled out. They may not speak as women or for women. Women newsreaders must search for a visual style that stresses their femininity yet defers to the seriousness of the news, that complements that of the man, yet takes care not to impinge on the male preserve. Hair that has not been 'done', lack of make-up, the less studied appearance associated with feminism, must be avoided. They must embrace the 'post-feminist' worked-on appearance of the young businesswoman of the 1980s, a style made current in advertisements and magazines directed at women executives. Their self-presentation must stress a rigid and unbridgeable *difference* between men and women, while distracting from the continuing process of *differentiation*.

However, it is not an eternal and unchangeable difference but the process of differentiation itself which works to secure and re-secure the relations of domination and subordination between men and women. It is a process which is flexible, able to change its ground, to adapt to circumstances, to re-establish new forms of relations of power. The invitation to speak with the voice of authority may be nothing but an invitation, yet again, to be a decorative performer. Women have become accustomed to being asked to identify with men and to express themselves through men. Any attempt to speak with a universal voice within a system grounded in deep divisions of domination and subordination is doomed to failure. The question may not be, 'Can women speak from this position?' but 'Do they want to?' The feminine position in which we have been placed is surely one we would wish to recover and make use of rather than to deny. If the cost of being offered a public voice involves giving up the right to speak specifically as a woman, is it a price worth paying? Should we not argue that the voice of those who are subordinated can reach for an expression of truth to experience that is denied to an authority grounded in domination? Theirs is 'the sound mind whose soundness is what ails it' (Adorno, 1973).

The appearance of women newsreaders is not necessarily a step towards women's liberation. In the contemporary style of news presentation where the reader may be recognised as a front, a mask, a performer, a transmitter rather than an originator of news, it is not difficult to imagine news reading becoming a 'women's job'. After all women are easy on the eye, speak clearly and still add that element of spice that the press found so exciting in Anna, Angela and the rest. If we are not watchful we will find that once more, with the infinite flexibility of effortless power, women will have been put in their place yet again.

References

Adorno, T. (1973), *Negative Dialectics*, trans. E.B. Ashton, London, Routledge & Kegan Paul.

Berger, J. (1972), *Ways of Seeing*, Harmondsworth, Penguin.

Blanchard, S. and Morley, D. (eds) (1982), *What's this Channel Fo(u)r? An Alternative Report*, London, Comedia.

Burns, T. (1977), 'The organisation of public opinion', in J. Curran *et al.* (eds), *Mass Communication and Society*, London, Edward Arnold.

Butcher, H. *et al.* (1974), *Images of Women in the Media*, duplicated paper, Birmingham, Centre for Contemporary Cultural Studies.

Cardiff, D. and Scannell P. (1981), 'Radio in World War Two', in U203 *Popular Culture*, Block 2, Unit 8, Milton Keynes, Open University Press.

Collett, P. (1986), 'Watching the TV audience', paper presented to the International Television Studies Conference, London.

Cook, P. and Johnston, C. (1974), 'The place of women in the cinema of Raoul Walsh', in P. Hardy (ed.), *Raoul Walsh*, Edinburgh, Edinburgh Film Festival.

Cowie, E. (1978), 'Woman as sign', in *M/F*, no.1.

Curtis, L. (1984), *Ireland the Propaganda War*, London, Pluto Press.

Daly, M. (1979), *Gyn-ecology*, Boston, Beacon Press.

Davis, A. (1976), *Television: the First Forty Years*, London, Independent Television Publications.

Dunkley, C. (1981), 'The news that fits the view', in *Financial Times*, 4 February.

Eddings, B.M. (1980), "Women in broadcasting (US) de jure, de facto", in H. Baehr (ed.), *Women and Media*, Oxford, Pergamon Press.

Ellis, J. (1982), *Visible Fictions*, London, Routledge & Kegan Paul.

Galtung, J. and Ruge, M. (1973), 'Structuring and selecting news', in S. Cohen, and J. Young (eds), *The manufacture of News*, London, Constable.

Glasgow University Media Group (1976), *Bad News*, London, Routledge & Kegan Paul.

Goldie, G.W. (1977), *Facing the Nation*, London, Bodley Head.

Goulden, H. *et al.* (1982), "Consciousness razing", in S. Blanchard and D. Morley (eds), *What's this Channel Fo(u)r? An Alternative Report*, London, Comedia.

Hall, S. *et al.* (1978), *Policing the Crisis*, London, Macmillan.

Jensen, E. (1982), 'Television newscasts in a woman's perspective', typescript from the E. Jensen and M. Kleberg report *Kvinders rolle i TV-nyheder og underholdningsprogrammer*, Stockholm, Nord-publikation.

Kramarae, C. (1985), 'Revolutionary statements about a communication revolution', paper presented to International Communication Association meeting, Honolulu.

Kumar, K. (1977), 'Holding the middle ground', in J. Curran *et al.* (eds), *Mass Communication and Society*, London, Edward Arnold.

Morley, D. (1986), 'Family television: cultural power and domestic leisure', paper presented to International Television Studies Conference, London.

Mulvey, L. (1973), 'You don't know what is happening, do you, Mr Jones?', *Spare Rib*, no.8.

Mulvey, L. (1975), 'Visual pleasure and narrative cinema', *Screen*, vol.16, no.3.

Mulvey, L. (1984), 'The image and desire', in L. Appignanesi (ed.), *Desire*, London, ICA.

Scannell, P. (1979), 'The social eye of television 1946–55', *Media, Culture and Society*, vol.1, no.1.

Scannell, P. and Cardiff, D. (1982), 'Serving the nation: public service broadcasting before the war', in B. Waites *et al.* (eds), *Popular Culture Past and Present*, London, Croom Helm.

Schlesinger, P. (1978), *Putting 'Reality' Together*, London, Constable.

Schlesinger, P. *et al.* (1983), *Television Terrorism*, London, Comedia.

Spender, D. (1980), *Manmade language*, London, Routledge & Kegan Paul.

Tuchman, G. *et al.* (1978), *Hearth and Home*, New York, Oxford University Press.

10 Entering the arena:
writing for television

Jill Hyem

In 1983 a women's committee was formed within the Writers' Guild of Great Britain (an affiliated trade union). This move, reached democratically after an open meeting and approval by the then Executive Council, was met with immediate opposition. Two years later the committee was still under constant attack. At the AGM in 1985 a resolution was proposed to abolish the committee on sexist grounds. This, in spite of the facts that all their craft meetings were open to members of either sex and that there was a male on the committee. The resolution was not proposed by male writers, although the main bulk of opposition came from them, but by two women, Rosemary Anne Sisson and Julia Jones. Both are prominent screenwriters who first made their names in the 1950s and 1960s and they maintained that a women's committee was unnecessary and divisive in a profession where all are treated the same and the quality of one's work is the only criterion. After a fierce but well-reasoned debate and a secret ballot (called for by the proposers) the committee, to which I belonged, survived. However, the opposition continues. We only have a reprieve.

The obviously sincere views of these two women, whose work I have long respected, made me examine my own recent experiences in television – which I shall chronicle in this account – and to pose certain questions to other women writers. Are we treated differently from men working in the same area of television? Are we able to work across the board in the same way that our male counterparts are? Are our ideas and work given the same serious consideration by producers, editors, critics?

The first point to remember is that things have changed since the days when those women made their mark. They were talented, but they were few. They presented no threat. They were not labelled 'women writers' because they were, in effect, honorary men. In 1952 when the Screenwriters' Association (the forerunner of the Guild) was formed, there were 173 full members, i.e. members who had actually sold a screenplay. Of these, 144 were men and 29 women. Of these women only a few worked regularly. One cannot draw any accurate comparison with today's figures since the Guild now incorporates radio, book and theatre writers as well as screenwriters. However, it is indisputable that an ever-growing number of women writers are seeking employment in the mainstream of television. Indeed, many need to do so as sole or main breadwinners. Twenty years ago a woman's meagre earnings gleaned from the occasional novel or radio play was probably only a supplement for the family income.

I shall restrict myself to the field of series and serials, since the single play market is becoming increasingly inaccessible to any but top established writers (mostly men). There was a time when a writer's entrée into television would be through a modest thirty- or fifty-minute play, as mine was (*Equal Terms*, TX BBC2, 1973). Now it is more likely that the aspiring television writer will be tried out on an episode of one of the soap operas. Commercial pressures are becoming a major influence on the type and scale of productions. No-one is likely to risk the considerable sums involved on a little-known writer with an idea that is not obviously marketable overseas. With co-production on the increase, writers are often encouraged to take into account the 'transatlantic factor' or told that their themes should be 'universal'. In this atmosphere the openings for 'experimental' (i.e. cheap) or studio-based drama are few. Yet the more intimate plays, often favoured by women writers, are well suited to less expensive forms of production. It is essential that these alternative methods of drama production are fostered and developed.

The other reason that I am concentrating on series and serials is that I believe strongly that if women are to change attitudes in television then this is where they should be operating. It is where they can command the largest audience. It is also where some of the best writing is now to be found. In the absence of a wider play market many writers are exploring progressive ideas in the guise of series episodes.

Although I sold my first television play in the early 1970s and also wrote some of the original episodes for BBC1's *Angels* (a series, script-edited by Paula Milne, that showed hospital life through the eyes of student nurses), my main work at that time was in radio, where women writers and their ideas were being actively encouraged by script editors such as William Ash. It was not until 1980, when Anne Valery and I were invited by the BBC to co-write the series *Tenko*, that I started to work regularly in television. Ironically both Anne and I were chosen on the strength of theatre and radio plays with all-women casts that had previously been turned down by television companies. *Tenko* followed a group of British women interned by the Japanese for three and a half years during the Second World War. It also dealt with their liberation and the after effects of their captivity. It was a heaven-sent chance for two women writers to explore a variety of female characters in depth and to dispel some of the clichés of past war dramas, as well as to show that war was not the exclusive province of male experience. It also gave us a unique opportunity to observe our male colleagues' attitudes towards the subject and our treatment of it.

Although the basic idea for the series came from a woman (Lavinia Warner), the two producers, five directors and the original script editor appointed to the series were all male, as were the designers, the composer and the person in charge of publicity. It is also worth noting that a man was commissioned to write the first two episodes before the women reached the camp. These dealt with the fall of Singapore. It was not thought that a woman writer could 'handle the military side', in spite of the fact that Anne Valery had been in the army at this period and that anyway events were meant to be seen through the eyes of the women. By the third series, when the women were liberated and the military figured again, this was not thought to be an obstacle.

Tenko was not expected to be a success – except by Lavinia Warner, Anne Valery and myself. The powers-that-be were singularly pessimistic – 'No one'll want to know about an all-woman cast looking their worst' and 'such a depressing subject, they'll switch off in droves'. When he was offered the series, the producer, Ken Riddington (as he freely admits), turned it down at first on the grounds that 'war drama has been done to death, there's nothing more to say' and 'anyway I couldn't stand the thought of working with all those neurotic women'. He was to change his mind on both scores. *Tenko* ran for three series (autumn 1981, 1982, 1984) after which a hundred-minute *Reunion* was commissioned as a Christmas special (December

1985). *Tenko* was nominated for most of the major television awards. It was repeated and sold all over the world. I shall therefore give specific examples from the series in the hope that readers will have seen at least some of it.

Every writer would like to create and write his or her own series or serial. It is the only way to have any control over your work. Even then such control is limited. One of the problems for women writers trying to sell their ideas for television is that most of the people who make the ultimate decisions are still male. You may find an enthusiastic script editor or producer who is willing to put your idea forward, but it is not they who will have the final say-so. Women colleagues tell me of formats rejected by male executives because 'the idea didn't grab me' or 'it would have limited appeal.' The words 'depressing', 'cosy' and 'feminist' recur with monotonous regularity in these rejection letters. The *Tenko* format did the rounds for some time before the BBC finally bought it. Its sale was no doubt aided by the fact that Lavinia Warner joined forces with a male producer then working within the BBC. He took a stake in the property and, in her words, 'put it on the right desk.'

One of the factors that must have gone against *Tenko* at that stage was one that prejudices many ideas. Most of the central characters were middle-aged. There is a tendency among men to dismiss women characters who are not young and attractive as 'unappealing' or 'uninteresting'. Unless, that is, they fulfil the usual stereotype of nagging wife or mother-in-law. In the event the four most popular characters in *Tenko* (Marian, Beatrice, Joss and Ulrica) were all over 40. A letter I received from a male viewer underlined the point. He wrote, 'I was impressed by your portrayal of women over 30 as human beings. Men usually find it easy to relate to a woman in her twenties, probably because their mothers were that age when they were young boys. We need to see older women more often if we are to perceive them as real people.' He went on to thank us for showing 'something of the special relationship that can exist between women. Perhaps we men need to be reminded sometimes that if male/female relationships were the only ones, they would be prisons.' The younger characters had an enthusiastic following among school-girls, starved for so long of war heroines with whom they could identify. It was encouraging too that their letters asked for background information on the characters and not just for photographs of the actresses playing them.

Hustling undoubtedly plays an important part in getting any project off the ground. This is an alien pursuit for most women, as is the continual in-fighting that goes on in television. It is interesting to note that many women writing for television series are, like myself, actresses or ex-actresses (Lynda La Plante, Anne Valery, Gilly Fraser, Julia Jones, Valerie Georgeson, Liane Aukin, to name but a few). We started writing in the first place because of the dearth of good parts for women and of subjects shown from a woman's point of view. A random search by the *Sunday Times* in December 1985 showed 803 men in TV cast lists compared with 381 women, while a report by Equity found that in only 14 per cent of mid-evening programmes were women the main characters – and most of those were under 30. Writer-actresses gain an automatic advantage from their knowledge of the medium. They are able to write speakable dialogue. They are also accustomed to the wear and tear of the business. Anne Valery, when asked by an interviewer what made her successful in this field, replied, 'A lot of people can write for television, but not many can survive the hassle.' Writer Jennifer Phillips, who had a television comedy series produced some years ago, asked me if I would be interested in collaborating with her on a new idea. 'I couldn't face that nightmare on my own again,' she said. In a profile in *Writers' Newsletter*, it was commented that the words 'fighting' and 'battles' loomed large in my vocabulary (Campbell, 1985). Perhaps that is the result of six years solid in television.

Most of the skirmishes on *Tenko* arose from the fact that the writers saw things from a different perspective than the men with whom we were working. This is not to say that our basic priorities were not the same or that we did not have a great deal of respect for their work. We all wanted the programme to stand as a tribute to the women who were interned and forgotten. We wanted to show, as faithfully as possible, this hitherto hidden area of history. After his initial reservations Ken Riddington had come to see that this was an area of war drama that had not been 'done to death'. However, we could not help feeling that time was wasted over issues that would not have arisen had we been working with women. Problems arose over apparently small things, but ones which together could have had a major effect on the style and content of the series. Anne Valery and I became aware, as we had both been on past occasions, of unconscious male censorship of our work. On the one hand we would be told 'Don't let's have any *Woman's Own* writing,' and on the other we would find dialogue or scenes softened and termed 'unfeminine'. I will give two examples. In the prison camps the lavatory was the only place the women could talk in comparative privacy. In the first episode in the camp I therefore set a scene between two of the central characters in the latrine. This was immediately reset in a more 'acceptable' environment – the cookhouse. I lost that battle. Yet there are often scenes in plays and series where men have a conversation while urinating. In another episode a woman died. The doctor told a nurse to put her teeth aside as 'they might come in useful for someone else'. Although this was an actual line gleaned from a diary, it was considered 'to be going too far'. I won that battle. It was the same with bad language, which we used very sparingly. Women, it seemed, did not swear or tell crude jokes. Often we would find that the producer's/script editor's pen had been at work. We always queried these omissions and retained most of our lines. When the series went into production we found that music and lighting would often be used to soften or romanticise scenes which we had intended to be stark. This softening process was certainly not peculiar to *Tenko*. Most of the women writers I spoke to had experienced it. Two cited instances when they had been told by men that 'Women wouldn't speak like that'. Both concerned scenes between women characters with no male present. One was between some women in the army whose language was considered too bawdy. The other showed two women discussing their boyfriends' sexual failings.

The main conflict I had on *Tenko* came in the first series and was a turning point in my relationship with the producer. It was over subject matter. I wanted to write a story about a relationship between two of the younger women. This was not such an unlikely occurrence in a camp with several hundred of them; indeed, ex-prisoners had told us of women who were 'special friends'. The idea was rejected out of hand. I was told that if we introduced such a subject it would be 'turn-off time' and that the characters concerned would lose audience sympathy. I argued my case. Anne Valery and Lavinia Warner supported me. The producer remained adamant. I said that if the series was going to dodge such issues I would sooner not work on it. A compromise was reached. I was told I could write my story provided I did not use the word 'lesbian'. It was probably one of the best episodes I wrote. The audience figures did not plummet, nor did the characters lose popularity. This was an important breakthrough. In the subsequent series we were allowed to deal with such controversial subjects as abortion, euthanasia and suicide. Our judgment was, on the whole, respected.

It was interesting to notice how the attitude of the producer changed towards us as the years went by. We worked together intermittently over a period of five years between 1980 and 1985. He learnt to treat us as writers rather than as women. His opening words to me at our original interview had been, 'I've never worked with a lady writer before.' As the series progressed we were allowed virtual control over the character development and storylines. There were still times when one felt that minor misunderstandings, which might have been sorted out over a pint with a male writer, became blown up by the time messages had been passed down the line.

Before I entered the arena of television series I had been warned of 'male mafias': programmes on which no woman writer had ever been employed or was likely to be. These were mostly of the police spy genre, often made largely on location. Women writers are not popular on location. They cramp styles. That is possibly why the original male writer on *Tenko* was taken on a recce to Singapore, although Anne Valery and I were not allowed out there till all three series had been completed, and then we had to pay our own air fares. Over the years some of the male-oriented series have started to use the odd token woman writer (*Juliet Bravo*, *Bergerac*, *The Bill*). She then has an awesome responsibility. If she turns in a less than good script she knows it will provide an excuse for not using another woman. As in many professions a woman has to be that much better, that much more reliable. Deliver late and all women are late deliverers. After the third *Tenko* series I was approached by just such a macho team. The producer and his script editor had worked together on a number of successful series in the past and were now setting up a new one to be centred on a rich sailing community (later to become *Howards Way*, BBC1). I went to see the producer. The buzz words were 'glossy', 'fast-moving', 'slick', '*Dallas*'. He told me that the other two writers were to be men but he felt they 'ought to have a feminine touch'. My first impulse was to run a mile, but I took the format home. I read it, and was so incensed by the biased and unsympathetic biography of the central female character that I determined to take the job, if only to redress the balance a little. I also felt that it had the potential basis of a good family saga that could be more than just a *Dallas* prototype. I made no secret of my feelings. Over the next eight months I progressed from being 'the feminine touch' to the 'personal touch' (when my script was the only one of the first four to be accepted) to 'our main writer' (when I had written five out of the first seven episodes) to 'that difficult bitch' when I disagreed with their future storylines and the cynicism behind them. They were surprised when I turned down the second series.

A recurring problem for me on that particular series was one which other women tell me they too have encountered: the interpretation of the word 'strength' in relation to a (usually male) character. The all-men team with whom I was working saw the hero's 'strength' (i.e. audience appeal) in terms of his physical superiority and his ability to 'rule the roost'. If I gave him an introspective scene I was told he was 'spineless' or 'wet'. If he expressed the same sentiments while shouting and slamming his fist on the table he was showing 'guts'. Of course these men do not represent all men in television. Yet even in *Tenko* a 'strong' scene was usually considered to be one where the characters shouted at each other.

As I said earlier, a likely start for would-be television writers is through one of the twice-weekly soaps. Unlike their American counterparts these series attempt to reflect accurately day-to-day life in Britain. The ratio of women to men writers on some of these programmes is notably higher than on most other series and serials, although a survey conducted by the Writers' Guild women's committee for the month of February 1985 showed that the long-running soap operas were still dominated by male writers: *Coronation Street* (ITV), seven men, no women; *Emmerdale Farm* (ITV), three men, no women; *Crossroads* (ITV), three men, one woman. In contrast the newer soaps, *Brookside* (Channel 4) and *EastEnders* (BBC1), employed more women than men writers in the same month: *Brookside*, two men, three women; *EastEnders*, one man, two women. A year later the figures remained much the same. *EastEnders*, which has a female producer (Julia Smith), and *Brookside* continued to employ a consistently high number of women writers. Perhaps this is why some of the most 'truthful' female characters are to be found in these two serials and why social issues are often dealt with in more depth than in a prestige play. *EastEnders'* script editor, Tony Holland, speaking at a Writers' Guild craft meeting, told us, 'We don't think about our writers as men or women, simply as good or bad.' That is all we ask. Having said that, writers on the soaps have virtually no control. The system varies from programme to programme, but there is usually a number of writers involved and detailed storylines are provided so that the pacing and long-term development of a story often lies in someone else's hands. There are regular script conferences, but the very pressure of production means that there is little room for manoeuvre.

Working as part of one of these writing teams can be an advantage or a disadvantage according to the prevailing atmosphere. Most of the women writers I know enjoy working closely with other people, pooling their ideas in a non-competitive environment. This was one of the joys of my collaboration with Anne Valery on *Tenko*. That is fine on programmes where this sort of teamwork is encouraged, but in some a spirit of aggressive competitiveness exists. A male writer who worked for a while on *Coronation Street* described 'the unnerving experience of competing openly with other writers at meetings to obtain commissions'. It is perhaps not surprising that few women have worked on that serial.

More publicity is given to soap operas than to any other television genre. Sadly, most of it is of the muck-raking variety that serves only to diminish the production as a whole. Soaps have more women in the cast than most drama series and therefore attract the sort of exploitative attention so often given to programmes that feature women prominently. *Tenko* suffered from the same problem. The BBC itself promoted the second series in the *Radio Times* with totally misleading cheesecake photographs. The popular press at large were only interested in photographs of the younger actresses cowering in front of Japanese guards or of boobs behind the barbed wire. The early reviews were predictable too: 'Soap opera rave' (*Daily Express*), 'Closer to Tesco than *Tenko*' (*Daily Telegraph*), 'Another load of sentimental tat' (*Scotsman*). While Richard Last, again in the *Telegraph*, wrote, 'Add the further inhibition of a nearly all female cast and some kind of disastrous cosiness would seem inescapable'. In a perceptive article on the representation of the Second World War in television fictions, Cary Bazalgette comments, 'the key to this categorisation seems to have been the recognition that a women's point of view was present in the drama and that the series would therefore appeal more to women than to men. A further logical consequence – at least for some reviewers – is that such a series does not warrant serious attention' (Bazalgette, 1984). Even after *Tenko* had been established as the top BBC series and hailed for having broken new ground, most critics were reluctant to discuss it seriously. Instead they chose to ignore it. I doubt that a series about men in the same situation would have been so cursorily dismissed.

There are still comparatively few women directors and producers in television drama. This has an obvious effect on women writers, not only in terms of having people with a shared outlook to promote their work, but also when it comes to interpreting their scripts. Anne Valery and I asked on several occasions if there could not be a woman director on *Tenko*. We were invariably told either, 'no-one is available' or, 'There are no women directors with enough experience'. This did not prevent their using two new male directors. On another major drama series a producer who purported to be an enthusiastic supporter of women told me, 'I'd love to use a woman director, but the leading lady feels more secure with a man'. Having come to know the actress concerned, I would doubt that. It is not the first time I have found these lipservice liberals in television. Many sympathetic noises are made, even in high places, but no radical changes have taken place. On the few occasions when I have worked with women directors in television I found it an extremely rewarding experience. There was an automatic understanding of my script and of the thoughts that lay between the lines. That is not to say that I have not worked with good male directors. All one asks for is a good representative mix. A handful of top writers are consulted about the choice of cast and director, or already have working relationships with particular producers and directors. The Writers' Guild is pressing for this kind of consultation to be the prerogative of all established writers. If this principle were adopted, as it has been in radio, it could improve the situation for women writers and directors.

Few women have worked in the mainstream of television comedy, where the decisions are made by male executives and there are even fewer women producers and directors than there are in drama. Carla Lane is the only woman writer to have established herself in the top echelons. Yet plenty of women attend comedy writing courses and workshops and there is no shortage of ideas. In 1984 BBC Drama produced a series of comedy plays under an umbrella title. The only limitation was that they should take place in the same time-share flat. The producer (Evgeny Gridneff) circularised agents. Later he told me, 'It's amazing. Most of the funniest ideas are coming from women'. So why are they not filtering through to Light Entertainment? Heads of Light Entertainment departments maintain that they would welcome more comedy series from women writers, but they have yet to break down some of the barriers that discourage them. It is now some years since Jennifer Phillips and I had a comedy format about a mother, a daughter and their gay lodger rejected on the grounds that, 'Alas, it is not for me and my boys.' It was subsequently produced on BBC Radio as *Three Piece Sweet*. Attitudes like this may now be better disguised, but they still prevail. I spoke to Arline Whittacker who had a successful television sit com produced (*Sharon and Elsie*, BBC1, 1984/85). Although it went to two series, had impressive ratings, a good audience reaction and was expected to continue, it was dropped because 'the new man up there didn't like it'. The same writer said that although she was encouraged to be involved in the production, she felt a natural reticence about 'being one of the boys in the bar'. She thought that the atmosphere of 'male camaraderie that exists in most Light Entertainment departments' deterred women writers. Their male colleagues had 'greater access to the general feel of what is required in terms of current demands from heads of department and producers'. In spite of the success of her two series, no-one had ever suggested they discuss what she should do next. Perhaps if she had been 'one of the boys in the bar' they would have. This view was echoed by a male writer (Roy Apps) who has worked in light entertainment as a sketch writer. He pointed to the long list of contributors to comedy programmes, almost entirely male. He admitted that he himself had found it 'very daunting to enter that Rugby Club atmosphere'.

In conclusion I will return to the question I posed earlier. Are male and female writers treated the same in television? From my own experiences and those of other writers to whom I have spoken, the answer must be that, for the most part, they are not. Prejudice is not always conscious and sometimes comes from people who dub themselves 'pro-women'. There are still areas of drama and light entertainment that are virtually inaccessible to women writers. Even allowing for a certain amount of persecution mania, their ideas do tend to be belittled and misunderstood, and so-called 'women's programmes' are seldom given the serious consideration afforded to the male equivalents. They suffer on one hand from the backlash of feminism and on the other from male protectivism.

Some men writers have expressed the view that it is they who are now discriminated against, and that women have become 'the flavour of the day' in television. One well-established writer was dropped from his own series because the producer decided to have only women writing on it. (The idea did centre round three young women.) Another sent an idea to a producer who was looking for plays with an erotic theme. Although she liked his idea she turned it down because she had decided to do all plays by women writers. This syphoning off can be counter-productive. After all, the flavour of today can become the sour taste of tomorrow. It breeds resentment among our male colleagues from whom we should be seeking support and co-operation. It also reinforces the idea of women being separate, thereby creating ghettos of our work. In this respect the women who opposed the Writers' Guild women's committee had a point. By labelling ourselves 'women writers' we are in some respects being our own worst enemies, for none of us wish to be thought of as a persecuted minority seeking special treatment. Yet unless we provide a forum for women writers to organise, to discuss problems and ideas, to liaise with women in other entertainment groups and unions, we will never be in a position to enter the arena on equal terms with men. For that is what we must do if we are to have any radical effect on attitudes of viewers as well as of employers. One only has to look at the women's publishing houses to see how the work of women can enrich society, challenging accepted ideas, rediscovering forgotten writers, providing fresh approaches.

Perhaps with a new generation rising there will come a day when the female point of view will be fully presented throughout television drama and all other areas of writing.

Acknowledgment

I would like to thank members of the Writers' Guild of Great Britain, male and female, for their help in the preparation of this article.

References

Bazalgette, C. (1984), 'TV drama goes back to front,' in G. Hurd (ed.) *National Fictions: World War Two in British Films and Television*, London, British Film Institute.

Campbell, P. (December 1985), 'Unassuming rebel with a cause,' *Writers' Newsletter*, Writers' Guild of Great Britain.

11 Women/acting/power

Gillian Skirrow

Attention to acting breaks something of new ground in film and television academic criticism. Since actor/esses are the most visible part of the performance, and in theatre criticism the most celebrated, this seems to demand some explanation. What is it about film and television criticism that has excluded a consideration of acting, or what is it about acting that has made it invisible to such criticism? This chapter begins with a polemic to open up these questions to discussion.

Authentically women

Film criticism has been concerned to distance itself from journalistic reviewing which accepted the way that the industry wanted itself talked about – that is, in terms of stars, their charisma and the relationship of their roles to their personal lives. Film criticism rejected such extra-textual concerns, but at the cost of throwing out the actor-baby with the star's bathwater. In its consideration of character the emphasis in film criticism was and still is on the function of the characters within the plot rather than on the performance or characterisation itself. Further, there was, and still is, in film criticism an emphasis on the construction of meaning through contrasts and differences within the codes and systems of a text, and it was not obvious what systematic contrasts there were within acting that could justify it as having meaning. What attention there has been to acting has focused on large-scale differences – for example, on the difficulties of the transition from silent film to sound, and on the different traditions of film acting coming from the Kuleshov-Brecht approach on the one hand and the Method on the other.[1]

164

Traditional discussions of acting, on the contrary, have emphasised its relation to emotion, feeling, intuition – lexical items which do not figure often in structuralist criticism. The traditional approach is a romantic one which sees acting as something natural, a quality rather than a system of signification, and perhaps this is why structuralist and post-structuralist criticism just avoids the whole area. The avoidance of feeling, however, seems to me to be one of the biggest problems with this kind of criticism. Given the way that feelings are linked with the feminine in our society, it is almost as if avoiding them is necessary to guarantee the hard-nosed, rigorous, virile image which helps make a system of thought academically respectable in these technological times. The possibility emerges then that there is something 'feminine' about acting which escapes the male frameworks within which film and television are usually considered, and feminism, which has never shrunk from the personal and the expression of feelings, may therefore be the potential deliverer of new theory, rescuing film and television criticism from its Oedipal blindness. Those feminists who hold that all theory and possibly all language is male might prefer to share a position with the 'romantic' critics and leave the experience as ineffable. But although acting is certainly unquotable – neither words nor a still frame can capture it – this need not mean that it cannot or should not be analysed. Acting does have meaning and produces effects, although they may not yet have been systematised. In future research it certainly seems worth looking at patterns within acting and exploring how they can be made to count within the structure of meaning in the whole text. However, for those of us who would like to reclaim theory for feminism there is even more urgent work to be done on the relationship between sex/gender, acting and power.

First it can be noted that film criticism has masked the absence of a consideration of the actor/esses by producing other, more powerful heroes. In auteur criticism the director was seen – and often saw himself – as the sole creative source. One of the more polite formulations of the insignificance of the actor was Sternberg's, 'the actor in films cannot function as an artist . . . he is little more than one of the complex materials used in our craft' (McGilligan, 1980). Svengali in the novel *Trilby*, which was published at about the same time as moving film appeared, seems to epitomise the mesmeric hold which a director can have over an actor/ess, and it is no coincidence that in this power relationship it is a woman whose consciousness is taken over.[2] In practice there are many well-documented cases of a bullying relationship between male directors and female stars, and very few – Mae West, possibly? – in which either the power relation or the sexual relation is the other way round. Perhaps this is part of the way in which male actors and even acting itself have become feminised, and therefore unimportant.

This may seem to be contradicted by the Method school of acting whose stars are celebrated as much for their maleness as for their acting – Hal Hinson in his article 'Some notes on Method acting' (1984), discusses Jack Nicholson, Humphrey Bogart, Paul Newman, Marlon Brando, Robert de Niro . . . whatever happened to the women in the Method school? Hinson talks of the Method characters as being surrounded by an aloof, wary silence, and Method acting as 'the language of a realistic American style'. Thinking of the parts played by the actors he mentions, and in particular of Marlon Brando in *The Godfather*, could he mean 'the language of power'? I suggest that the reason why Method acting is discussed at all by Hinson is that it is a kind of acting which is about power, albeit often the power of the 'alienated loner', which therefore makes it important and male. The author seeks to de-feminise it still further by leaving out reference to Method actresses. But the linking of realism and power is interesting. What makes a powerful performance seems not to be a characterisation's contribution to the development of the narrative but its verisimilitude, relating power/authority to authenticity. Men being 'authentically' men are powerful.

This suggests that it might be interesting to see if women who act authority roles derive some of their authority or power simply from being authentically women. Some of the clearest examples of such roles are in the television crime series, where having women police officers seems to be a popular way of bringing the crime series up to date. I have selected one of these, *Juliet Bravo*, to look at more closely, and to contrast with a different example of the same genre, *Widows*.[3] These programmes have interesting similarities in that they show women in positions of power, which presents a challenge not only to the actresses involved but, as I shall hope to show later, to the routines and procedures of television production within which the role of the actor/esses is usually clear-cut. But the differences between the programmes are interesting too. *Juliet Bravo* is a police procedural – showing the audience, from a police point of view, how the police operate. It is a series, in which we meet the same characters week after week, but each time they are involved in a different story which is finished at the end of each episode. It was made by the series and serials department within the BBC and is mostly a studio production with some film inserts. It was scripted almost entirely by men, and had a male producer. *Widows*, on the other hand, is written from the point of view of the criminals. It is a serial, that is, it has a story which develops over six episodes in the first series, and over another six in the second series. It was made by Euston Films for transmission on ITV and was shot entirely on film and on location. It was written and produced by women. For this study I have interviewed Anna Carteret, who played Inspector Kate Longton in *Juliet Bravo* for three years, and Ann Mitchell, who played Dolly Rawlings, the leader of the female 'gang' in both series of *Widows*. I have also interviewed most of the cast and crew of *Widows*, and Joan Clark, who is the script editor for *Juliet Bravo* and many other BBC crime series before and since.

Before starting the examination of these productions I should perhaps try to define more closely what I understand by 'power' and 'authority', which have been used interchangeably up to this point. According to dictionary definitions and commonsense usage, 'power' seems to be related to the freedom and intrinsic ability to express oneself. It also has connotations of vigour. 'Authority', on the other hand, seems to represent the right to enforce obedience, to hold delegated rather than intrinsic power. This is how I use the two terms in the following analysis. Just to complicate matters, 'authenticity', although it looks as if it has something in common with 'authority', actually has a different derivation, and most of its connotations are closer to the definition of 'power' above. I shall later consider in more detail the implications of its quite widespread use in the broadcasting industry, where 'authenticity' tends to be synonymous with 'truth', which in turn is seen as something intrinsic rather than produced.

Acting the part

Because of the differences in mode of production of the two texts it is not possible to make a direct comparison between the roles of the actresses. Rather, I shall look at the two characters intended to be representations of powerful women to explore what aspects of the characters are determined by the script and shooting procedures, to describe what attributes of the characters and what audiovisual techniques are seen as giving power, and particularly to examine the ways in which actresses have real power over their character in the production situation. A proper analysis of 'power' as represented in acting would be enhanced by a study of how power is indicated in real-life situations, and it would be interesting to know if women indicate their power in ways different from men. However, this kind of work is only beginning to be done in linguistics and sociology, and as far as the analysis of acting as such is concerned the present paper simply aims to be suggestive of ways it can be looked at.

In contrast to film acting, television acting often seems to assume a relationship between characters and actor/esses – particularly in series and serials – an identification which is exploited in the popular press. Although this does not mean that an actor/ess is playing only him/herself, obviously a production team is looking for the possibility of this type of identification at the casting stage, and must be aware of how the actress will carry the narrative image of the programme, by appearing on the cover of the *Radio/TV Times*, for example. In the casting of both *Widows* and *Juliet Bravo* there was an idea of 'authenticity' operating which meant that the real-life and past experience of the actresses was particularly important.

In *Widows*, the production team were looking for actresses to realise parts already written in a script about working-class women who were born and bred in the east end of London. They favoured 'authentic' casting, so they looked for actresses with a similar background. One of the actresses who was not a bona fide Eastender had to lie – or 'act'? – at the interview in order to get the part. I do wonder whether 'authenticity' would have been such an important concept if the script had been about middle-class housewives. As Lionel Trilling points out, in the nineteenth century novel a character's authenticity was clearly linked to class structure, 'the person who accepts his class situation, whatever it may be, as a given and necessary condition of his life will be sincere beyond question. He will be sincere *and* authentic, sincere *because* authentic' (Trilling, 1972, pp.114–118). Perhaps in the twentieth century the working class, because of its otherness in relation to media culture, has itself become the guarantee of authenticity? I also have the feeling that in *Widows* authenticity was all the more important because women were involved, but I have no evidence for this. The production team certainly went to some lengths to find the right women. They wanted the actress to look like the part even before the actress knew what the part was. In this way the procedure was, from the production team's point of view, more like casting non-actors. They wanted to 'recognise' the characters, not create them. The casting director, however, knowing what the producer would be looking for, gave candidates tips about what to wear at the interview. (The casting director is the actor/ess's best friend but seems to have an ambiguous role as the producer's friend too.) Even from the production point of view the process of 'authentic' casting may be complicated by the persona the actress has built up, as opposed to her personality. For example, although in *Widows* it was quite important that the actresses should not be readily recognisable from other television productions, Ann Mitchell had been seen on television and in the theatre, often playing mothers, and in *Juliet Bravo* some of Anna's authority, and therefore suitability, may have come from her prestige in being connected with the National Theatre and some roles she had played there. She had also played mothers in television productions.

In *Juliet Bravo* the producer was looking for someone who would be close to a real-life model – in this case a policewoman whom they already knew. ('We have an exact model on whom to base our fiction series' – Ian Kennedy Martin[4]). But only the first four scripts out of a series of thirteen were already written, so they were looking for someone whose personality would influence the development of the later scripts. In this sense the interview was something like an actual police interview for putting someone in charge of a police station. One wonders how important it was that both Kate Longton's father and Anna Carteret's father had been in the army!

Ann Mitchell was also cast by interview rather than audition. She was interviewed first by the casting director Marilyn Johnston, then by the director, Ian Toynton, who was later joined by the producer, Linda Agran. This must have been one of the few casting teams in mainstream television with a majority of women. At the time Ann was co-directing a play she had written with another woman about being a single parent. All three of the

Widows casting team she had met so far came to see the play, and the next week she was called in to meet Verity Lambert, to whom she talked about what she had done in her life and what she felt. She was told she had got the part on the same day. She had not been asked to read any of the script aloud. This suggests that what was important, aside from her undoubted acting ability, was her curriculum vitae. The fact that she wrote and directed plays perhaps showed that she had the kind of initiative and organisational ability that Dolly Rawlings had.

One of the implications of 'being yourself', or appearing to be, at an interview is that the way you behave at one interview may affect your chances at the next. For example, Ann Mitchell had been interviewed a few years before by Ian Toynton at Euston Films for a part which she turned down because it was too small, although she was out of work at the time. He told her later that he did not forget her sense of pride and ability to say 'no' at that interview. Luckily this worked in her favour when it came to the casting of *Widows*. The casting teams seem to believe that the system works and that they have indeed cast authentic 'personalities'. The actresses involved, at least in this study, felt that the characters they played were quite far from their own personalities and that a great deal of effort had gone into the construction of the personalities the production team had wanted to see at the interview.

Both *Widows* and *Juliet Bravo* provided their actresses with background to the character but left the realisation of the character very much to the actress. This meant a good deal of hard work by the actress to decide how the character would move and express herself in ways which went beyond the script, and this is of course the very place where power is expressed visually. For example, in *Widows* the lines provided the actress with a lot of information about the strength of Dolly's character but there was a lot more in what she did *not* say but must have been feeling. Ann Mitchell said she tried to capture this excess in a tenseness of manner and speech. In *Juliet Bravo* the police jargon limited the way character could be expressed in speech, and Anna Carteret said she tried to use her eyes to express herself as being something more than the lines she was saying. Directors/producers of series and serials, once they have done the casting, seem to be happy to leave interpretation to the actress, but there are of course still many constraints on this interpretation. Anna

Carteret's use of the eyes, for example, is only possible in the context of the television close-up. Different formats, different kinds of direction, the choosing of wardrobes, and different ways of scheduling rehearsals and shooting, have different effects on character before the individual actress can put anything of herself into it.

Widows as a serial with one writer and one director throughout might seem to offer a great deal of stability to the actresses, but since the script called for most of the characters to develop or change, and the shooting was done out of sequence and with no rehearsals (as is usual in film production), it did present continuity problems for the actresses even though they had the scripts two months before filming. The director, however, had a strategy for helping the actresses to have a sense of where they were, emotionally as well as physically, at any time. He chose to shoot first all the sequences in the lock-up, the women's regular meeting place which appears in nearly every episode, so that the actresses could concentrate on character development at the one time, and after that they would be able to use their past performances as a yardstick for how the character was behaving in any episode. This director seems to have great respect for actors and actresses and gives them a lot of space, seeing his job as talking a good deal with the actresses about the characters before the shooting starts and then, during shooting, only reminding them of what their characters had just done or just been feeling in the immediately preceding part of the script. The fact that the director allowed some democracy to the actresses once he had cast them, and did not try to impose his ideas about performance, did not in any way seem to hinder the development of a clear identity for the serial. His non-sexist attitude towards the women set the tone for the rest of the crew, so that, for example, the stuntmen who showed the women how to do things they had not done before did not patronise them but were positively helpful. The kind of power that Ian Toynton had is very different from the charismatic bullying relationship of some of the more celebrated Hollywood film directors, and perhaps more characteristic of director-actor relations in British 'made-for-television' drama, with the exception of the single play. Still it is power, because in the end he has the responsibility.

Juliet Bravo, as a series with different writers and different directors, did not so much develop Kate Longton's character as bring out different aspects of it, or sometimes evacuate it altogether in favour of the role: Anna was several times told by directors that she was 'too involved', and should be cooler or more objective. Mostly, however, the directors left interpretation entirely up to her. Only occasionally would a director say 'you always seem a bit po-faced to me, let's try and get a bit of humour'. She says she would have liked more direction like this because in a long-running series the danger is that you become stale. But since such series seem almost to run themselves they are often given to trainee directors, who on the whole are reluctant to stir things up. They are also more likely to have to concentrate harder on technical matters and so not be able to give the performance or the actress so much attention; this neglect obviously has a very different effect from the freedom and space given by a confident director, even though in both cases the actress is given a great deal of responsibility. Anna Carteret stresses, 'You've got to fight for yourself. . . . I got friendly with the cameraman, who would say things like "Could you move more slowly, then your face will end up on the screen".' In this situation, 'authentic' casting would seem to have the practical advantage of giving the director a feeling of safety.

On *Juliet Bravo* all the filming for four episodes is done first, then each programme is rehearsed as a separate entity, and then shot in the studio. One director usually does two episodes, e.g. one and three, both the film inserts and the studio. Certain directors tend to pair with certain writers, so alternate episodes are often alternately written. As if this were not enough discontinuity, the producer can sometimes decide to transmit the episodes in a different order after they have been shot, so the plots have to be written with minimal character development. In fact the character is one of the few continuities. The fact that the character is an authority figure in some way makes the lack of development more credible. Kate Longton's power seems to be indicated by a *lack* of normal human emotions and an emphasis on the office held. The most human thing about her is her north country accent, which was Anna's idea. Most of the time the background is one of the five studio sets representing the police station. Kate's clothes are police uniform, her hair is shorter than her collar, her whole appearance neat and tidy, and her 'business' involves looking at files or brushing her uniform or writing in notebooks. Other people give her a lot of her power. Anna

Figure 11.1 *Juliet Bravo* (1983): Anna Carteret as Inspector Kate Longton, surrounded by the supporting cast, 'playing a leading part with five men in supporting roles took some courage'.

Carteret said she tried to build up authority by letting other people come to her both psychologically and physically rather than her going towards them. This made her very dependent on her fellow actors and some of them used to 'tease' (harass?) her a lot. She admits that to play a leading part with five men in supporting roles took some courage. Her on-screen authority was not reflected in the real-life shooting situation, even though she eventually gained some control over the scripts.

There seems to be something of a contradiction built into the authority role, even on-screen, however. Kate has to represent the stability, not to say staticness, of an authority figure, but at the same time what is felt to give the series its edge, its element of risk, is the fact that she is a woman. 'Because she is a woman she tackles the job in a very different way from a man,' say the background notes, and 'she can let fly when frustrated'. The notes for her predecessor, Inspector Jean Darblay, specify that 'there's unquestionably a little anarchy in her make-up'. The woman spells disruption and chaos even here. The series format, written by Ian Kennedy Martin in 1979, also emphasises the woman as the object of an almost sadistic curiosity. 'The primary focus of the series is to observe this woman operating in the all-male world of our fictional police section. How she functions, copes with and controls a town and the men under her command.' So the whole basis of the series is in fact questioning her authority, which perhaps accounts for the lack of risk in her behaviour as it appears in the scripts. Whenever she is shown to be wrong, it is because she has let her 'womanly' emotions interfere with her judgment. And sexual riskiness is quite out of the question. Kate Longton is single, and this is obviously felt to be risky enough. Anna Carteret once suggested that she might be lesbian, which was greeted by nervous laughter from the production team. The early evening slot and what is referred to as the 'baked bean' audience were given as the reasons for the rather rigid moral boundaries of the series. Even her relationship with a male social worker had to be terminated because he was married, though separated. A later relationship with Detective Inspector Mark Perrin was supposed to give added interest because he was a chauvinist, not because he was sexy. Her position of authority seems to demand a renunciation or innocence of sex, like that of a celibate queen or a boy king. But even this aspect of her authority leaves a space for her to be undermined by male viewers' fantasies. From her fan mail asking for full length photographs of her in uniform to hang in the bathroom, and the disappointment from admirers when she appears in real life not wearing black stockings, it is clear that uniformed authority is no protection for a woman against being seen as a sex object. In one episode Kate was made to partially undress at gun point. One of the letters on the *Points of View* programme asked to see that bit again – for which Anna got a tiny per cent of a repeat fee.

Although she has authority as a police person, the audience is denied any access to knowledge of her as a woman and so can only conjecture about her personal strength. She has no woman friend in whom she confides. Sometimes she would be seen playing badminton with a woman (she is the Police Athletics Association National Ladies Badminton Champion) and in one episode she got friendly with a single mother. But neither of these relationships developed, presumably because the male script-writers either were not interested in them or were diffident about writing women's parts. Anna constantly tried to negotiate for more actresses to be involved and in the last four episodes a woman PC was written in. Her isolation from other women, rather than adding to her power, seems to me to underline the series' intention of looking at her as an unusual specimen under a microscope. The camera increases this impression by looking at her and the environment in a descriptive rather than an expressive way. It does not help to build up personal strength, but it emphasises the coolness and distance associated with authority.

Ann Mitchell's character in *Widows*, Dolly Rawlins, had a much riskier kind of power. She had no authority to start with except as the widow of the leader of a gang, but this association with death and the grief of bereavement perhaps gave her the freedom and strength of one who has nothing left to lose. Here again, being outside of the family was unusual enough for her to gain a kind of strength by it, but she had no position of authority in society. Dolly's appearance was recognised as important by everyone concerned, and was the cause of most disagreement between the actress and the production team. Ann Mitchell says it has been her life's ambition to play a working-class cockney woman who was not stereotyped. She slimmed for the part because she thought it was important for Dolly to be streamlined. She was conscious of using a very strong cockney accent and of wanting working-class women to identify with some dignity. She wanted to present the contrast between being elegant and at the same time very working class: 'These were conscious political decisions – the result of a lifetime of watching my class rubbished on television.' Ann wanted Dolly to be the height of elegance in Armani outfits rather than the practical Jaeger trouser suits that the production team preferred. In her identification of elegance and dignity there seems to be some reference to the power of the film noir femme fatale[5] which was undoubtedly one of the references for Dolly in the script and in the acting. Ann says both she and Lynda La Plante, the writer of *Widows*, watch a lot of old movies on a Saturday afternoon. Also, from a very young age Ann went to the cinema five times a week, and so has seen a lot of Bette Davis and Joan Crawford movies. The director also admires the noir style – particularly the modern versions of it, such as *Klute* and *Chinatown* – so although Ann mostly lost the battles over wardrobe, some of the charisma of a film noir heroine was achieved for her by lighting, camera angles, shot composition, and non-standard lenses.

Ann discussed the character of Dolly, and Dolly's relationship with husband Harry, with Ian Toynton over a number of dinners. She was quite surprised that Ian Toynton actually listened to what she said and accepted the authority of her interpretation. In fact dinners seemed to be Euston Films' substitute for rehearsals. She met the other actresses only once before shooting started, and that was at a dinner. She didn't see the sets at all before shooting and the rehearsals before the takes were mainly for the lighting.

Unlike the distancing effect of Kate Longton's lack of emotion, we are invited to identify very strongly with Dolly's grief and the way she controls it. Ann Mitchell says of Dolly, 'Although she is very maternal, like a lot of child-free women, I didn't want to use that side of myself too much because Dolly's grief had made her brittle. She is tight, tense, close and bound.' This sounds a little like the 'aloof wary silence' which goes with male Method acting, and achieving this tenseness had a lot to do with gestures, timing, pace and the allowing of silences.

Because Dolly had no socially given authority such as a policewoman would have, her characterisation needed the support of careful camera work and editing. The whole atmosphere of risk, as produced by an undertone of violence in the sub-plots and by physical chaos in many of the sets, gave the world in which she moved excitement and power. There was a build-up of power from the long shot of Dolly as a tiny figure when she first went into the lock-up, to her being shown as dominating the space as the episodes progressed; there was also a power in her being free to look dreadful dressed in old clothes when the female gang was working in the lock-up, which contrasted with Dolly's more elegant image in other spaces later on; a wide angle lens made her home look more spacious and at the same time gave her more presence in it; she was shot running uphill rather than on the flat or going down because it gave more of an impression of strength. As with Kate Longton, Dolly Rawlings derived some of her power from the way others behaved towards her. She was active, whereas other characters reacted to her. Her behaviour as a leader was contrasted with the behaviour of the bullying policeman who was heading the enquiry into the robbery in which Harry Rawlings died. The police officer was often seen in single shot, from a low angle. By contrast Dolly was shown as quite democratic – by means of group shots and eye-level camera – although in the second episode she behaved in a very male way and even slapped people. One of the difficulties Ann found was that the director would exhort her to 'be natural'. But how does a female gang leader naturally behave? The age difference between her and the other women meant that her relationship to them had something of the power of a mother even if she refused that role. At the same time she derived considerable strength from the presence of the other women. She was not isolated either on or off the set. In relating to the police and rival male gangs she showed a confidence which the audience knew, from scenes which only they had witnessed, to be a faked confidence. Thus the audience were invited to admire the character's 'acting' strength.

Dolly's sexuality plays a major part in the narrative. It is the answer to the enigma that the serial sets up: what is driving her? She is in love with her husband. When she finds he is not dead but has left her, we do not see her rage but we do see the results of it in Harry's slashed clothing. We also see her vulnerability at the end, where her capacity not to deny her feelings gives her another kind of strength not often seen in the male acting tradition, and not often thought of as power. Her position of power in relation to the younger women also makes for a relationship of 'difference' onto which sexuality can be mapped. Particularly in the second episode, where Bella is introduced into the group by Linda, there are undertones of sexual attraction, even though of a sado-masochistic kind, between the women. It is not obvious in the original script but seems to have been produced by the acting.

Both Ann Mitchell and Anna Carteret agree that what is most important in determining the attributes of the characters and their strength is the script. Ann Mitchell had no control over the *Widows* script, but it was written by a woman writer who is also an actress and who wrote it out of frustration with the parts normally written for actresses in television plays. So Ann Mitchell found herself in almost complete agreement with it, except that she felt there was too much slapping. She would have liked to talk to the author about this but the production team had decided that it would be better if Lynda La Plante did not go on location. The reason given was that as she had been an actress herself her presence might make the actresses nervous. The producer, the director and the writer had talked about the script a great deal and all of them really cared about it. It was the first major production for Linda Agran, first serial for Ian Toynton, first TV script for Lynda La Plante and first major TV part for most of the actresses. This meant that everyone discussed every detail, which was a help to Ann in that she was not getting conflicting interpretations from producer, director and writer, and was able to work in an atmosphere of enthusiasm.

Anna Carteret's relation to the scripts was more complicated. She was in the series for three years, and since only four scripts had been written before the first series started she was able to affect the writing. In the last year she was in quite a powerful position because she had become a household name, and so had it written into her contract that she could attend script conferences and contribute ideas. Some of her ideas which were taken up by the writers were domestic violence, drug abuse, and old women being robbed of their savings by con men. Ideas which were not taken up included the miners' strike and the police use of arms. With one exception the scripts were all written by men. The producer did commission one woman writer at Anna's suggestion but only one of her scripts was used, as it was felt she did not understand police procedure well enough and the male actors complained about their parts. Often a particular writer would pair up with a director he got on with. This was a relief to everyone. Anna said she sometimes felt caught in the middle when it was clear that the director did not like the writing, and she felt she had to support the writer against the director, or *vice versa*. There were some times when she found her character saying things she was diametrically opposed to, which caused her a real dilemma. There were two major examples of this. One was an episode about a community setting up a committee to decide how they wanted their police force to deal with certain things. Kate had a speech to her Commissioner which ran, 'I lose patience with the assorted amateurs who form committees to try to tell police officers how to run their police force'. Anna felt that communities do have a right to decide how their police force should act, and because the viewers had come to associate her with Kate they might think that what she said in the part reflected her personal view. She almost refused to say the words, but the writer, who in this case was ex-CID, pointed out that it was a conflict between amateurs and professionals and any professional police person would support the 'professional' view. He asked her whether she was interested in playing herself or the character. Her dilemma was about the relation between the two, but the most important consideration in *Juliet Bravo* was not the authenticity of the woman or the character but authenticity in portraying the police and their values. There was also clearly a desire not to upset the police, whose co-operation and advice the BBC relied on for this and other series.

The other major disagreement was about the end of the series. It is interesting that Ann Mitchell's only major quarrel with the production team of the first series of *Widows* was also about its closure. This is usually the place where the enigma of the female character is resolved and she is often returned to the family or some other traditional woman's role. In *Juliet Bravo* it was Anna Carteret's idea for the penultimate episode of the series that Kate Longton should go for promotion, be given a sexist interview and leave the police force on a question of principle. But the writer, who was again the police adviser, produced a script in which Kate lost her temper at the interview, walked out, and so lost the job. Anna argued that this was a sign of weakness and that after sixteen years in the police force Kate would have been able to cope with the sexist questions. The police adviser said that if she had done that she would have got the job, and so would not have left the force. So the actress's experience of being a woman and understanding of what her character would have felt and done in that situation was again sacrificed to the 'reality' of the police. The producer did not want Kate to leave the force anyway. He wanted to keep his options open for another series and said he thought her leaving would be betraying the audience – like slapping them in the face. But Anna was able to convince them that as an actress she wanted people to know that the series had come to an end. And so, for this professional reason, it did. As it happened, Kate's revealing of her vulnerability by losing her temper proved to be very powerful for thousands of women viewers who wrote in to say that they would have done, or had actually done, the same thing.

In the final episode of *Juliet Bravo*, Danny, the 'boy' policeman on the station, who often seemed closest to Kate, died in a fire. This was given as a final reason for Kate to leave the force and allowed her to cry on the shoulder of DI Perrin, whose proposal of marriage she had refused earlier in the series. This refusal was undermined in the last episode, where before Danny's death she was seen flirting with Perrin under the mistletoe at a Christmas party. Anna again expressed her misgivings about this change of 'no' into a possible 'yes', but the production team thought that with so many 'negative' things happening in the last two episodes there was a need of something more positive and 'nice'. As someone else had proposed that she might be raped at the end of the series and therefore be too destroyed to go on, perhaps we should be thankful for the ending we had!

At the end of *Widows* Ann Mitchell's character, Dolly, also admits to being in love and being vulnerable. But she confesses it to the other women, not to a man, and she does not cry. In the shooting script this confession was followed by what could be interpreted as a more fighting statement about the future, which was cut at the editing stage. Ann Mitchell agrees that the ending that was transmitted worked quite well, but what made her anxious was that she might have wanted to say the lines, 'I still loved him – and even worse – I still do,' rather differently if she had known they were to be the final ones. She had worked out very carefully in the long final speech where she would be vulnerable and where she would build up to strength. Suddenly to find that the strength had been cut was a blow to her feeling of control over the character.

Acting power

One thing that emerges from these two case studies is that, for women on British television, representing authority is different from representing power. Authority, at least in an early evening slot, is characterised by lack of emotions, lack of sex, and a descriptive camera. Power is characterised by the presence of emotions and sexuality, and an expressive, perhaps even excessive, *mise-en-scène*. It is a pity that this study could not include *The Gentle Touch* (Jill Gascoine was away filming during the research period) because this might have complicated the relationship between sexuality and authority a little. In the real world, authority may not be signified very differently by men and by women, although it is so generally associated with the male gender that women are more often obliged to state the grounds of their authority and have had little chance of developing their own style, except to add a little of the maternal.

Another thing to emerge from the study is that representing the police on BBC television seems to mean that the final authority is not only beyond the individual actor/ress but outside of television. Being a woman gave Anna a certain negotiating position, though it was hardly recognised as a strong or even a significant one in comparison with that of the police adviser, whose authority came from the fact that his *wife* had been in charge of a police station.

In film and television, it is doubtful whether acting on its own can carry power. The study of *Widows* suggests that, at least as far as women are concerned, it needs a sympathetic relationship between acting and camera to convey power. A close examination of the para-linguistic features of the actor/ess's performance of the script – gestures, body movement, and particularly pausing and the look, and the relationship between these two – would no doubt produce some significant material on the representation of power, but the camera and editing can either reinforce what is being built up by this performance or destroy it. The two series of *Widows* provide good evidence for this. In the first series, directed by Ian Toynton, the director and the actresses shared a sense of timing which built up the strength of the characters as opposed to emphasising the action. In the second series, which had mostly the same actresses but a different director and producer, the cuts came closely on the end of speeches and the impression of power was destroyed.

Watching Godard's *Passion* I always feel uncomfortable at the demonstration of the total powerlessness of the actresses. I hope that what this study has shown is that this need not always be the case. The involvement of the actress in suggesting stories for her character in *Juliet Bravo* and the conditions created for the actresses in *Widows* did, I think, allow the relation between acting and the institution of television to be influenced by feminism, even if ever so slightly,[6] as opposed to acting being totally feminised in these productions. These concessions were mainly due to a respect for 'authenticity' which, however doubtful, led to an acknowledgment on the part of the institutions that women's experience is largely outside the former's understanding. The corresponding concession on the part of criticism – which, strengthened by psychoanalysis, is now becoming interested in such things as the relationship of power and pleasure – would be to look beyond the obvious structures of power in the shaping of the film or television text, to make visible the contribution of the actor/esses whom it has too often regarded as powerless puppets.

Notes

1 A Day School on Acting and the Cinema in February 1986 which was sponsored jointly by the Society for Education in Film and Television and the National Film Theatre reviewed many approaches to acting, and I should like to thank the presenters of papers, particularly John Caughie, for starting me thinking how these approaches would or would not apply to women. The Day School was itself based on an issue of *Screen* (vol.26, no.5, 1985) which dealt with acting in the cinema mainly from a structuralist point of view.

2 In this novel, Trilby, a young woman, is hypnotised by Svengali first in order to cure her of depression but later to train her as a singer, La Svengali, so that he could live on the profits of her performance. She was completely unaware of everything that happened while she was hypnotised, including Svengali's often physically brutal methods of rehearsing.

3 *Juliet Bravo* was first broadcast in August 1980. The series of sixteen episodes went out on Saturday night at 7.35 pm on BBC 1. The programme had an average rating of 10 million per episode and a second series was transmitted in September 1982. Stephanie Turner, who played Inspector Jean Darblay,

was replaced by Anna Carteret as Inspector Kate Longton in the third series which began in September 1983. The fifth series was broadcast in 1985 and repeated in 1986.

Widows was first shown on ITV in spring 1983 in six episodes. A second series was made in 1985 and broadcast after a repeat showing of the first series at 9 p.m. on a Wednesday night. For a detailed discussion of *Widows* as an example of a television crime series in relation to women, see Charlotte Brunsdon's chapter 'Men's genres for women' in this volume (chapter 12).

4 This is taken from the series format for *Juliet Bravo*, written by Ian Kennedy Martin in 1979. The model was a woman in charge of a police station in the North of England who apparently surprised everyone by being quite glamorous. Her *husband* became police adviser to the series.

5 For a discussion of the role of women in film noir (a critics' term for the black and white thrillers of the 1940s) see Kaplan, E. Ann (ed.) (1978).

6 I discuss the 'progressiveness' of *Widows* in a chapter in Alvarado and Stewart (eds) (1985).

References

du Maurier, G. (1894), *Trilby*, Leipzig.

Higson, A. (1985), 'Acting Taped – an interview with Mark Nash and James Swinson', *Screen*, vol.26, no.5.

Higson, A. (1986), 'Film acting and independent cinema', *Screen*, vol.27, nos 3–4.

Hinson, H. (1984), 'Some notes on Method acting', *Sight and Sound*, vol.53, no.3.

Kaplan, E.A. (ed.) (1978), *Women in Film Noir*, London, British Film Institute.

King, B. (1986), 'Screen acting – reflections on the day', *Screen*, vol.27, nos 3–4.

McGilligan, P. (1980), *Cagney, the Actor as Auteur*, New York, de Capo Press.

Skirrow, G. (1985), '*Widows*' in M. Alvarado and J. Stewart (eds), *Made for Television: Euston Films Limited*, London, British Film Institute.

Thompson, J.O.L. (1985), 'Beyond Commutation – a Reconsideration of Screen Acting', *Screen*, vol.26, no.5.

Trilling, L. (1972), *Sincerity and Authenticity*, London, Oxford University Press.

12 Men's genres for women

Charlotte Brunsdon

> Rough stuff, this female macho (headline, Last Night's View, *Daily Express*, 17 March 1983, p.21.)

The Euston Films series *Widows* was first shown on British television in spring 1983. Following the success of this first series (six episodes), in which four women successfully carry out a robbery which was planned by their husbands, three of whom died in a similar raid, a follow-up series was made. The two series were then broadcast in the spring of 1985, at 9 p.m. on a Wednesday evening. The first series had been successful and cultish. The second series had more problems, which I discuss below, but still the June 1985 issue of *Spare Rib* enthused:

> What is it about *Widows* that had us abandoning half-made cups of coffee in the kitchen at the sound of the . . . theme music? Not just a female version of *The Sweeney* – *Widows* was brilliantly scripted, dazzlingly performed and had a great plot. (Alison Whyte, *Spare Rib*, June 1985, p.41)

Feminist enthusiasm for television crime series is uncommon, and indeed the genre is generally thought of as one which appeals to a male audience. Gillian Skirrow opens up some questions of the appeal of *Widows* in her analysis of the first series (Alvarado and Stewart [eds] 1985) in which she is particularly concerned with the way in which masculinity and femininity are shown to be constructed by the text.

Early feminist criticism was concerned to document available images *of* women. Argument that the proper object of study should instead be the system(s) of representation in which women are produced as a meaningful and different category shifted the emphasis from a comparison between images and real women to the construction of gender within a given text or set of texts.[1] *Widows*, a man's genre with women, offers a rich text for either or both of these approaches. A traditionally masculine genre which attracted a strong female following, the series also provokes questions about whether we can speak of masculinity and femininity in relation to practices of television viewing.[2] The series is, I would argue, not only a man's genre with women, but also a man's genre for women. It is thus also an exemplary site for thinking through some of the connections of gender and genre.[3]

Skirrow argues for the progressive potential of the series being located not so much in the representations of women, but in a plot which necessarily brings performance to the foreground and the commentary this new plot makes on both existing genre and gender conventions. There is certainly a level of generic self-consciousness and play within the first series, which potentially opens up questions of appropriate gender behaviour, in a way that is quite different to the self-congratulatory generic reference – and rather trying archness – of, for example, the American *Moonlighting* (in which a woman owns a private investigation agency).

In the hard world of the crime series, Skirrow looks on the bright side. I agree with the substance of her analysis, but want to take a bleaker perspective, to look for the troubles of the text. My main motivation is the disappointment I felt during the second series of *Widows*. The comparative failure of the second series is linked to some of the difficulties and uncertainties of the first. As a critical operation, I am not trying to provide another reading, or to challenge Skirrow's, but to use different emphases to point to some of the major problems which arise in the attempt to produce different, popular, pleasurable and recognisable representations of women.

The first and second series

> And speaking of mysteries, the new series of *Widows* (ITV) is a major disappointment, having *somehow* failed to capture *something*. (Danny Kelly, 'On the box', *New Musical Express*, 20 April 1985, p.21)

All sequels and follow-up series face the problems of building up new, but familiar, excitement after the denouement of the first, as well as attracting new audiences while satisfying the old. This demand for 'the same but different', which has been argued to be one of the characteristics of television programming, is more difficult to satisfy when the original is, as *Widows* was, premised on a 'novelty' story line. If *Widows I* offered some different pleasure to the sameness of the crime series, what could *Widows II* offer? I want to suggest that the second series, in its differentiation from the first, inexorably returns to some of the traditional patterns of the genre, particularly in relation to the representation of gender.

Sympathising with criminals on a weekly basis is a complicated project and British television series based on the wrong side of the law have either had a humorous edge, like *Minder*, *Budgie* and *Porridge*, or else have had a limited and completable narrative structure, like Euston's *Out*, or the BBC's *Law and Order*. There was comment in the press reviews on the fact that the widows got away with the money at the end of the first series, and I think it would have been too much to expect that they would be living happily ever after in the second.[4] It is significant, though, that the retribution of the second series comes not from the classical opponent to the criminal (the law), but from the mastermind of the original plan (Dolly's husband Harry). Arguably, this retribution in fact comes at the end of the first series, which I discuss below. The point here is that having 'got' the money in the first series, the women have to spend their time and energy in keeping it in the second. I want now to concentrate on some of the particular strains that the original dramatic premises for the first series put on the continuation in the second.

As a television genre, the crime series is seen to have a privileged relation to reality (Alvarado and Stewart, *op.cit.*, Hurd, 1981). A range of newspaper critics made reference to the realism of *Widows* – thus Bronwen Balmforth in the *Sun* wrote, 'The six part series is so tough and realistic it could give real criminals a few ideas. . . . The three actresses . . . are all relatively new faces to television and this adds to the realism' ('Big job for the girls', 16 March 1983). Peter Ackroyd in *The Times* commented, 'The series . . . is really the feminist answer to *The Professionals* and as a result is couched in a more realistic and less sentimental manner' ('Ladies in liberation', 17 March 1983). Ackroyd also compared *Widows* with *Minder*, 'the same mordant realism in its depiction of "cops and robbers"'. The titles and vocabulary of these reviews point to an opposition between that form of femininity known as being a lady, and realism, which is made explicit in this comment from the *Daily Star* (6 April 1983), 'There is nothing very ladylike about the four stars of Widows (ITV 9p.m.). They are rough, tough and very believable'.

The realism of a television programme is constructed through a range of devices and conventions which derive their significance primarily from generic and textual histories, rather than from any direct relation to the real. *Widows* has an oblique relation to these conventions, which means that the series teeters on the edge of implausibility in its most ambitious moments. 'I've heard chaps quibbling about its authenticity. They can't believe that women would turn to crime like that. Indeed they would' (Nina Myskow, 'Crime queens steal the show,' *Sunday People*, 20 March 1983). The central protagonists are precisely not the usual male protagonists – but related to them, of the same sub-culture in terms of class and milieu, but with different attributes (femininity) – a production company's dream for adding zest to an audience-pulling genre which needs new angles. However, the plot availability in a realist genre of these new, different protagonists is premised on their sudden, tragic widowing, and plot interest, in the first series, is partly founded on their unfamiliarity with their generic role as male criminals. The pre-credit sequence of the first series shows the fatal raid in which the men die, and the episode opens with an introduction to the women at three different funerals.

There are thus two disruptions which set the narrative of the first series going, neither of which can be re-used in the second series. Firstly, the widowing. This, and divorce, have been relatively common narrative devices to produce central female protagonists to whom things can happen (they can meet men) but who are thus also affirmed as being properly feminine (men have wanted them).[5] This first disruption constructs and makes available the heroines of the series. The second disruption is not so much a narrative event, although it exists as that, but a breach in the normal order of the crime series – the widows' world – brought about by their audacious decision to carry out the next robbery. It is this decision which moves the widows into the narrative space of heroes. It is also this decision which delightfully makes them, in the first series, undetectable, because they are, within the terms of the genre, inconceivable. Detective

Inspector Resnick approaches closest to the truth, not because he has any intimation of it, but because of his obsession with Harry Rawlins.

The neatness of the storyline is that it does not try to make its audience believe in four fully fledged mistress criminals. After the double disruption sets the story going, the plot is largely pre-ordained, literally planned and written by Harry Rawlins. As Skirrow has observed, the pleasure of the series lies partly in the way in which the familiar visual imagery of the genre is 'made strange' as we watch women mastering the skills and physical postures of the crime series. This pleasure is in the first series articulated through and with the iconographic familiarity of the triangle of police, criminals and rival gang. The elegance of the deployment of these familiar narrative elements is that all are in pursuit of something that they cannot find, for it is the women (in that narrative other space of the crime series, the domestic) who are the perpetrators of crime.

These structural relations, inevitably, are changed in the second series. The second series has none of the goal-oriented simplicity of the first. The double structure of suspense in the first – 'Will the women pull off the raid, as men?' and 'Will they get away with it, from men?' is reduced to only the second question. The first series had Harry's plan, a known structure, and the women's performance, the unknown realisation. The second series has 'living with the consequences'. These consequences necessarily involve more conventional organisation of the relation of gender and genre.

Heroes and heroines

It is safe to say that beside the Widows, *Minder* looks effeminate.
(Daniel Farson, guest critic, *Mail on Sunday*, 17 April 1983)

Linda is not the sort of girl you would like to meet in a dark alley.
(Peter Ackroyd, 'Ladies in liberation', *The Times*, 17 March 1983)

Much of the interest of the first series came from the way in which the widows were called upon to occupy two roles, those of heroes and those of heroines. The narrative placing of these women is as heroes, those who do, rather than those who are done to. This different placing of the women, in a broadly or associatively realist genre, produces certain problems. Centrally these are to do with the conflicts between the demands of generic realism, and the plausibility of the different placing of the women. The problem can be taken two ways. Either the women are not perceived as plausible in their new roles as criminals, or, using the femininity and competence contradiction (mutually exclusive terms outside certain limited spheres), if successful as criminals, the women have their femininity thrown into doubt. The question is one of plausibility in both cases, once in relation to genre and once in relation to gender.

This coalescence of gender and genre into issues of plausibility can be seen in a range of critical response to both series. In the first series, a realism of effect was usually granted, despite a recognition of the 'difficulty' of the original widowing device. Thus Herbert Kretzmer in the *Daily Mail*, 'The whole premise of *Widows* strikes one as most unlikely, but it's carried off with confidence and looks good for a run' ('An equal right to do wrong', 17 March 1983). Stanley Reynolds wrote in the *Guardian* (21 April 1983), 'If anything, it got better as it went along. I suppose one dropped the original barrier of disbelief at the preposterous plot'. This device is crucial, as I have already argued, in establishing the women in the genre milieu – but also in establishing them *as women*. However, as the comments at the head of this section indicate, women as heroes are often perceived as threatening or unpleasant – or not women. There are a range of additional narrative devices in the first series which function to guarantee the femininity of all the women, although in different ways. As Gillian Skirrow has observed, particularly the beauty competition and the strip show, to the extent that they involve the performance of femininity, can in this context be read as investigations of the signifiers of gender. There are ironies too in Linda's choice of lover, in that he is also shown to be having an affair with Arnie Fisher, from the rival Fisher Brothers gang. However, if read like this, it is important that femininity is also guaranteed for each of the four women, in ways which are generically consistent with the iconography of the crime show and, indeed, with Euston's particular, rather seedy world. Thus we have Shirley appearing in a beauty contest, and Bella in a strip show (see below). Linda is shown to be heterosexually active through her affair with Carlos. Dolly's case is slightly different, and I shall discuss it in more detail in the context of the ending of the first series. However, the paradox of the programme's necessary 'double guarantee' is rather neatly pointed by this letter to the *TV Times* during the transmission of the first series:

> I didn't believe that bank robbery on ITV's *Widows*. I'm not being sexist, but I think a group of women like those in the programme, would have chosen a far more straightforward crime with less bravado and one which involved no other people. The action packed heist on the security van may have been suitably dramatic but it was hardly credible.
>
> P. Wilson
> Luton, Bedfordshire
> (*TV Times* 28 May 1983)

This writer accepts the femininity of the widows, and thus finds the 'physical and complicated' crime implausible. The plausibility cover provided by the narrative – Harry planned the crime – is ignored, and there is an invocation of femininity as necessarily leading to a less spectacular, and more humane ('no other people') choice of crime. The double placing of the women (as heroes and heroines), with the plausibility problems this entails in the first series, are shifted by the second series when the narrative come-uppances of the first series 'get' the women, and push them back to much more traditional feminine narrative roles. Possessors of the profits from the raid, the women become the object of pursuit. It is this (necessarily) changed narrative structure, when the women are returned to the sort of roles which are more familiar in crime series, which partly accounts for the disappointment of the second series. One of the people interviewed by David Morley in a series of interviews about family viewing commented on the second series as follows:

> It's [*Widows*] gotten silly – they should have left it. When it was first on it was really good. You didn't know whether he was dead – it wasn't until the end that you found out he was alive. Now it's gotten silly because, I don't know, when you bring women into it, I mean I'm not a feminist and I should really be, but *when you start bringing women into it, it gets silly because they don't write good enough parts for them.*
> (Morley, 1986;[6] my italics)

This speaker, a woman, becomes almost incoherent in her

attempt to say *something* about the problem of the second series. She is engaging directly with the mismatch, the sense of disappointment produced by the tension of the innovation in a generic form. I don't wish to over-read this comment, to sweep the woman in Morley's survey into my own world view, but I think she is talking about the same disappointment that I felt in *Widows II*, the inadequacy of dramatic role in relation to the perceived and remembered strength and performance of the actresses. What is important is the change in direction in her argument. She starts off almost as if she's going to say it gets silly because it's got women in it, but this causes a crisis in the sentence which leads her to make external, apologetic, framing reference to her own politics, and the problem becomes one of scripting, some perceived mismatch between the women and the parts.

There are other factors leading to the difference between the first and second series, one of which, a cast change for the character Bella O'Reilly, I discuss in more detail in the next section. There were also a number of changes in the production team, the most significant probably being the direction, from Ian Toynton (first series) to Paul Annett. The script for both series was written by Lynda La Plante.

Bella

> She claimed sexual and racial prejudice with the production crew of the series, but she was more emotional and upset about that than depressed. (Mr Anthony Earlham, stepfather of Eva Mottley, quoted by *The Times* in its report on the post-mortem of Ms Mottley, 21 March 1985)

Although all publicity for *Widows* showed four women, three white, one black, in the first episode we are introduced only to the three white women, widows of the men who died in the underpass raid. Of course, we later learn that Dolly Rawlins, one of these women, was not in fact widowed in the raid, the third widow was in fact Jimmy Nunn's wife, Trudie. The fourth widow of the credits, Bella O'Reilly, is recruited by her friend, Linda Perelli, in the second episode. The original three have discovered that they will need a fourth, and Bella's suitability occurs to Linda when her co-worker, Charlie, comments of Bella that 'she looks too much like a fella', to be attractive. It has earlier been established that Bella too is now a widow ('My old man did the final load three months ago') and is working as a prostitute and in strip clubs. It is for this work that Dolly abuses her ('tart', 'slag') when first introduced, but there is no racial abuse for Bella in the first series as there is for the 'rhymed' Afro-Caribbean male character Harvey in the second. He cannot comment that a uniform is a bit small without being called 'ape man', and is shown to be recruited to Harry's gang only as a last resort. In the first series, it is only when Bella is taken for a man that she is referred to as black, by a security guard and the police, trying to identify 'the black bloke' after the Widows' raid.

There is no verbal discourse on race in the first series, although racial difference is marked in a range of ways (see below). The second series introduces two new Afro-Caribbean characters, Harvey Rintle, and a girl friend of Bella's, Carla, as well as a stereotypical Jewish antique-dealer/'fence' (pawnbroker figure), Sonny Chizzel. It also returns to a more conventional 'realist racism'. Harvey becomes the site for the display of the normal and casual racism (realism) of the Rawlins world, threatened because he has a relationship with a white woman and subjected to *Black and White Minstrel Show* jokes when he joins the gang. Carla is mistaken for Bella, and brutally beaten up in the second episode of the second series. When Bella tells the others of this, she loses her temper with Linda for failing to grasp the racist element in the attack: 'Of course he did [think it was Bella] – I'm black, she's black, we all look alike in the dark, stupid bitch!' This comment works very curiously with the most noticeable feature of the Bella character, which is that she is played by two different actresses: Eva Mottley and then in the second series, Debby Bishop. This substitution, itself uncommon in British television drama, stands in relation to the national, unsympathetic and uninformative coverage of Eva Mottley's death in February 1985, shortly before *Widows I* was repeated, and several months after she left the set at the beginning of shooting *Widows II*.[7]

The crime series offers particular problems for the representation of race if the production company wishes to move away from the stereotypical presentation of black villains. The problem lies in the way in which the effect of realism is created in a genre.

If we take what we might call the internal realism of the genre – its inter-textuality, its construction of the 'reality effect' through particular codes and conventions – the way in which realism as an effect has more to do with the reality constructed in other crime series than with reality as such (out there), we can only conclude that sympathetic characters are white. There are exceptions, like *The Chinese Detective*, but the very title of the series indicates the exceptional juxtaposition of 'Chinese' and 'Detective'. *Wolcott*, with an Afro-Caribbean policeman in the title role, was not extended after the pilot.[8] Sympathetic black characters aren't in this genre at all, except in the USA – they are (or were) over in *Ebony*, *Eastern Eye* and *Black on Black*, or, since *Widows* was first transmitted, in Albert Square. The realist codes and conventions of the genre are homologous with those of television as an institution, in which 'ethnicity' applies only to the non-white.

I am thus suggesting that there is little generic support for Bella as a sympathetic, realist character, which increased the demands made, in the first series, on Eva Mottley as an actress. The strength of her acting was arguably undercut, during the first transmission of *Widows* I, by the repeated blurring of character and actress in press features.[9] By implication it wasn't acting, it was just natural, as Eva Mottley had served a prison sentence for a drug offence and had started acting while in prison. Bella, in the first series, is characterised as particularly tough. Shirley and Linda are both, in different ways, *girls*. They are quite frequently shown as weak, hysterical, frightened and vulnerable. Dolly, a *woman*, does not reveal the same weaknesses but does have vulnerability in relation to Harry. Dolly is shown to be stern and brusque (one reviewer commented on wishing to cross the road to get out of her way), and even slaps the hysterical Linda at a meeting during the second episode. Later in the same episode, in a rhyming gesture, Bella too slaps Linda (who is at that point drunk). It is this gesture which is shown to cause Dolly to reconsider her original rejection of Bella. Bella, in the first series, is never shown to be out of control. The repeated guarantees of 'femininity through vulnerability' which are used in relation to the other widows are not employed in relation to Bella. It is perhaps this uncompromising representation of a strong, cool, tough woman which led to many critics referring to her as 'threatening' and 'androgynous'. It is this latter appellation that is the more revealing, hinting at the proposition that a woman without vulnerability might not be one.

Bella's difference – apart from her later narrative arrival – is most noticeably marked in the opening pre-credit sequence, which partly reflects her different route in. Each week, viewers are brought up-to-date by a male voice over a series of images, some from previous episodes. After Bella's appearance, for episodes three and four the audience is introduced to the widows with an image which offers the simulcrum of a page from a family photographic album. In individual snaps, Linda, Shirley and Dolly appear, not 'now' (alone, or with each other), but with their husbands, happy and relaxed in their socially legitimate past. Bella, on the other hand, appears alone. There are, to an extent, narrative reasons for this – Bella's husband, unlike the others, has no plot significance. To have given Bella the same socially legitimate past, coupleness, could well have been confusing to viewers. But the effect is to mark her difference, to offer her without the visual guarantee of a heterosexual past.

Although all the women were married to criminals, and Linda's job in the amusement arcade is fairly rough, Bella is clearly perceived as less respectable than the others. There seems to be a division between good clean family crime and drugs and sex, with Bella on the dirty side, and this despite the fact that Audrey's first explanation of her daughter Shirley's sudden wealth is that she is 'doing tricks'. Linda asks Bella about her drug use on greeting her, and while Shirley enters for the rather affectionately ridiculed Miss Paddington competition, Bella wears a dog collar, black leather and brandishes a whip to earn money from that favourite post-colonial strip show theme, black woman as dominatrice.

Debby Bishop, who had worked with Eva Mottley in *Scrubbers* and apparently had Mottley's full support, played a very different Bella. Mottley's Bella had real hauteur and style – she was completely believable at the end of the first series when asked about their celebratory meal: 'Book a table? Did I book a table – we are taking over the joint!' In the first episode of the second series, Bella is shown to have become engaged to an evidently rich Brazilian aristocrat who knows nothing of her past. He treats her like a princess, and looks very much like a Mills and Boon hero (see Figure 12.3). Bella – and it is slightly difficult to imagine Mottley in this role, given the strength of the Bella she

Figure 12.1   The title line-up from the *first* series of *Widows* (1983) with Eva Mottley as Bella.

Figure 12.2   The title line-up from the *second* series of *Widows* (1985) with Debbie Bishop as Bella.

played – is quite correctly very anxious that her past might catch up with her and ruin her happy ending. This it does, and for the rest of the series Bella is portrayed as one who has loved and lost. In episode four she confides to Dolly, 'I reckon I lost my chance'.[10] Bishop's Bella, although still tough and at points rather unpleasantly bossy, is vulnerable in ways which make her seem much more like Linda and Shirley. This is partly a quality of performance, but is also a result of the very different narrative structure and positions of power in the second series, in which the women really are more vulnerable.

The end of the first series

I like *Widows*, now that's a thing we both sit and watch together.
(Morley transcripts)

Crime series are traditionally programming for men. *Widows* was innovatory not only in its cast and storyline, but in its appeal to women as audience. An identifiable product of an industry which has noticed feminism not so much for its politics but for its constitutive power in relation to a new, attractive-to-advertisers audience, *Widows* makes a bid for *Guardian* readers, as well as offering more pleasure for women in a genre which they probably have very little choice about watching in the first place.[11] As recent television research has alerted us to the power struggles in the home over programme choice, *Widows* can be seen as a text which tries to negotiate this dynamic context of viewing. It tries to maximise its audience by offering gendered pleasure for both men and women. Its traditionally generic elements offer conventionally 'masculine' pleasures, while some of its innovatory elements – with some difficulty – offer more feminine pleasures. The tension of this double gender appeal, together with many of the other elements already discussed, can be seen clearly in the ending of the first series.

The last scene of the first series takes place in a suite in the Hilton Hotel in Rio de Janeiro. All the women have managed to escape from England. The scene opens on classic, indeed clichéd, images of criminal success: champagne and piles of money. This is the moment of the pay-off, not only for the women, but also for the programme-makers and audience, in that

Figure 12.3

the new element – women as criminals – permits the (re)use of
these images which would otherwise signify 'caper movie', or
comedy. Also, because conventional femininity is, historically,
partly constructed and signified through conspicuous consumption, women as successful criminals are a much more glorious
sight than men. The banter among the women is all about their
clothes, and their spectacular outfits and make-up are a
counterpoint to the unmade-up, black clothed 'heroes' of earlier
episodes. The moment of celebration, indeed the mode of
celebration, is a return to femininity.

This return – and the irony of their route – is articulated by
Shirley in a moment which condenses the strengths of the series,
and would have provided a triumphal end. The three younger
women are toasting their success, and Shirley, champagne glass
in one hand, cigarette between her lips, parodies her own entry,
desperate for money, in the Miss Paddington competition in the
first episode, 'And now, for the next contestant, Miss Shirley
Miller'. Shirley continues, now acting herself in a very little girl

voice, 'I like reading, writing and robbing banks.' This moment, which offers parody of both femininity and genre, and concludes a narrative in which the women functioned as both heroes and heroines, is followed by Dolly's entrance and a scene in which success is turned to bitterness. Dolly reveals that she knows that Harry is still alive, and that despite his humiliation of her, she still wants him. The series finishes with the rising of Dolly's loss theme, the lament from *Orfeo and Eurydice*, as the camera pans slowly across the young women's faces, to finish on Dolly – also restored to femininity, but with the knowledge of loss and grief that this position properly entails. This final, conclusive feminisation of Dolly, the 'strong man' of the series, also shifts the final register of the series from heist to romance. In order to conclude this rather unfamiliar story, the unfamiliar element – women as heroes – must be transformed. The move is from man's genre to women's genre, the women's genre at its most masochistic.[12]

It is this restoration, this clarifying of the gender of the genre, which marks the starting point of the second series. In the second series, the women are demoted to accessories, and hindrances, to Harry's quest. The grammar of one of the voice-overs which

Figure 12.4   Dolly, the 'strong man' of the series.

introduce and up-date each episode reveals this clearly, 'the Widows know they cannot be safe until they get Harry Rawlins off their trail' (voice-over opening titles, episode four, second series). Although the widows are the subject of the sentence, that is their only active moment. The active agent is Harry Rawlins, the widows' desires are all to do with stopping being the object of his agency. The narrative structure of the second series allows the widows to have no goal of their own. Their relation to the money becomes completely displaced, as Ann Mitchell observed in an interview, 'in the second series, the money becomes quite incidental. We are forever dropping it, flicking through it – no-one wants to hold onto it' (Ann Mitchell – Dolly – interviewed by Nicola Roberts, 'Not so merry widows', *New Musical Express*, 11 May 1985). The only plausible goals that can appear are completely conventional – Shirley wants to be a model, and Dolly might, just might, get something going with Vic. However, these women would clearly make unlikely housewives and by the end of the second series two of them are dead, one is in prison, and Bella has left the country.

Credits

Widows I

Executive producer: Verity Lambert. *Executive in charge of production:* Johnny Goodman. *Producer:* Linda Agran. *Director:* Ian Toynton. *Script:* Lynda La Plante. *Production manager:* Stephen Pushkin. *Location manager:* Ray Freeborn. *Director of photography:* Ray Parslow. *Camera operator:* Mike Proudfoot. *Supervising editor:* Roger Wilson. *Assistant editor:* Colin Chapman. *Art director:* Christopher Burke. *Sound mixer:* Derek Rye. *Boom operator:* David Pearson. *1st assistant director:* Ted Morley. *Casting director:* Marilyn Johnson.
Cast: Ann Mitchell (*Dolly Rawlins*), Maureen O'Farrell (*Linda Perelli*), Fiona Hendley (*Shirley Miller*), Eva Mottley (*Bella O'Reilly*), David Calder (*Det. Insp. George Resnick*), Paul Jesson (*Det. Sgt. Alec Fuller*), Maurice O'Connell (*Harry Rawlins*), Stanley Meadows (*Eddie Rawlins*).

Widows II

Executive producers: Linda Agran, Johnny Goodman. *Producer:* Irving Teitelbaum. *Associate producer:* Ron Purdie. *Director:* Paul Annett. *Script:* Lynda La Plante. *Production manager:* Ron Holtzer. *Location managers:* Micky Moynihan, Nick Page. *Director of photography:* Dusty Miller. *Camera operator:* John Boulter. *Editor:* Roger Wilson. *Art director:* Christopher Burke. *Music:* Stanley Myers. *Sound mixer:* Bill Burgess. *Boom operator:* Simon Hayter. *1st assistant director:* Simon

Channing Williams. *Casting director:* Ann Fielden.
Cast: Ann Mitchell (*Dolly Rawlins*), Maureen O'Farrell (*Linda Perelli*), Fiona Hendley (*Shirley Miller*), Debby Bishop (*Bella O'Reilly*), Maurice O'Connell (*Harry Rawlins*), Stephen Yardley (*Vic Morgan*), David Calder (*Det. Insp. George Resnick*).

Acknowledgments

Elements of this essay were first presented in Copenhagen (Women and the Electronic Mass Media Conference, Centre for Massekommunication, Kobenhavns Universitet, April 1986) and East Lansing (Fifth International Conference on Television Drama, Michigan State University, May 1986). I should like to thank the organisers of both conferences for inviting me to participate.

Notes

1 For an early example of the first approach see King and Stott (eds) (1977); Kuhn (1985) provides examples of the latter.
2 Feminist film criticism has been much concerned with the question of the gendering of the gaze. See 'Is the gaze male?' in Kaplan (1983), and the essays by Doane and Williams in Doane, Mellencamp and Williams (eds) (1984). Kuhn (1984) provides a very useful summary of theorisation of the female spectator. See also Flynn and Schweikart (eds) (1986) in relation to feminist literary criticism.
3 For a preliminary discussion of gender and genre see Batsleer *et al.* (1985). With specific reference to television, see Curti (1986) and Deming (1986).
4 'In the old days evildoers were always seen to be punished. But times have changed and it would not surprise me if the widows get away with it in next week's final instalment' (Herbert Kretzmer, *Daily Mail*, 14 April 1983).
   'What's more, they get away with it. Dolly and her gang lifted £700,000. They stashed £600,000 behind the lockers in the convent school and last night we saw them get away clean scotfree to Rio with a cool thou.
   I always thought there was some law about crime not being seen to pay on the telly' (Stanley Reynolds, '*Widows*' in the *Guardian*, 21 April 1983).
5 I argue this point at more length in a discussion of 1970s films for women (Brunsdon, 1982).
6 This, and the later quotation from this research, are taken from the transcripts of Morley's interviews, which were conducted while *Widows* was being broadcast.
7 The report in *The Voice* (23 February 1983) was an exception to the general 'Eva's web of tragedy' tone.
8 The second series of *The Bill*, transmitted in the autumn of 1985, featured the rather low-key introduction of an Afro-Caribbean police constable. He partly functions to reveal the racism of some of his colleagues.

9 Eva Mottley received considerable publicity in March 1983, just after the first series started, which included a profile in the *Sunday Telegraph Magazine* (26 April 1983). 'Black beauty' and 'Black widow' seem to have been irresistible headlines.

10 British racism reserves a special place for rich South Americans and the sort of women who marry them. The rather embarrassed press coverage in 1986 of the fact that Sarah Ferguson's mother was married to not just a South American but an Argentinian provides one example, as does the plot and particularly the sex scenes in Jill Tweedie's novel, *Bliss* (1984). I would want to argue that *only* Bella, of the four women, could 'plausibly' fall in love with a South American.

11 See Morley, *op.cit.*, and Ann Gray's chapter 'Behind closed doors: video recorders in the home' in this volume (chapter 3).

12 There has been extensive discussion of 'endings' in relation to film melodrama. See Gledhill, (ed.) (1987).

References

Alvarado, M. and Stewart, J. (eds) (1985), *Made for Television: Euston Films Limited*, London, British Film Institute.

Batsleer, J. *et al.* (1985), *Rewriting English*, London, Methuen.

Bennett, T. *et al.* (eds) (1981), *Popular Television and Film*, London, British Film Institute and Open University Press.

Brunsdon, C. (1982), 'A subject for the seventies', *Screen*, vol.23, nos.3/4, pp.20–9.

Curti, L. (1986), 'Genre and gender', paper presented to the Television Studies Conference, London.

Deming, C. (1986), 'Gender and genre: the criticism of television melodrama', paper presented to the International Communications Association Conference, Chicago.

Doane, M., Mellencamp, P. and Williams, L. (1984), *Revision*, Los Angeles, American Film Institute.

Flynn, E. and Schweikart, P. (eds) (1986), *Gender and Reading*, Baltimore, Johns Hopkins University Press.

Gledhill, C. (1987), *Women and Melodrama*, London, British Film Institute.

Gray, A. (1986), 'Women's work and boy's toys', paper, presented to the International Television Studies Conference, London.

Hurd, G. (1981) 'The television presentation of the police', in Bennett, T., *et al.* (eds) (1981), *Popular Television and Film*, London, British Film Institute and Open University Press.

Kaplan, A. (1983), *Women and Film*, New York, Methuen.

King, J. and Stott, M. (eds) (1977), *Is This Your Life?* London, Virago.

Kuhn, A. (1984), 'Women's genres', *Screen*, vol.25, no.1, pp.18–28.

Kuhn, A. (1985), *The Power of the Image*, London, Routledge and Kegan Paul.

Morley, D. (1986), *Family Television*, London, Comedia.

Skirrow, G. (1985), '*Widows*' in Alvarado, M. and Stewart, J. (eds) (1985), *Made*

for Television: Euston Films Limited, London, British Film Institute/Methuen, Euston.
Tweedie, J. (1984), *Bliss*, London, Penguin.

13 The case of Cagney and Lacey

Julie D'Acci

The meanings of 'woman' on television

This chapter will examine several aspects of the relationship between women, 'woman' and television. I will be employing the distinction between women and 'woman' formulated by Teresa de Lauretis in her book *Alice Doesn't: Feminism, Semiotics, and Cinema*. She writes:

> By 'woman', I mean a fictional construct, a distillate from diverse but congruent discourses dominant in Western cultures. . . . By women, on the other hand, I mean the real historical beings who cannot as yet be defined outside of those discursive formations, but whose material existence is nonetheless certain. (de Lauretis, 1984, p.5)

The relationship between 'woman', produced by discursive practices such as television, and women as historical/empirical subjects, is neither direct nor natural, but always primarily cultural. On a general level my purpose is to investigate some of the meanings of 'woman' that are produced and negotiated in the interaction of television representations, viewer receptions, and the historical/industry context. In speaking of meanings in this way, I am drawing from Annette Kuhn in her book the *Power of the Image* when she says that 'meanings do not reside in images. They are circulated between representation, spectator, and social formation' (Kuhn, 1985, p.6). The interaction of various meanings is what I will be referring to as the 'negotiation' of meanings.[1]

On a more specific level, I will examine the series *Cagney and Lacey* as a particular instance of the cultural production and negotiation of the meanings of 'woman'. A study of the series's development demonstrates the ways in which several discourses and discursive practices, each with their own investments in specific ideals of 'woman' and 'femininity', interact to produce the representations of the characters Cagney and Lacey. They construct a variety of interpretations of the characters, a general discourse of multiple definitions of 'woman' and 'femininity', as well as a woman's audience for the series. I will be producing a type of history of the series by investigating several discourses and discursive practices: the television industry; publicity; the contributions of the individual participants in the production process; the mainstream press; the reception of the television audience; the liberal women's movement and several interest and pressure groups. I will not be focusing directly on the narrative parameters of the programmes, but on what have traditionally been called extra-narrative or extra-textual factors.

Cagney and Lacey is a mainstream American television series with wide international distribution. It is about two white, middle-class and upper-middle-class women detectives in the New York City Police Department. It was the creation of writers Barbara Avedon and Barbara Corday and is produced by a Los Angeles-based company, Orion Television, with Barney Rosenzweig as executive producer.[2] It stars Sharon Gless as Christine Cagney and Tyne Daly as Mary Beth Lacey, and was first transmitted in March 1982. I became interested in studying *Cagney and Lacey* because the series was specifically targeted at a working women's audience; it was constructed as a 'woman's programme' and was received by a large number of vocal woman viewers. It also interested me because it was the first dramatic narrative programme in television history to star two women. The characters were represented as active subjects of the narrative who solved their own cases both mentally and physically. They were rarely represented as 'women-in-distress' and virtually never rescued by their male colleagues. As well as functioning in both the public and private spheres, they were portrayed as active subjects, rarely as objects, of sexual desire. Chris Cagney, a single woman, was shown as having an active sex life which she would often initiate. Similarly, Mary Beth Lacey, the married woman, was shown as a sexual initiator with her husband, Harvey. Mary Beth was, furthermore, the breadwinner of the family, and Harvey an out-of-work construction worker who cooked and took care of the house and the two kids. The actresses and characters were in their mid-thirties and there was a distinct minimisation of glamour at the levels of clothing, hairstyles and make-up. Originally (and I will discuss this change in more detail) the characters were from middle to lower-middle-class backgrounds and were both working women. They were represented as close friends who took a lot of pleasure in one another's company and spent a lot of screen time talking.

Cagney and Lacey was conceived in 1974 solidly within the discourses of the US liberal women's movement. When speaking of the 'US liberal women's movement', I am referring to a number of things: the determination by this part of the women's movement to achieve material gains for women in both the public and private spheres, the focus on conditions of women's everyday lives and the attention to issues such as the representation of women in the media, and women's friendship. I am also referring to two assumptions of the liberal women's movement regarding social change and representation, which I find problematic and which figure in the history of *Cagney and Lacey*. The first is the basic assumption that representational practices (film, television, print material) can promote social change for women by producing representations which reflect more accurately and more positively the 'real-life' changes and conditions of 'real-life' women'. This 'reflection theory' of representational practices assumes both a non-problematic acceptance of the concept 'real life' and a non-problematic correspondence between 'woman' as represented in cultural texts and empirical women. It assumes these things, I would argue, because it does not examine the ideological character of the concept 'real life' or the ideological, mediational and industrial aspects of representational practices.

The second assumption which I find problematic follows from the first. It is the tendency to carry over the basic tenets of liberalism regarding social change into the area of representational practice. Appeals for equal rights, equal pay and individualism become appeals for equality of representation. The result is a call for pluralism of representation, the practice of role reversals and the focus on individual accomplishment. Women on television – black, white, Hispanic, Asian etc. – then come to be shown as having 'made it' by being portrayed as doctors, lawyers, businesswomen and so forth. The lack of examination of the relationship of these representations to the support and production of social power structures is highly problematic when speaking about social change, or 'difference' regarding the representation of 'woman'. All of these issues from the liberal US women's movement, those which I read as enabling change and difference and those which I read as limiting them, play, as I hope to show, active roles in the history of *Cagney and Lacey*.

The female 'buddy movie'

According to Avedon, Corday and Rosenzweig, in interviews I conducted with them and in published articles, *Cagney and Lacey* was specifically conceived as a response to an early and influential book from the women's movement – Molly Haskell's *From Reverence to Rape: The Treatment of Women in the Movies* (1974). Avedon and Corday were engaged in the literature and politics of the early US women's movement and both were in women's groups. Rosenzweig was 'setting out to have his consciousness raised'. They read Haskell's book and were intrigued by the fact that there had never been a Hollywood movie about two women 'buddies' comparable to *M*A*S*H* or *Butch Cassidy and the Sundance Kid*. According to Rosenzweig:

> The Hollywood establishment had totally refused women those friendships, the closest thing being perhaps Joan Crawford and Eve Arden in *Mildred Pierce*, the tough lady boss and her wise-cracking sidekick. So I went to my friend Ed Feldman, who was then head of Filmways [now Orion], and I said, 'I want to do a picture where we turn around a conventional genre piece like *Freebie and the Bean* with its traditional male situations and make it into the first real hit feminist film. (Rosen, 1981, p.49)

Corday says:

> Barney came to this conclusion not so much, at that time, as a feminist [because he was very new to all of those ideas then], but came to the conclusion as a commercial producer, that it was *extraordinary* that there had never been a female buddy movie; and at that moment in history it would probably be a great idea. (personal interview, 1984)

One of the main motivations behind *Cagney and Lacey* from its inception was the creators' notion that two women could, in fact, be represented as friends who worked and talked together, rather than as conventionally portrayed competitors – in Rosenzweig's words, 'as buddies not bitches'. Both Avedon and Corday acknowledge the ways in which the relationship between Cagney and Lacey was modelled (if somewhat unconsciously) on their own eight-year relationship as writing partners and friends. Ed Feldman, an executive at Filmways, was, in fact, interested in the idea Rosenzweig had pitched to him, and gave him the 'seed' money to hire Avedon and Corday as writers (Rosen, 1981, p.49; Corday, 1985, p.12). Barbara Avedon recalls that although Filmways was 'excited' about the idea, they had difficulty understanding the view of women involved. 'They [Filmways] told us things like, when [Cagney or Lacey] rips her shirt back and shows her badge to the guys, they can all stare [at her breasts]'. 'That', continues Avedon, 'was the level of consciousness, even though they [Filmways] were doing a women-buddy movie'.

The original script, entitled *Freeze*, was a spoof in which Cagney and Lacey uncover the existence of the Godmother, the female intelligence behind a brothel where men are the prostitutes and women the patrons (Rosen, 1981, p.49). The major narrative device was the early women's movement notion of role reversals. The limitations of difference with regard to the representations of 'woman' on *Cagney and Lacey* can therefore be seen from the outset. It is important to address this issue here because in the history a great deal is made of the magnitude of the difference regarding *Cagney and Lacey*'s representation of 'woman'. The practice of role reversals essentially accepts uncritically the basic societal structures and power arrangements.

After getting the script financed by Filmways, Rosenzweig needed a major motion picture studio to pick it up and do the actual production. He took the original property to every studio in Hollywood and got such responses from the industry as 'these women aren't soft enough, aren't feminine enough' (Rosen, 1981, p.49). At MGM, Sherry Lansing (who was later to become the first woman head of a major motion picture studio, Paramount) persuaded her boss, Dan Melnik, to make the movie. MGM said it would but only if well-known 'sex symbols' Raquel Welch and Ann Margret starred. (Welch and Margret had not yet demonstrated their versatility as actresses at this point in Hollywood history.) The other stipulation was a $1.6 million budget which, in a kind of catch-22 fashion, prohibited the hiring of such high-priced actresses (Rosen, 1981, p.49). The property, therefore, lay dormant for the next six years.

In 1980 Rosenzweig decided to have another go. According to Avedon and Corday, it was only because of his dogged perseverance that *Cagney and Lacey* ever got into production. Corday and Avedon rethought the script to update it and make it less of a spoof and more of a 'realistic' crime drama (Rosen, 1981, p.50). Because Corday, by this time, had taken a job as vice-president of Comedy Development at ABC, Barbara Avedon wrote the script herself. This time, Rosenzweig took it to the television networks as a pilot for a weekly series. Although CBS would not pick it up as a series, it decided it would take it as a less costly, less risky, made-for-TV movie and suggested that Rosenzweig cast 'two sexy young actresses'. According to Rosenzweig, he told CBS:

> You don't understand, these policewomen must be mature women. One has a family and kids, the other is a committed career officer. What separates this project from *Charlie's Angels* is that Cagney and Lacey are women; they're not girls and they're *certainly* not objects. (Rosen, 1981, p.50)

During this impasse, CBS, which had an outstanding made-for-TV-movie commitment to Loretta Swit of *M*A*S*H*, asked Rosenzweig to cast her as Cagney. Avedon and Corday, who had recently worked with Sharon Gless on the TV series *Turnabout*, wanted her for the part. Because Gless could not be released from her contract to Universal, Rosenzweig cast Swit as Cagney even though her contract to *M*A*S*H* would preclude her availability should the opportunity to turn *Cagney and Lacey* into a series arise. Tyne Daly was cast as Lacey.

The movie was shot in Toronto with a budget of $1.85 million and was scheduled for broadcast in October 1981. It was publicised by the television industry, the mainstream press and the women's movement. The representations were seen as important for the causes of the women's movement especially with regard to women's friendship, women's independence and women working in non-traditional jobs. Gloria Steinem at *Ms* magazine had been sent a script by the creators and was so enthusiastic that the cover of the October 1981 issue of *Ms* pictured Loretta Swit and Tyne Daly in police uniforms as Cagney and Lacey (see Figure 13.1). The issue also contained a feature article on *Cagney and Lacey* written by Majorie Rosen, a well-known feminist film critic and author. It retold the troubled history of the property and emphasised its importance for feminism. A pitch for a weekly series was included at the end of the article, 'If you would like to see *Cagney and Lacey* expanded into a TV series write to Richard Rosenbloom, Filmways, 2049 Century Park East, Los Angeles, California 90067' (Rosen, 1981, p.109). Gloria Steinem appeared with Loretta Swit on *The Phil Donahue Show* to plug the movie, 'in tones,' according to one media critic, 'so reverential it sounded as though they were promoting the first woman president' (Rosenthal, 1983). These were only the first of many interventions on behalf of *Cagney and Lacey* by representatives of the women's movement and by feminist journalists both in the feminist and mainstream press.

The movie was publicised by CBS according to a standard television industry advertising practice (especially for made-for-TV movies and mini-series), called 'exploitation advertising'. This is a practice, with precedents in the Hollywood film industry, in which a sensational, usually sexual or violent, aspect of a programme is highlighted for the purposes of audience attraction. The *Cagney and Lacey* movie advertisement from *TV Guide* (see Figure 13.2) has a large close-up of Loretta Swit, with

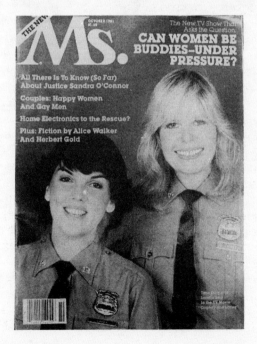

Figure 13.1

209

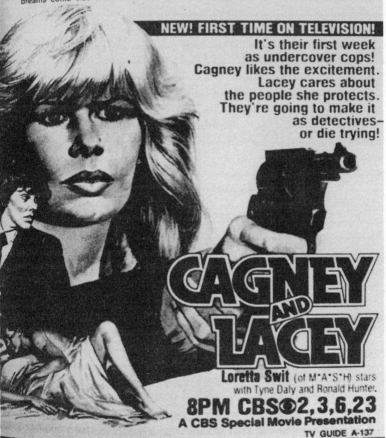

Figure 13.2

long blonde hair, lipstick and eye make-up, dominating three-quarters of the left side of the ad. Her clasped, outstretched hands contain a pointed revolver which dominates the right side of the ad. A significantly smaller medium shot of the (then) lesser-known Tyne Daly in police coat, shirt and tie is under the Swit close-up. On the far left of the page, under and smaller than the Daly image, is a shot of Swit lying on her back (presumably naked) with a sheet draped over her. One bare shoulder and arm, and one bare leg bent at the knee are exposed. A man, seen only from the waist up (also naked) is leaning over and on top of her; his arm is over her body. The copy reads, 'It's their first week as undercover cops! Cagney likes the excitement. Lacey cares about the people she protects. They're going to make it as detectives – or die trying.'

A number of meanings of 'woman' are in play here and there are, no doubt, many possible readings and interpretations of this one ad. One interpretation is that the television industry, in dealing with a movie about 'woman' in non-traditional roles, is careful in its advertising to invoke not only meanings regarding the 'new woman', but meanings regarding the conventional woman as well. I would argue that the inclusion of this image of 'woman' as spectacle for and object of male desire as one of the three images in an ad for a movie about women in new roles, carries a particular charge. It not only fulfils the formula for exploitation advertising by suggesting sexual content to the audience, but also reassures it with regard to 'woman's' conventional role and position regarding societal power.

The movie was also publicised in the mainstream press. In an article, 'Real policewomen view the TV variety,' (*New York Times* 7 October 1981), the day before the airing of the movie, Barbara Basler interviewed three New York policewomen who were shown a preview of the movie. It praises the representations of Cagney and Lacey as 'true-to-life'. A few months later, however, Howard Rosenberg interviewed three Los Angeles policewomen for the *Los Angeles Times*; they severely challenged the reality of *Cagney and Lacey* in favour of their own definitions of 'woman' and 'femininity' (Rosenberg, 1982). The Basler article generally demonstrates the ways that the representations of Cagney and Lacey begin to generate discourses regarding not only the characters in the series but also the possibilities of 'woman' in the social context outside the series.

The movie was aired at 8 pm on 8 October 1981 and captured

an astonishing 42 per cent share of the television audience (CBS had been getting a 28 or 29 share in this period). Within thirty-six hours, CBS was on the telephone to Barney Rosenzweig asking him to put a weekly series together. Gloria Steinem and *Ms* magazine staff members had already lobbied members of the CBS board urging them to make a series out of the movie.

The second phase of *Cagney and Lacey*'s history, the television series starring Tyne Daly and Meg Foster as the new Chris Cagney, dates from March 1982 to August 1982. The first script was written by Avedon, Corday and Rosenzweig. The main characters were publicised by Filmways in press releases as 'two top-notch female cops who fight crime while proving themselves to male colleagues'. Gloria Steinem and *Ms* magazine, keeping alive the link between the women's movement and *Cagney and Lacey*, organised a reception for the stars and creators in early March. The angle, emphasised both in the publicity for the series and the scripts, was of women working in non-traditional jobs and fighting sexism. It is important to see this within the context of the television industry trying to attract a working women's audience. The very night and hour *Cagney and Lacey* was first shown (Thursday 25 March, 9 p.m. Eastern Standard Time), the series *9 to 5*, based on the hit movie of the same name, was premiered on another network, ABC. Six months later, in the autumn of 1982, four other working women-oriented programmes (*Gloria*, *Remington Steele*, *It Takes Two*, and *Square Pegs*), were also added to the schedule. The fact that *Cagney and Lacey* and *9 to 5* were scheduled opposite one another would prove costly for both series in terms of ratings. Gloria Steinem, speaking at a Hollywood Radio and Television Society luncheon a month before the premières, had in fact protested at this scheduling, saying it might 'split the audience and hurt each other's [the two series'] chances' (Bierbaum, 1982).

Despite the favourable press, and without much consideration for the fact that it was scheduled in competition with *9 to 5* (a programme that attracted the same target audience), the network wanted to cancel *Cagney and Lacey* after two episodes. CBS did not, in fact, allocate advertising money to promote the series' third episode in *TV Guide*. ABC's *9 to 5* had a half-page ad. The series would have been cancelled abruptly had not Rosenzweig persuaded Harvey Shephard, vice-president in charge of pro-gramming for CBS, to give *Cagney and Lacey* a spot on Sunday,

25 April at 10 p.m. Rosenzweig argued that *Cagney and Lacey* was an adult programme rather than one which would also attract children, and that it required a time-slot later than 9 p.m. Shephard reluctantly agreed, but once again voiced CBS's ambivalence by telling Rosenzweig to 'save his money' (Turner, 1983, p.53) when Rosenzweig said Filmways would put up $25,000 to send Meg Foster and Tyne Daly across the country to stump for the series prior to the Sunday night airing. Filmways did send Foster and Daly on the road. In a one-week campaign, the two actresses gave approximately fifty radio, television, and print interviews including a television talk show on women's rights with Betty Friedan.

Playing safe with Cagney

The Sunday 25 April episode of *Cagney and Lacey* pulled in an impressive 34 per cent audience share and ranked number seven in the overall ratings. Despite this success, Harvey Shephard told Rosenzweig that many members of the CBS board (responsible for the final renewal of decisions) would consider this share 'a fluke'. He said he would fight for the series renewal only if Rosenzweig made a significant change in the programme. The required change centred on the character of Cagney and Meg Foster's portrayal of her.

At this point in the history of *Cagney and Lacey* other factors regarding CBS' ambivalence begin to emerge. In a *Daily Variety* article on 25 May 1982 and a *Hollywood Reporter* article on 28 May, Harvey Shephard spoke publicly about the replacement of Meg Foster and the renewal of *Cagney and Lacey*. Shephard is quoted in both articles as saying that 'several mistakes were made with the show in that the stories were too gritty, the characterisations of both Cagney and Lacey were too tough and there was not enough contrast between these two partners'. A few weeks later, however, other factors were made public. According to statements by a 'CBS programmer', published in the 12–18 June 1982 *TV Guide*, CBS thought the characters were 'too tough, too hard, not feminine . . . too harshly women's lib' and perceived them as 'dykes'. It would appear that the association of *Cagney and Lacey* with the 'masculine woman' and with lesbianism gave CBS a way in which to think about and cast its objections with regard to the non-conventional and apparently threatening representations of 'woman' in the series. The public explanation by CBS was that audience research had discovered objections to the representations. According to Arnold Becker, Chief of Research for CBS, evidence – drawn from a sample of 160 persons – had picked up such comments on *Cagney and Lacey* as, 'inordinately abrasive, loud and lacking warmth,' and, 'they should be given a measure of traditional female appeal, especially Chris' (Rosenberg, 1982). The differential treatment given to the characters and the actresses during this incident underscores some of the dimensions of the network's anxiety. The evidence points to an extreme discomfort on the part of the network with 'woman' represented as non-glamorous, feminist, sexually active *and* working-class and single. 'Woman' in the case of the original Chris Cagney manifested too many markers of 'non-feminine', according to the network's definition of the term. She also had no acceptable class, family or marriage context to contain, domesticate or 'make safe' those differences. Lacey, on the other hand, was 'less threatening' because married.

It is plausible and even predictable that a portion of viewers would find the representations of Cagney and Lacey problematic. The viewer reaction in any letters I have seen, was, however, critical of CBS, and *TV Guide* printed a series of angry responses in its subsequent issue. A sample of excerpts from audience letters from the *Cagney and Lacey* files reads as follows, 'The programme *Cagney and Lacey* is being ruined. I have thoroughly enjoyed it: the actresses had good chemistry and I enjoyed seeing a tough female.' And, 'With Cagney and Lacey, Meg and Tyne, we at least have a programme that shows two women doing a hard job, but we also see an honest and warm friendship. . . . We can see they care for each other, there isn't much about a good friendship between women on TV.' And, 'I read in last week's *TV Guide* something about replacing Meg Foster for such reasons as she is too threatening? . . . I get the feeling there's a card game at the Hillcrest Country Club called "let's go with the path of least resistance when it comes to women on TV".' And a final one, 'Foster and Daly did a marvellous job of portraying strong, confident women living through some trying and testing circumstances. Too strong? Too aggressive? Come on! They are cops in the city. They aren't supposed to be fragile, delicate wimps.' Two months after the removal of Meg Foster, CBS may have, in the words of one reviewer, 'shuddered a little' when a new Meg Foster-Tyne Daly episode, aired on 21 June, ranked number two in the overall ratings.

CBS' ultimate decision on *Cagney and Lacey* was that the series should be revised to 'combine competency with an element of sensuality' (Arnold Becker quoted in Rosenberg, 1982). Its solution was twofold: to replace Meg Foster with someone more 'feminine,' and to change Chris Cagney's socio-economic background. The replacement was Sharon Gless, and instead of being working-class, Cagney was now said to have been raised by a wealthy Westchester mother and grandmother. A new CBS press kit was issued to publicise the series in a new way. 'Cagney and Lacey,' it reads, 'are two cops who have earned the respect of their male counterparts and at no expense to their femininity' (DuBrow, 1983). Cagney also underwent a radical fashion change to accompany her class change. A memo in the *Cagney and Lacey* production files reads as follows, 'the new budget will include an additional $15,000 for wardrobe costs, the revised concept for character calls for Cagney to wear less middle-class, classier clothes so that her upward mobility is evidenced.' The overt feminism of the scripts was, after the original series, for the most part removed. The new Chris Cagney is more of a rugged individualist than a feminist and is actually conservative on many social issues. Mary Beth Lacey carries on most of the feminism and the liberal politics.

The new series with Sharon Gless and Tyne Daly began in the autumn of 1982. Viewers, according to audience letters, were at first reluctant to accept Gless but within two months an avid and large viewer following began to develop. Gless was seen by the press as bringing 'humour', 'vibrance' and 'softness' to Cagney's character, while still, according to some journalists, maintaining the 'toughness', or being 'very pretty and at the same time a jock'. An irony in the history of the series, which also demonstrates the operation of multiple and contradictory viewer receptions, is that Sharon Gless, according to recently published articles, and viewer letters, has a large lesbian viewing audience. This development, seen in relation to the viewer-response letters surrounding the removal of Meg Foster and the press comments on the appeal of the friendship between Cagney and Lacey, demonstrates quite concretely the ways in which the television industry's investments in particular notions of 'woman' or 'femininity', are at odds with

Figure 13.3   Sharon Gless and Tyne Daly as *Cagney and Lacey*

certain viewer investments at least. The potential homo-erotic overtones in the representation of the two women which formed the basis for the TV industry's discomfort are, in varying degrees, the bases of certain viewers' pleasure. However, despite a good deal of critical acclaim, the first season of the Gless/Daly *Cagney and Lacey* did not do well in the ratings, not even with a women-only target audience. Its competition during much of the season came from women-oriented prime-time movies.

Promotable stories

Several strategies were proposed to save the show. One was to develop more 'exploitable' stories and publicise them in an 'exploitation' manner. A May 1983 episode on wife-beating, entitled 'A cry for help' (the ratings from which were considered crucial to the network's decision of whether to renew or cancel *Cagney and Lacey*), was one of the few (after the 1981 made-for-TV-movie) to employ not only an exploitation topic but also exploitation advertising in *TV Guide*. I will say more about the practice of exploitation or 'promotable' programming later, but here I want to point out that the contradictions and complexities of the practice are underscored by the fact that 'A cry for help' pulled in high ratings, won several awards from social programmes for its treatment of the issue, and was praised in many letters from women viewers.

Another strategy to save the series and engender a larger women's audience was to send Tyne Daly and Sharon Gless on a publicity tour to promote the series. Barney Rosenzweig co-ordinated a large letter writing campaign to save the series,[3] and CBS and major newspapers throughout the country were deluged with volumes of unprecedented and appreciative viewer mail. The series, however, was cancelled in the spring of 1983 but several factors combined to cause CBS to reverse its decision and bring it back on the air. First, the audience letters continued to come in, and mostly from the desired target audience: women between the ages of 18 and 54. Secondly, after cancellation *Cagney and Lacey* received four Emmy nominations and Tyne Daly won an Emmy for best dramatic actress. Third, *Cagney and Lacey* scored number one ratings for the first week of the summer re-run period and remained in the top ten throughout the summer. After the programme was revived, the press, and *Cagney and Lacey*'s own publicity, stressed the importance of the audience in saving the series. Such headlines as 'Flood of mail from women viewers revives *Cagney and Lacey*' and 'Viewers hollered loud enough to be heard', were commonplace. In this way the audience, which already had a lot invested in the series, was, unlike any other audience in the history of television, represented as being part of the actual production process. This fact, of course, was somewhat exaggerated by the publicity. The audience, although a key factor in the decision to revive the series, would not have caused CBS to reverse its decision without the high summer ratings.

At this point, some of the principals involved in the production process struggled over the representations of Cagney and Lacey on the levels of hairstyle, make-up and clothing. Barney Rosenzweig, set on getting the series renewed beyond the limited seven episodes, wanted a general upgrading of the styles and 'looks' of the two characters. He wanted a renovation of the Cagney 'look' to include more 'stylish', 'glamorous' outfits, and a new hairstyle that would 'move' and 'bounce'. Sharon Gless, reluctant about making Cagney 'too frilly', objected but finally agreed to the new hairstyle. For several months, Rosenzweig had wanted to change the Lacey wardrobe, and make it and the character 'more fashionable'. Tyne Daly, however, who had designed the Mary Beth Lacey 'look', refused to change Lacey's plain and eccentric style. Rosenzweig and Daly argued over issues of make-up, Rosenzweig wanting more and Daly less. They also battled about Lacey's hairstyle. Rosenzweig would ask her hairdresser to get to her between takes and tease and spray her hair. During one such incident Daly shouted to the crew and production staff, 'Can anyone tell me why my producer wants me to look like Pat Nixon?'.

The practice of developing 'promotable' stories aimed specifically at target audience women surfaces again during this period and remains part of *Cagney and Lacey*'s future practice. Of the seven programmes produced during this period, four could be considered 'promotable': a male stripper club and wife-murder, pornography, a Cagney pregnancy scare, and illegal baby-selling. In a *New York Times* article of 5 July 1984, which praises *Cagney and Lacey* as a 'class act', John J. O'Connor says, '*Cagney and Lacey* hasn't yet found the perfect balancing mechanisms for dealing with subjects that are still considered sensational or controversial. . . . It's not that any of this is completely objectionable. It's simply that the wheels of exploitation can be heard grinding off camera.' Exploitation vehicles or 'promotable stories' emerged, it seems, to combat the other networks' women-oriented movies which were luring away *Cagney and Lacey*'s target audience women. On the one hand, the use of exploitation stories may be seen as part of the territory of popular commercial programme production. With an innovative programme such as *Cagney and Lacey*, their use may be seen as one of many moves necessary simply to keep the series on the air. On the other hand, the choice of such material quite literally 'cashes in on' – and subjects to the demands, constraints, and distortions of television – issues of enormous complexity for women. Rape, wife-beating, incest, child molestation, pregnancy and unmarried women, breast cancer and abortion are all issues that have formed the material for *Cagney and Lacey* episodes. Yet again, some producers in the television industry consider the exploitation vehicle a way to attract a large audience and then in the programme itself present a well-researched and socially useful treatment of a problem. The positive audience reaction to *Cagney and Lacey*'s treatment of certain women's issues, while not exonerating the practice of exploitation topics, certainly makes the complex, contradictory character of this practice clear.

The promotable episode of Cagney's pregnancy scare, the last of the seven trial episodes in May 1984, is an interesting example of negotiations, at the level of script development, regarding the representations of an unmarried woman's pregnancy. Originally the story, conceived by Terry Louise Fisher, had Cagney discover in Act I that she was pregnant and then have a miscarriage in Act IV. Terry Louise Fisher had struggled with how to resolve the pregnancy. Knowing that the network would never allow abortion as a possibility for Cagney, she self-censored the consideration and was less than satisfied in resorting to the clichéd miscarriage route. Tony Barr, an executive at CBS, rejected the script, saying that the network did not 'want to shine the spotlight on pregnancy' and the problems of a pregnant unmarried woman. CBS had suggested that they turn the episode into a biological clock story in which Cagney is faced with the decision of whether or not she will ever have children. Fisher felt that the biological clock angle was not dramatically sound because it would offer no 'resolution' or 'closure'. She asked Rosenzweig if he would fight for the original story with the network. Since the sub-plot of the script involved the officers at the precinct preparing for the sergeant's exam, and since attaining the rank of sergeant was one of Cagney's immediate ambitions, it was suggested that the issue get cast around a 'my job or having a baby' kind of choice. Fisher said she refused to do that to working women, 'it sounds too much like waiting for Prince Charming to come'. Rosenzweig thought that they should leave the first act exactly as it was – Cagney *thinks* she's pregnant. In reality, however, she is not. The network agreed that Cagney could *think* she was pregnant, but only on condition that Lacey accuse her of being totally irresponsible. There then followed much discussion on how they would cast Cagney's irresponsibility – 'Should we say it was a night of passion?'; 'Cagney could say something like, "I know it was my fault, I was acting like a teenager," or "well, it happens, I mean the diaphragm is not foolproof".' Rosenzweig objected that 'as the father of four daughters, I don't want to put down the diaphragm'. In the final episode, entitled 'Biological Clock', Cagney thinks she is pregnant, but is not, and Lacey is only mildly accusatory. There is no mention of specific birth control technologies or how the 'mistake' might have happened. There is no mention of what Cagney would do if she were pregnant, although Lacey strongly pushes marriage. Cagney seems to be developing a relationship with the alleged baby and abortion is never mentioned.

During this period, the producers and writers also talked about where, in general, to go with the Cagney character. The discussions revolved around making Cagney a more 'sympathetic' character. According to Terry Louise Fisher and Barbara Avedon, the word 'sympathetic' is industry jargon directed almost exclusively towards a female character. It means to portray her in traditional ways and situations, 'show her in the kitchen', 'show her as warm'. The decision to make Cagney sympathetic by having her in a committed relationship with her boyfriend Dory was unpopular with viewers. One of the reporters on *Sixty Minutes* during the 'letters-from-viewers' segment read a viewer-letter which called for the removal of Dory from the *Cagney and Lacey* series.

The series was picked up by CBS for a full season renewal in the spring of 1984. In the 1984–85 and 1985–86 seasons it won the Emmy award for best dramatic programme. Tyne Daly won for best actress in 1983–85 and Sharon Gless in 1986. It has won many other awards, including the award for best programme by the National Committee on Working Women in 1985 and the Humanitas Award in 1986. Moreover, 12 April 1984 was declared 'Cagney and Lacey Day' by the mayor of Washington DC and the Commission on Working Women. During the 1984–85 season, the Cagney character was associated with some conventionally feminist actions: against many odds she files sexual harassment charges against a captain in the police department, she urges Lacey to get a second opinion on a mastectomy treatment and introduces the option of a lumpectomy, she is the only one in her precinct to make the rank of sergeant and continues emphasising the importance of her career and her goal to become the first woman chief of detectives. Critical and industrial acclaim, a more secure place in the ratings (at least with target audience women), and the requisite changes in class and glamour, it seems, made the network less nervous about the representation of 'woman' on the series.

A two part programme from the 1984–85 season and an episode from the 1985–86 season gave *Cagney and Lacey* a good deal of publicity and are interesting examples of convergences of discourses regarding 'woman'. They both could be considered exploitation topics and were aired during ratings sweeps periods.[4] The episodes (11 and 18 February 1985) on Lacey's breast cancer centred on early detection of breast cancer, getting quick medical attention, and lumpectomy as an alternative to mastectomy. However, they worked within the parameters of the medical establishment and did not address such issues as 'disfigurement' and the fetishisation of women's bodies. Tyne Daly, in an article in *People*, was overtly critical of the medical institution with regard to breast cancer. She said that after some hesitation she decided to do the part because, 'I realised that as long as there are women being led astray by the medical establishment, women getting hacked up into pieces, it's important that I tell the story' (Ryan, 1985, p.96).

An episode about abortion, broadcast 11 November 1985, became a central part of the public struggle over a woman's autonomy and control over her body. Anti-abortion groups, led by the National Right to Life Committee, appealed to CBS to pull the episode which centred on the bombing of an abortion clinic and the support by Cagney and Lacey (after considerable debate) of a woman's right to choose. The NRLC called the programme a 'piece of pure political propaganda' (Associated Press, 1985). When CBS, saying that they found the programme to be 'a fair and well-balanced view' (CBS vice-president George Schweitzer quoted in Hellmich, 1985), refused to pull it from the schedule, the NRLC asked CBS affiliates to black it. If the affiliate did not want to black it, NLRC asked it to offer NLRC a half-hour film of their choice (such as the anti-abortion film *Matter of Choice*) or a half-hour to 'put some of our folks on to rebut this' (John Wilke, president of NRLC, on *MacNeil/Lehrer New Hour*, 1985). Tyne Daly and Barney Rosenzweig flew to Washington DC for a luncheon co-sponsored by the National Abortion Rights Action League and Orion Television to 'counter opposition' to the episode. According to Daly, 'we feel we've done something very balanced. . . . I don't think I know a woman who hasn't struggled or knows someone who has struggled with this issue' (Hellmich, 1985). John Wilke and Barney Rosenzweig debated the issue on the *McNeil/Lehrer News Hour*. To Wilke's charges that 'this programme is the most unbalanced, most unfair programme we've seen in a number of years . . . we did not hear a single right-to-life answer properly given', Rosenzweig answered, 'a year ago we had an episode in which Christine Cagney believed she was pregnant, and never once considered abortion as an alternative. I didn't hear from the National Organization for Women or the Voters for Choice then about banning the show or boycotting us. I just got some rather nice letters from the pro-life people.'

Closing and re-opening the case of Cagney and Lacey

There is, I would maintain, a good deal of difference with regard to the representation of 'woman' on television in *Cagney and Lacey*, and television viewers, coming from a variety of social contexts, with a variety of interpretive strategies, produce many different meanings of the representations. But the ways in which the series has been talked about in the mainstream and feminist press, and the support it has generated from representatives of the women's movement have, I think, caused the series itself and its representations to become invested with *more* difference than may actually exist. The differences represented, rooted as they are in liberal notions of politics and representation, imply that social change and difference for women is simply a matter of equal roles, equal jobs and equal representation. And the practices of exploitation themes and exploitation advertising, although complex and contradictory, make problematic the whole notion of 'woman', women, and television representation. Also, I think it can be demonstrated that the *Cagney and Lacey* narratives have progressively come to portray Mary Beth's and Harvey's situation – the traditional family, and the role of mother and wife – not simply as *one* of many possibilities but as *the* satisfying, healthy norm for 'woman'. Chris Cagney in several narratives has in fact been represented as alone and on the outside of this normal, healthy and moral unit.

On the other hand, although *Cagney and Lacey* is basically rooted in liberal notions of social and feminist change, it manages to keep in play alternative and even oppositional political discourses. Issues such as single, working mothers, federal cutbacks in social service programmes, nuclear irresponsibility and inhumane treatment of 'illegal aliens', as well as race, class and gender, have also been addressed. Certain of the 'exploitation' episodes have made such issues as rape and wife-battering matters of wide public attention and communicated to women in the audience that their experiences are not isolated ones. The Lacey character, at the same time as working to tack down the moral 'healthy' norm for 'woman' as wife and mother, also works to keep in play alternative and oppositional discourses in her pro-labour, pro-abortion, anti-nuclear, and anti-racist dialogue. And the Cagney character, particularly the shifting conceptualisation of her role, generates non-conventional possibilities for 'woman' – 'woman' as the autonomous subject rather than the object of action, desire, humour and intelligence.

Cagney and Lacey has also provided jobs and consequently a forum for a significant number of women in the television industry. Forty-six of the eighty-two scripts aired at the time of writing have been written or co-written by women. Sixty of the eighty-two episodes have one or more women credited as producer and all have had a woman co-producer. Women also function as creative consultants, executive story editors, executive story consultants and first assistant directors for the series. With regard to acting, in addition to providing two of the few leading dramatic roles for women in television, the series has tried to offer a good share of its minor roles (some recurrent) to women.

The representation of friendship between Cagney and Lacey, their conversations and arguments in the women's room, the locker room and the squad car, opens on to spaces of women's culture and women's communities and offers moments of well-documented pleasure for women viewers. And the series itself, at various points in its history, has functioned to test the limits and define the conditions of possibility for the representation of 'woman' on television.

Acknowledgments

This article is part of a longer project on the representation of 'woman' on prime-time American television. A version was presented to the International Television Studies Conference, 1986.

Notes

1 See S. Hall (1980), p.137 for a different yet related use of 'negotiation', upon which much of my notion is based.
2 I want to thank Barney Rosenzweig, executive producer of *Cagney and Lacey*, for generously granting me interviews and access to the set, production files and production and staff meetings from January to March 1984. I also want to thank Barbara Corday, Barbara Avedon, P.K. Knelman, Terry Louise Fisher, Peter Lefcourt, Tyne Daly, Sharon Gless, Stewart Lyons, Ralph Singleton and the cast, crew and staff of *Cagney and Lacey* for granting me interviews, information and the opportunity to observe them at work. I am grateful to Todd Gitlin for taking an afternoon to discuss this project with me. Finally, I owe special thanks to Fran Breit and Biddy Martin for their suggestions, discussions and indefatigable help with all aspects of this article.
3 After receiving a large volume of viewer mail, Rosenzweig sent return letters to the writers asking them to write to major newspapers such as the *New York Times* and the *Los Angeles Times*, as well as to Bud Grant, president of CBS.
4 November, February and May are called 'sweeps' periods in the US television industry. These are periods during which the network affiliated stations are rated by the Nielsen and Arbitron ratings companies. Networks typically run special programming during these periods to attract as many viewers as possible. The practice is called 'hypoing.'

References

Associated Press (1985), 'An episode of *Cagney* under fire on abortion,' *New York Times*, 11 November.
Avedon, B., Corday, B., Adams, C. and Green, P. (1985), story, part I, 'Breast cancer' episode, *Cagney and Lacey*, airdate: 11 February.
Bierbaum, T. (1982), 'Steinem takes right turn on TV violence,' *Daily Variety*, 2 February, p.25.
Cagney and Lacey offices (1982), 'Analysis of costs for CBS for *Cagney and Lacey*,' Rosenzweig files.
Corday, B. (1985), 'Dialogue on film,' *American Film*, vol.10, no.9, pp.11, 12, 60.
D'Acci, J. (1986), 'Women, "Woman," and prime-time American television,' paper presented to Cornell University Women's Studies Program and Middlebury College, 13 and 14 March.
de Lauretis, T. (1984), *Alice Doesn't: Feminism, Semiotics, and Cinema*, Indiana, Indiana University Press.
DuBrow, R. (1983), 'Cagney and Lacey hang tough,' *Los Angeles Herald Examiner*, 25 January, pp.C–1 and C–4.
Filmways News Release (1982), 'Meg Foster to join Tyne Daly as CBS *Cagney and Lacey* duo,' Rosenzweig file.

Green, P. (1985a), teleplay, part I, 'Breast cancer' episode, *Cagney and Lacey*, airdate: 11 February.

Green, P. (1985b), script, part II, 'Breast cancer' episode, *Cagney and Lacey*, airdate: 18 February.

Hall, S. (1980), 'Encoding/decoding' in Hall, Hobson, Lowe, and Willis (eds.), *Culture, Media, Language*, London, Hutchinson, pp.128–38.

Haskell, Molly (1974), *From Reverence to Rape: The Treatment of Women in the Movies*, London, Penguin.

Welmich, N. (1985), 'Daly defends *Cagney* show on abortion,' *USA Today*, 6 November, section D, p.1.

Kuhn, A. (1985), *The Power of the Image: Essays on Representation and Sexuality*, London, Routledge and Kegan Paul, p.6.

MacNeil/Lehrer News Hour (1985), Public Broadcasting Service, 8 November.

Malleck, B. (1982), 'Real women at last: punch-hitter *Cagney and Lacey* is a mid-season bonus,' *Kitchener-Waterloo Record*, Kitchener, Ontario.

Ms (1981), cover photo, vol.10, no.4.

O'Connor, J. (1984), '*Cagney and Lacey* – indisputably a class act,' *New York Times* News Service to *The Patriot Ledger*, 5 July, p.42.

Rogers and Cowan Inc, Public Relations (1982a), letter to Barney Rosenzweig, 8 September, Rosenzweig files.

Rosen, M. (1981), 'Cagney and Lacey', *Ms*, vol.10, no.4, pp.47–50,109.

Rosenberg, H. (1982), 'Cagney and (Uh) Lacey: a question of a pink slip,' *Los Angeles Times*, 23 June, Calendar Section, pp.1,7.

Rosenthal, S. (1983), 'Cancellation of *Cagney and Lacey* to mean loss of "rare" TV series,' *New York Daily News*, 3 June, pp.31,35.

Ryan, M. (1985), 'A Method in the madness,' *People*, 11 February, p.96.

Soho News, (1982), 9 March.

Stephen, B. (1982), 'Policewomen: TV show on the case,' *Los Angeles Times*, 11 April.

Turner, R. (1983), 'The curious case of the lady cops and the shots that blew them away,' *TV Guide*, vol.31, no.41, 8–14 October, p.52.

TV Guide advertisement (1982), *TV Guide*, 3–10 April, pp.A–116–17.

TV Guide advertisement (1983), *TV Guide*, 30 April–6 May, p.A–75.

TV Guide letters (1982), *TV Guide*, 10–16 June, p.A–4.

Index

227

Index

Index

Scandinavia, 20, 26
Schlesinger, P., 93, 133, 138, 141
Scotsman, 159
Screen, 182
Screenwriters' Association, 152
Seear, Baroness, 63
series/serials, 152, 154, 168; *see also* drama, soap operas
sex discrimination, 56; positive action against, 56–8, 61–2, 68
Sex Discrimination Act (1975), 57
sexism, 89, 211
sexuality, 6, 133, 135, 137, 140, 175, 177–8, 181
Sims, M., 59–60, 62, 65, 120
Sixty Minutes, 219
Skirrow, G., 9, 15, 184, 185, 188, 189
Sky Channel (Windsor TV), 20, 25, 26–7, 32
Smith, A., 20, 147
soap operas, 11, 45, 49, 50, 114; function, 30–1; narrative in, 12–13; single person households and, 113; social/cultural context, 13–14; writing, 152, 158–9
social change, 92; media representations and, 205–6, 221–2
Society for Education in Film and Television, 182
Somerville, J., 135–6
Spain, 24, 25
sports programmes, 7–8, 101
Steinem, G., 208, 209, 211, 212
Stephens, D., 83–4, 87, 88, 89, 94
stereotypes, 7, 9, 105
Stewart, J., 183, 184, 186
subject positions: in film/soap opera, 11–13, 49; gender and, 44
Summerskill, E., 93
Sun, 135, 186
Sunday Telegraph, 135, 137, 201
Sunday Times, 155
Superchannel, 21
Sweden, 26
Switzerland, 21

technology: gender and, 34, 42–3, 68, 114; information technology, 22, 25–7, 35; sports programming and, 8; of video, 42–3

teleshopping, 32
teletext, 20, 25–6
television: as background, 112; early history, 73–4
Television Audience Measurement, 114
Tenko, 153–7, 158, 159–60
Thames Television: childcare, 62; personnel, 57–9, 63
Times, The, 134, 186, 188, 191
Toynton, I., 169, 170, 171, 176, 178, 182, 191
Trades Union Congress (1980), 56
trade unions: feminism and, 66–7, 68; male domination, 55, 61, 66; weakening of, 55
training (for women), 57, 58–9, 63, 64–5
TV-am, 127
TVEye, 124
TV Guide, 109–10 (*210*), 212, 213, 214, 215
TV Times, 86, 94, 168, 189

unemployment, 55, 98, 107
United Nations Decade for Women, teleconferences, 28–9
United States of America, 19, 21, 23, 25, 32, 33; advertising, 31; cable TV, 28; equal opportunity, 56, 61; race and drama, 193; satellite transmission, 28–9; soap operas, 114, 158; teleshopping, 32

Valery, A., 153, 155, 156, 157, 159, 160
video cassette recorders, 20, 38, 107, 109; access to, 38–9; potential for choice, 40, 51; uses, 39, 114
video games, 25
video libraries, 39–40, 48–9; women and, 44
video 'nasties', 40
Video Recordings Bill (1984), 40
videotex, 25–6
viewers, *see* audience
viewing contexts, 40–1, 46–50
viewing patterns, 107–9, 110–11
violence, 33, 103